ADVANCING
in the
World of Work

Grady Kimbrell
Educational Consultant
Santa Barbara, California

Ben S. Vineyard
Professor and Chairman Emeritus
Vocational and Technical Education
Pittsburg State University
Pittsburg, Kansas

M. Valorie Putnam
Workforce Entry Coordinator
Comstock, Michigan

GLENCOE
Macmillan/McGraw-Hill

Lake Forest, Illinois   Columbus, Ohio   Mission Hills, California   Peoria, Illinois

Send all inquiries to:
GLENCOE DIVISION
Macmillan/McGraw-Hill
15319 Chatsworth Street
P.O. Box 9609
Mission Hills, CA 91346-9609

ISBN 0-02-675591-2
1 2 3 4 5 6 7 8 9   97 96 95 94 93 92

Teacher Reviewers and Consultants

Charlotte E. Curtis
Vocational Education Consultant
Stanislaus County Department of
Education
Incline Village, Nevada

Jeanne England
Career Investigation Teacher
DeSoto West Junior High School
DeSoto Independent School District
DeSoto, Texas

Christine Krueger
L.D. Teacher/Vocational Instruction
Coordinator
Franklin High School
Franklin School District 5
Franklin, Wisconsin

Kevin M. McCarthy
Law offices of
Miller, Canfield, Paddock and Stone
Kalamazoo, Michigan

Michael Shipley
Pre-vocational Experience Coordinator
Kokomo Center Township
Consolidated School Corporation
Kokomo High School
Kokomo, Indiana

David J. Uher
Occupational Work Adjustment
Coordinator
Circleville High School
Circleville City Schools
Circleville, Ohio

Catherine A. Williams
Career Guidance Consultant
C.L.A.S.S. Consulting
Sisters, Oregon

Beth E. Zitko-Peters
Educational Consultant
Little Rock, Arkansas

○ Contents

O Introduction

The world of work is exciting! It is filled with new challenges. This book will show you how to meet these challenges with confidence. And it will provide knowledge you will need to advance in your career.

You will explore the skills you will need on the job such as communication, math, and computer skills. You will learn how to face social issues at work such as discrimination, peer pressure, and drug abuse. You will discover how to make wise decisions about your life-style. These include decisions about where to live, how to act on the job, and how to afford your life-style.

You will use the skills and knowledge you learn from *Advancing* every day in the working world. It will give you the keys to life-long success.

Now, browse through the following photos and take a look at your future.

▲ *Communication is how we convey thoughts and ideas from one person to another. Learning good communication skills will help you to succeed in the working world.*

▲ *Math skills are used every day on many jobs. Having good math skills will make your job easier.*

▶ *Computer skills are used in almost every career field today. Your computer skills may help you get the job you want.*

◀ *Many important decisions must be made both on and off the job. The decisions you make today will affect you tomorrow.*

▶ *Learning how to get along with people is important on every job. How well you get along with others is a key to your success.*

▲ *Your job may depend on your work values. Are you honest? Are you loyal? Positive work values often lead to promotions on the job.*

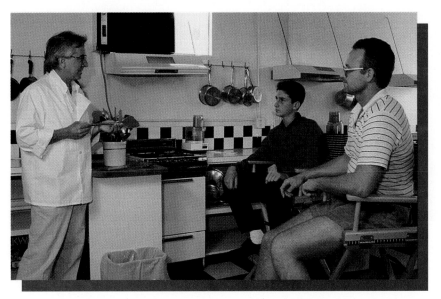

◄ *There are many opportunities to further your education. Further education will help you to advance on the job.*

▲ *Almost everyone will change jobs sometime during his or her career.*
Knowing when and how to change jobs will make the decision easier.

► *Living on your own will be a big change in your life. Learning to make wise decisions about where you will live will make the change easier.*

◄ *You will need transportation to take you to and from work each day. Knowing how to judge your transportation needs will save you time and money.*

► *Finding time in your day for leisure and recreation is as important as finding time for your job. Learning to maintain a balanced life-style will improve your health and happiness.*

◄ *There are many expenses when you live on your own. You will feel most comfortable knowing how to afford your life-style.*

► *If you are not healthy, you cannot work. Learning to stay healthy is important to your work and overall life.*

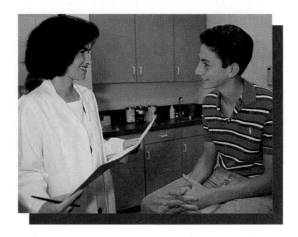

◄ *Social problems are present in almost any job. You may face peer pressure and discrimination. How you handle social issues will determine how well you do on the job.*

◀ *Most people must deal with legal matters sometime during their life. Understanding the law and how it affects you will help you face legal matters in your life.*

▲ *There will always be changes in your life. Learning to prepare and plan for change will help you to feel positive about your life.*

Part One
Basic Job Skills

Chapter 1
Communication Skills

Chapter 2
Math and Calculator Skills

Chapter 3
Introduction to Computers

Chapter 4
Decision Making

Communication Skills

Words to learn and use

Here are the new terms you will learn in this chapter. Challenge yourself. Read through the list to see if you know what they mean.

communication
body language
inflections
distractions
emotional blocks
standard English
pronunciation
enunciation
pace
pitch
volume
previewing
skimming
topic sentence

Build on what you know

You already know...
- you learn by listening to others.
- you speak to inform others and ask questions.
- you read to learn and for fun.
- you write to record information.

In this chapter you will learn...
- how to get more out of listening.
- how to get others to listen when you speak.
- how to remember more of what you read.
- how to get others to understand what you write.

Communication is sending and receiving messages. But just hearing or reading a message is not enough. A message is communicated only when both the sender and receiver *understand* it in the same way.

The four basic communication skills are listening, speaking, reading, and writing. In this chapter, you will learn how to use these skills to send and receive messages.

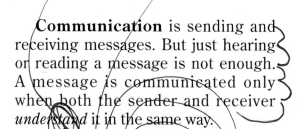

O Listening

In communication, we spend half our time listening. Yet sometimes we hear the words without getting the full meaning of the message. A good listener is an *active listener.*

An active listener gets involved in the message. This makes the message easier to understand. Being an active listener will help you succeed in the world of work. How can you become an active listener?

1. Know the purpose of the message. Know the reason you are listening.
2. Signal that you understand. Use eye contact and body language to show you understand.
3. Ask questions. If you do not understand the speaker, say so.
4. Notice voice inflections. These are the rising and falling sounds in the speaker's voice.
5. Look for the speaker's body language.
6. Decide what is important in the message.
7. Take notes on the message.
8. Listen for a conclusion to the message.

Here is a closer look at these points.

▷ Know the Purpose

You will often know the purpose of a message before the person begins to speak. Sometimes the speaker will tell you the purpose first. If he or she does not, listen for details. Think about the reason you are listening. Knowing the reason for the message will help you concentrate on it. This will make the message easier to understand.

▷ Signal Your Understanding

Let the speaker know that you understand his or her message. For example, when you are in a small group, signal your understanding of the message. You might say, "Oh," or "I see."

In a larger group, you may want to use *body language.* **Body language** is using the body to communicate meaning. For example, nod your head to show you are getting the message. If you do not understand, give a puzzled look.

▷ Ask Questions

On a new job, your boss will talk to you about how to do your work. You will listen, but you may not always understand. When you are not sure about something, say so. Ask your boss to clarify what was said.

As you learn your job, you will be given new duties. Your boss or your co-workers will give you more directions. Whenever you do not understand them, ask questions until you understand the message. Do not guess at what they mean. If you guess, you might be wrong.

▷ Notice Voice Inflections

Inflections are the rising and falling tones in a person's voice. As you listen, notice the speaker's inflections. They add meaning to the words. They help you know what the speaker feels is most important.

Inflections can sometimes help you tell whether a person is in a good mood. For example, suppose your boss greets you with "Good morning." If this is said with a rising inflection, he or she is probably in a good mood. If it is said with a falling inflection, your boss is probably not in a good mood. (Do not always assume that a falling inflection indicates a bad mood. It may simply mean that the person has other things on his or her mind.)

▲ *People often use body language to communicate. Can you name some examples of body language in this photo?*

▷ Look for Body Language

Body language adds meaning to words. A person's face often tells how he or she really feels. A smile usually means approval. Wide open eyes usually mean surprise.

Be careful not to misread body language. A person speaking to you with crossed arms, for example, might mean the person is defensive. However, it could also mean the person is focusing on giving you a message. Crossed arms do not always mean that the person is angry.

Keep your eyes on the speaker while you are listening. Look the speaker in the eye most of the time. Watch for body language while you listen. This will help you understand much more of the message.

▷ Decide What Is Important

You will not remember every point in the spoken messages you hear. No one can. So try to decide what is most important. Think about how the important points will affect you.

Here is a good way to remember important points. Picture yourself doing what the message calls for you to do. For example, suppose that your boss is describing a new project. Where will you fit in to the project? Will you be working with others? Will you be working by yourself? See yourself doing the things your boss is describing.

▷ Take Notes

Some messages will include important points about how to do your job. This is the time to take notes. Be prepared. Keep a notebook and pen handy. Write down the most important points. You can review them later. Even a few notes will help you remember much of what was said.

▷ Listen for a Conclusion

The person speaking may end the message with a conclusion. This may be a short statement about the action you or others should take. If no conclusion is given, refer to your notes. Then draw your own conclusion. If you have not taken notes, review the main points of the message.

As we listen, we all hear words that we may not know the meanings of. If this happens, write down the words. Later, look them up in a dictionary.

✔ Check Up ✔ ✔ ✔

1. List eight ways to become an active listener.
2. How can you signal that you understand a message?
3. What are voice inflections?
4. What is body language?
5. Tell one good way to remember the important points in a spoken message.

○ Blocks to Understanding

Some things keep you from being a good listener. They are called *blocks to understanding.* If you know what to look for, you can often avoid them. Watch out for these three blocks.

1. Distractions.
2. Emotional blocks.
3. Planning a response.

Here is a look at each of these blocks.

▷ Distractions

Distractions are things that take your mind off what is being said. They keep you from listening. Noise is often a distraction. For example, you probably cannot listen well when someone is cutting the grass nearby.

Another type of distraction is daydreaming. When you allow other thoughts into your mind, you will miss much of the message.

▷ Emotional Blocks

Sometimes you may have to listen to a person or to ideas you do not like. In these cases, you may find it hard to listen. So you may *block* your understanding of the message. This is called an **emotional block**. On the job, you may not do your job right if you block messages.

▲ *Distractions can prevent you from understanding what is being said. What are the distractions here? How can they be overcome?*

Suppose you disagree with the speaker's ideas. You feel that your ideas are better. How can you get them across? The first step is to listen and to understand the other person. Then you can use your speaking skills to get your ideas across. (We will look at speaking skills in the next section.)

□ **Case Study** □ □ □ □ □ □

One day, Maria allowed less than enough time to get to work. When she arrived at work, her boss scolded her for being late. She had missed a meeting.

Later in the day, Maria's boss told her exactly how to set up a new display. He thought Maria understood. But Maria had trouble listening. She was thinking about how her boss had scolded her.

After her boss left, Maria realized she did not know how to set up the display. She had blocked her boss's message. She wished she had asked him some questions.

▲ *You may want to plan your response while another person is speaking. Why should you wait until he or she has stopped talking to plan your response?*

▷ **Planning a Response**

When someone is talking to you, listen to every word. Keep tuned in. Wait until the person has stopped talking before you plan a *response* (what you will say).

You may attend some meetings at work. In these small groups, people often take turns speaking. You may want to plan your response while another person is still speaking. But if you do this, you miss much of the other person's message. Listen to the entire message. Then plan a response.

✓ **Check Up** ✓ ✓ ✓

1. What are three blocks to understanding?
2. What is an emotional block?
3. When should you plan a response?

○ Speaking

Some jobs require you to use more speaking skills than other jobs. You may not like speaking in front of others. Maybe your job will not require you to do so. Yet you still have to talk with your boss and co-workers. You will ask and answer questions. Sometimes you will try to persuade or inform people. Sometimes you will talk simply for fun.

In each situation, you will want your message to be understood. So you will need to speak clearly by using these four tips for proper speech.

- Standard English.
- Good speaking habits.
- Good voice qualities.
- Good telephone techniques.

Here is a closer look at each of these tips.

▷ Standard English

When you talk with your friends, you probably use informal language called *slang*. It is fun to use. But slang words do not mean the same thing to everyone. Do your parents always understand the meaning of words you and your friends use? Do you always understand the words your parents use?

On the job, it is important that your message is understood. When you are talking to your boss, then, do not use slang. When talking with co-workers on the job, do not use slang. Instead, you should always try to use *standard English*.

Standard English is the formal English you have learned in school. It is standard because the words mean the same to everyone. Standard English words are listed in the dictionary.

Standard English also means using good grammar. This means putting words together correctly in a sentence. For example, "Ann *has* a good job" is standard English. "Ann *have* a good job" is not. Using words such as *you know* and *like* over and over is not standard English either.

You have another advantage when you speak standard English on the job. Your boss will think of you as an educated person. He or she will think that you are capable of doing a more responsible job. This will help you advance in your career.

▷ Good Speaking Habits

Your message is only communicated when the listener understands it. Using standard English will help the listener understand you. You can also do some things to get others to be good listeners. This includes using *PEP*. PEP refers to three words that describe good speaking habits.

These are the three words.

- Pronunciation.
- Enunciation.
- Pace.

Pronunciation. How do you say the word *girl*? If you say "gurl," your *pronunciation* is correct.

Pronunciation is the way a word sounds. Learn the correct way to say words.

Enunciation. Do you speak clearly? **Enunciation** is saying each syllable clearly. Some people have lazy speaking habits. They do not say every syllable of some words. Have you ever heard someone say "didja" instead of "did you"? This is poor enunciation.

Many people drop the last sound of certain words. Have you heard "workin" instead of "working"? Again, this is poor enunciation.

Do you speak clearly? Just knowing how you sound can help you improve your speaking habits. You might try reading into a tape recorder. Then play back the tape. How well did you pronounce each word? How well did you enunciate?

Pace. How fast or slowly do you speak? **Pace** is the speed at which you speak. Some people speak so fast that you miss much of the message. It is hard to listen carefully to someone who speaks at a fast pace. You want others to understand what you say. So do not speak too fast.

★ **Tricks of the Trade** ★

PEP Tips

To pick up tips on PEP, listen to the news readers on TV. They are trained to pronounce and enunciate each word. They may speak just a little fast because they are trying to say a great deal in a short time. You can use a little slower pace when you are speaking.

On the other hand, do not speak too slowly. This will bore your listener. His or her mind will wander while you speak.

Pick a medium pace and vary it. That is, do not talk at the same pace all the time. Speak a little faster to show excitement. Speak a little slower when you want your listener to think carefully about what you say.

▷ Voice Qualities

You can also make others listen more carefully by using your voice actively. Again, try speaking into a tape recorder. Play your message back and listen to how you sound. Pay special attention to these qualities.

- Pitch.
- Volume.
- Inflections.

Pitch. Do you have a high or low voice? **Pitch** is how high or how low your voice sounds. Have you listened to someone with a highly pitched voice? His or her voice might have been annoying. So you may have blocked what that person said. It is much easier to listen to a lower pitched voice.

Both men and women can control the pitch of their voices to sound more pleasant. Practice speaking in higher and lower tones. Then find the pitch that sounds best for you.

Volume. Do you have a soft or a loud voice? **Volume** is how loudly you speak. If you speak too softly, people will not hear you. If you speak too loudly, people will not want to listen to you. Try for a volume between high and low. People will listen to you if you use correct volume.

Inflections. As you learned, inflections are the rising and falling sounds in your voice. Inflection means changing the pitch while you speak.

Most people will not listen very long to someone who does not use inflections. So use slightly rising and falling tones in your voice. This will make you a more interesting speaker. Do not overdo this, though. Using too many inflections makes your voice a boring sing-song.

▷ Speaking on the Telephone

Good telephone skills are important on the job. When you speak on the telephone, your listener cannot see you. So you cannot use body language to help get your message across. Your voice has to do it all.

◀ *Good telephone skills are important on the job. Why should you use your voice actively on the phone?*

When your telephone rings, answer right away. Callers can become unpleasant if they are kept waiting. You will be happier talking with people who are in a good mood. You will be more successful, too.

Suppose all calls come to your company through a switchboard. In that case, the operator answers with the company name. When the call is transferred to you, give the name of your department first. Then give your own name. You might say, "Service department, this is Charlotte."

If your company has no switchboard, your calls will come directly to you. Answer with the name of the company. Then give your own name. You might say, "White's Auto Shop, this is Lisa."

Some companies have their own way of answering the phone. If you are new on the job, ask your boss how you should answer calls.

How should you sound on the telephone? Always use a pleasant pitch, medium volume, and varied inflections. Most importantly, never interrupt the other person.

You will probably have to take phone messages like the one shown in Figure 1-1. Write down everything your boss wants you to write. You may have a company message pad for taking phone calls. After you write down the caller's name and number, repeat them to the caller. If you have either one wrong, the caller will correct you. If the name is long, spell it so the caller can tell you if it is right.

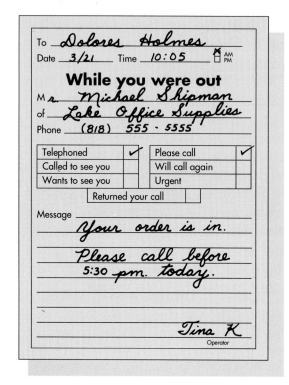

▲ *Figure 1-1*
For many jobs you will have to take phone messages. What information would you repeat back to the caller after taking this message?

✔ Check Up ✔ ✔ ✔

1. Why should you speak standard English on the job?
2. What are three good speaking habits?
3. What are three good voice qualities?
4. Why is your voice so important when you speak on the telephone?

⭕ **Reading**

Reading is much like listening. When we read, we think about the meaning of words and thoughts. We are trying to understand a message.

Reading is an important skill both on and off the job. Much of what we know we learn by reading books, magazines, newspapers, letters, and memos.

Knowing why you are reading helps you know *how* to read. For example, some things must be read carefully. Think of job application forms. You need to understand every word.

Some things, though, do not need to be read so carefully. Then you can use two skills called *previewing* and *skimming.*

▷ Previewing

When you go to a movie, you see previews of other new movies. Each preview shows just enough to give an idea of what the movie is about. **Previewing** when reading gives you just enough information to learn what the writing contains. Outlines, tables of contents, indexes, and summaries help you preview.

Suppose your boss asks you to find out what type of computers the company should buy. You will have to know how your company plans to use computers. Then you will have to read about different types of computers.

When you begin reading anything, preview it first. Read the table of contents of books and magazines. Check book indexes for specific topics. Find chapters and articles about the things you want to learn. See if they have summaries. If they do, read the summaries before you read the entire chapter or article. The summaries will tell you if the chapter or article has the information you need. Such previewing will save you time.

▷ Skimming

When you are short on time, try *skimming.* **Skimming** is reading something very quickly and picking out the main points. You are skimming when you read only the headlines in the newspaper. Sometimes you just skim articles or chapters, picking out the main points.

When you are skimming an article, look for topic sentences. A **topic sentence** is often the first sentence in each paragraph. It states the paragraph's main idea. Sometimes the topic sentence is about something you already know or something that does not interest you. In either case, skip that paragraph and look for the next topic sentence. When you find one that is of interest, read the whole paragraph. By skimming, you can read more of the information you need.

▷ Reading for Meaning

Reading for meaning is very important on the job. It is a skill that improves with practice. These three tips will help you read for meaning.

1. Focus your mind.
2. Use your mind's eye.
3. Use the dictionary.

Focus Your Mind. This means to think about what you are reading. Sometimes this is easy to do. It is easy when you are rested and when you have an interest in what you are reading. What happens when you are tired? What happens when you have no interest in what you are reading? Your mind wanders to other thoughts. Learn to notice when this happens. When it does, force your mind to think about what you are reading.

Use Your Mind's Eye. You may have heard people speak about the mind's eye. This means using your mind to form a picture. Close your eyes and think about your best friend. Can you picture his or her face? When you read short stories or novels, you form pictures in your mind about the story and the people in it. Learn to do this when you are reading for meaning. It will help you remember the message.

▶ *When you are tired, it is hard to read for meaning. Why is it important to focus your mind when you read?*

Use the Dictionary. When reading, do you sometimes skip over words you do not know? Many people do. This is a bad habit. It can keep you from understanding the message.

When you see a word you do not know, look it up in a dictionary. It takes extra time. But it is worth the time. It will help you to understand the message. Also, you will know the meaning the next time you come across the same word.

▲ *When reading, use the dictionary to look up any words you do not know. What might happen if you skip over the words you do not know?*

▲ *Using your mind's eye when you read will help you remember the message. What has this person done to help him remember the message?*

✔ Check Up ✔ ✔ ✔

1. What are two skills that can help you read faster?
2. What would you preview in a book?
3. When should you skim your reading?
4. What are three things you can do to help you read for meaning?

A Desire to Succeed

Bree Walker

Bree Walker is a TV news reporter in Los Angeles. When she goes out in public, people notice her. She never knows exactly why. Do people recognize her from TV? Or are they looking at her hands?

Bree was born with many of her toes and fingers joined. Kids teased her and called her names. She hated wearing the special shoes she needed. But her parents would not let her feel sorry for herself.

Bree wanted to be a reporter. She applied for a job at a newspaper. She was not hired because she could not type. So she worked at radio stations as a disk jockey. Sometimes she was given the opportunity to read the news.

After eight years in radio, Bree tried to get a job in TV. News directors said the public would not accept her appearance. So she had a pair of artificial hands made. Still, no one hired her.

Finally, a news director in San Diego hired her. She wore her false hands on the air a few times. But she just did not feel comfortable wearing them. So one day, she simply took them off. The public response was good. Many people called the station to encourage her. She is now a successful and respected TV news reporter.

Bree feels it is important to respect people for what they can do. She makes national speeches about issues facing the disabled. Her work has earned her several awards. She has used her communication skills to help show the world that desire and hard work help people achieve despite their challenges.

⊙ Writing

Speaking to someone is an easy and quick way to send a message. But most people forget about half of a spoken message within 24 hours. So it is often better to write your message. When you do so, you have more time to plan what you want to say. If the message is not clear, you can change it. In fact, you can rewrite it several times.

People remember what they read longer than what they hear. When you speak to someone, you only say it once. So the other person only hears the message once. When you write your message, the receiver can read it over and over. It is a permanent record. For these reasons, written messages are very important in the world of work.

During your working life, you will write many messages. If you write clear messages, the receiver will understand them. You can write clear messages if you do these things.

- Know your reader.
- Know the purpose.
- Use a direct style.
- Use correct form.

▷ Know Your Reader

Before you begin writing, think about who will read it. Suppose you are writing the same message to several people. Who are they? What do they know about your topic? Suppose they do not know much at all about it. In that case, you may need to introduce them to it. This will help them understand the main points of your message.

What if you are writing to someone who knows a great deal about the topic? Then you will not need much of an introduction.

▲ *Good writing skills are important in the working world. Can you name some ways writing skills are used on the job?*

▷ Know the Purpose

Every message has a purpose. Before you begin writing, think about why you are writing. Most of your writing will be for one of these four reasons.

1. To inform.
2. To request.
3. To complain.
4. To persuade.

▷ Use a Direct Style

The owner or top management of a business often sets the style of writing for company messages. You will probably get copies of some company memos and letters. Save them. You can look at the style in which they were written when you write your own messages.

Most companies today prefer a direct writing style. It uses only the words needed to write a clear message. Do not use big words to show off your vocabulary. Remember, you want others to understand your message.

▷ Use Correct Form

The two written forms used most often in business are memos and letters. Write a memo when you send messages to someone in your own company. Memos are usually short. Most are only one or two pages. They cover only one topic. Memos have five

parts. These are the date, the receiver, the sender, the subject or topic, and the body.

Write a letter to anyone outside your own company. Most business letters include these seven standard parts.

1. Return address.
2. Date.
3. Inside address.
4. Salutation.
5. Body.
6. Closing.
7. Signature and typed name.

Study the samples of a business letter and memo in Figures 1-2 and 1-3 on page 21. They will guide you as you prepare your own memos and letters. Use a typewriter or a computer to write your letters. If you use a computer, it will be much easier to make any desired corrections.

✔ Check Up ✔ ✔ ✔

1. Why is it sometimes better to write a message than to just say it?
2. What are four things you should do in order to write clear messages?
3. What are four reasons for writing messages?
4. What writing style is best for most messages?

JTC
Jones Tire Center
212 Oak Street, Austin, TX 78710
(412) 654-3210

Date — | June 6, 19 - -

Inside
Address — | Mr. John Wolf
Bates Rubber Company
12 East Fern Street
Dallas, TX 75221

Salutation — | Dear Mr. Wolf:

I have reviewed your company's listings of tires. You have many sizes and styles of tires from which to choose.

Body — | Can you allow your usual 40 percent discount on orders of 12 tires of each size? Over a period of a year, I would expect to buy about $30,000 worth of tires from your company.

Thank you for your consideration. I look forward to hearing from you.

Sincerely,

Carole Jones

Closing
Signature
and Typed
Name

Carole Jones

▶ *Figure 1-2*
Most business letters contain seven standard parts. What part contains the message?

▶ *Figure 1-3*
Memos are messages you write to someone in your company. What is the purpose of this memo?

M E M O R A N D U M

Date: June 9, 19 - - |—— Date

To: Ann Byers

From: Don Walter |—— Sender
          President

Subject: Staff Meeting |—— Subject or Topic

Our next staff meeting will be held in the conference room on June 18. We will start the meeting at 8 a.m. We will go over our sales plans for the coming year. |—— Body

Chapter 1 Review

Chapter Summary

- Communication is sending and receiving information.
- In communication, the sender and receiver must understand the message in the same way.
- The four basic communication skills are listening, speaking, reading, and writing.
- A good listener is an active listener.
- People speak to inform, persuade, or entertain.
- A good reader knows why he or she is reading.
- Good writers know their readers and their purpose for writing.
- Written messages are remembered longer and provide written records.

Reviewing Vocabulary

Listed below are the important new words that were used in this chapter. Next to each word is the page on which you will find the word. Turn to that page and read the paragraph in which the word is printed in **bold** type. On a separate piece of paper, write the word and its meaning. Then write a sentence of your own using each word.

1. communication (5)
2. body language (6)
3. inflections (7)
4. distractions (9)
5. emotional block (9)
6. standard English (11)
7. pronunciation (12)
8. enunciation (12)
9. pace (12)
10. pitch (13)
11. volume (13)
12. previewing (15)
13. skimming (15)
14. topic sentence (15)

Looking at the Facts

1. What is communication?
2. What are the four basic skills of communication?
3. List eight activities that can help you to be an active listener.
4. What are three common blocks to understanding what a speaker is saying?
5. What four tips will help you to speak clearly?
6. PEP refers to what three words?
7. What two reading skills are helpful when you do not have to read carefully?
8. List three tips that can help you read for meaning.
9. List four rules to follow in order to write clear messages.

Thinking Critically

1. Suppose you are a supervisor. You need to inform employees about an important meeting.

Which method of communication would you choose to do this? Why would you choose this method?

2. You are to read several trade journals and gather information for an important talk. You need to have the material ready by the next day. What skills would you use to do this?

3. You are giving a talk. You see that few people have their eyes on you. What might that tell you? What are two things you could do to get their attention?

4. You have to write a report on a project you are managing. What four things will you need to do to write a clear report?

Discussing Chapter Concepts

1. Name five careers in which the ability to speak well is important.

2. List three careers in which people need to be good listeners in order to succeed.

3. This chapter discussed four basic methods of communication. What other forms of communication can you name?

Using Basic Skills

Math

1. You work at a pizzeria. You just took a phone order for 16 sausage pizzas, 12 mushroom pizzas, and 3 cheese pizzas. What will the total be if each pizza costs $8?

Communication

2. Suppose you are applying for a job you would really like. The application asks you to write a paragraph about why you would be a good person for the job. Write the name of a job you would like. Write a 25-word paragraph to complete the application.

Human Relations

3. Your boss has given you and your co-workers written instructions. You read the instructions carefully. You notice several spelling errors. You also notice some instructions that you think are wrong. What would you say to your boss?

Activities for Enrichment

1. Record a passage from a book on a tape recorder. What do you notice about your pronunciation, enunciation, and pace? Record yourself again. Listen for improvements.

2. For the next week, write down ten words from your reading that you do not know. Look each word up in the dictionary. Write a short definition of each word.

3. Clip three examples of body language in magazines. Bring them to class. Talk to your classmates about the body language in each photo. Do you all agree on what the body language is saying?

Math and Calculator Skills

Words to learn and use

Here are the new terms you will learn in this chapter. Challenge yourself. Read through the list to see if you know what they mean.

percent
discount
shipping charge
cash drawer
reimburse
fraction

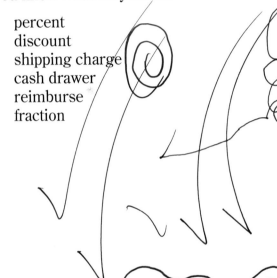

Build on what you know

You already know...
- calculators solve problems fast.
- math is required on many jobs.
- making change is required on many jobs.
- many companies pay travel expenses.
- weighing and measuring are a part of many jobs.

In this chapter you will learn...
- how to use a calculator to solve math problems.
- how to use math skills in sales.
- how to make change.
- how to record travel expenses.
- how to weigh and measure.

Math skills are required on more jobs today than in the past. Think of any job you could do. There is probably some math involved in it. You may have to use a calculator. You may also make change. You will probably have to solve some basic math problems.

In this chapter you will brush up on how to use a calculator to solve math problems. You will learn how math skills are used on the job. You will learn how to make change. You will also learn how to solve some of the math problems you might face on the job.

O Using a Calculator

Calculators are used in many types of work. You may have already used one at home or at your job. You may have noticed that not all calculators are the same. Some are for solving simple problems. Others are for solving business or science problems.

Each type and brand of calculator looks different. Some of the keys may be in different places. But all calculators add, subtract, multiply, and divide. Most have percent and memory keys, too.

Besides number keys, most calculators have these keys.

ON/OFF	Turns the calculator on and off.
+	Addition
−	Subtraction
x	Multiplication
÷	Division
=	Equals
%	Percent
CE	Clears last entry only.

C	Clears calculator.
·	Decimal point
CM	Clears the memory.
RM	Recalls the total amount in the memory.
M+	Adds the number showing on the display to the number in the memory. The amount showing on the display is not changed. The amount in the memory is increased.
M−	Subtracts the number on the display from the number in the memory. The amount showing on the display is not changed. The amount in the memory is decreased.

▷ Clearing Your Calculator

To begin using your calculator, first turn it on with the ON/OFF key. Then enter numbers by pressing the number keys. If you enter the wrong number, press the CE key. This will clear only your last entry.

Suppose you want to add 87 and 25. You press ⑧ and ⑦. Then you press ⊕. Then you press ③ and ⑤. The last entry, 35, was a mistake. So press the CE key, then press ② and ⑤. Press the = key. The answer is 112.

Sometimes you will want to redo the whole problem. If so, press the C key. This will clear all entries. Then you can start over. On some calculators, the clear key is marked AC (all clear).

▷ Percents

Many jobs require working with *percents*. **Percent** means parts per hundred. A penny is one cent. It is also one-hundredth of a dollar. So a penny is 1 percent of a dollar.

Most calculators have a percent key. Use the percent key to solve problems like the one below.

To find 35 percent of $500, enter ⑤ ⓪ ⓪, press ✕, enter ③ and ⑤, and press the % key. The answer 175 is shown.

What if your calculator does not have a percent key? Then you must change the percent to a decimal number. Do this by moving the decimal two places to the left. Thus, 35 percent becomes .35, and 2 percent becomes .02.

To find 5 percent of $315, enter ③ ① ⑤ and press the ✕ key. Change 5 percent to .05 and enter ⋅ ⓪ ⑤. Press the = key. The answer 15.75 is shown.

▲ *In many jobs, you will have to figure percentages. When would this waitress figure percentages?*

✓ Check Up ✓ ✓ ✓

1. What are four things that all calculators do?
2. What do the CE and C keys do?
3. What does percent mean?

O Math in Sales

More than 25 million people in the U.S. work in sales. Salespeople use math daily. The math skills they use are also used in many other jobs.

▷ Sales Slips

Most businesses record their sales on sales slips. Even some businesses that use the newest types of cash registers use sales slips.

When you write a sales slip, you will add and subtract numbers. You may multiply and divide numbers, too.

Look at the sales slip on this page. The customer bought three shirts and six pairs of socks. The shirts were $25 each. The socks were $2 per pair. What math skills are required to find out how much the customer paid? Follow these five steps.

1. Find the total price for the shirts. Multiply the number of shirts by the price.

$$3 \times \$25 = \$75$$

2. Find the total price for the socks. Multiply the number of socks by the price.

$$6 \times \$2 = \$12$$

3. Find the total for the clothing. Add the prices for shirts and for socks.

$$\$12 + \$75 = \$87$$

4. Figure the sales tax. Multiply the total price of the goods by the sales tax. Suppose the rate is 6 percent.

$$\$87 \times .06 = \$5.22$$

5. Add the tax to the total price of the goods.

$$\$87 + \$5.22 = \$92.22$$

▲ *Figure 2-1*
Sales slips are used to record a purchase. What would the final total be if the sales tax was 5 percent?

☐ Case Study ☐ ☐ ☐ ☐ ☐ ☐

Marco was a sales clerk. He was eager to learn other tasks at the store where he worked. He was pleased when his boss asked him to write an order for some store merchandise. His boss asked him not to spend more than $300 for the order.

Marco carefully selected items he thought would sell well. He wrote the order out neatly on a special order form. He added up the amount he had spent and mailed the order that afternoon.

A week later, the order arrived. Marco's boss asked him to unpack the merchandise.

Marco opened the box and the bill for the merchandise. The total on the bill was $440. Marco checked the bill. The company that sent the merchandise had made a mistake. It had charged $165 instead of $16.50 for two shirts that were priced at $8.25 each!

Marco told his boss about the mistake. Marco's boss praised him for checking the order. If Marco had not done this, his boss would have overpaid for the order. Marco saved his boss from losing $148.50. Marco realized that it was very important to check the math on sales slips before paying for the merchandise.

▷ Discounts

Some businesses offer *discounts*. A **discount** is a reduced price. Some businesses give discounts to their employees. Some stores have special sales. They may give a discount to everyone who buys during the sale.

There are many types of discounts. Most discounts involve two steps.

1. Multiply the price times the percent of discount.

2. Subtract the amount of the discount from the price. (Subtract discounts before adding sales tax.)

For example, suppose the price of a CD player is $250. A special sale gives customers a discount of 25 percent. What is the discounted price? To figure the discount, follow the two steps.

1. Multiply the price times the discount.

$$\$250 \times .25 = \$62.50$$

2. Subtract the discount from the price.

$$\$250 - \$62.50 = \$187.50$$

The discounted price is $187.50.

▷ Shipping Charge

A **shipping charge** is the cost of sending goods to the customer. The customer usually pays the charge.

Some businesses charge a percent of the total order. To figure the cost for shipping, multiply the price of the goods by the percent charged.

Suppose a company charges 5 percent of the total order for shipping. What would the shipping charge be if the total order is $78? Multiply the total amount by the percent charged.

$$\$78 \times .05 = \$3.90$$

Many businesses use a chart to find shipping charges. In these cases, you will have to weigh the package. Then you will find the weight on a shipping chart. The chart will tell you how much to charge for shipping.

★ Tricks of the Trade ★

Figuring Sales Slips with Shipping Charges

Figure the math on sales slips in this order.

1. Find the amount for goods.
2. Figure and subtract any discount.
3. Figure and add sales tax.
4. Find the total for the goods.
5. Figure and add shipping charges to the total.

▷ Making Change

If you take a job in sales, you will probably use a cash register. The money you collect from sales and use to make change is placed in the *cash drawer.* The **cash drawer** is the name for the money drawer of the cash register.

The cash drawer is divided into ten sections. Five large sections in the back of the drawer are used for checks and bills. Five small sections in the front are used for coins. The placement of checks, bills, and coins in a cash drawer is shown in Figure 2-2 on page 31.

In making change, you need to be accurate. You need to be quick, too. Customers want to pay and leave.

To make change, enter the sale in the cash register. Then say aloud the total amount of the sale, such as "$8.68." Some customers will pay the exact amount. In these cases, you will not have to make change. Most customers, though, will offer you a larger amount. They may hand you a $10 bill or a $20 bill.

Suppose the customer hands you a $10 bill. Say, "that's $8.68 out of $10." Place the $10 bill on the shelf above the cash drawer. Leave it there until you have given change to the customer. Then the customer cannot say he or she gave you a larger bill.

Count the change in your head as you take coins and bills from the cash drawer. Count up from the purchase

▲ *Figure 2-2*
Most cash drawers are organized as shown here. Bills are placed in the back and coins in the front. How does this arrangement help you to make change?

price. Begin with pennies if needed. Stop when you get to the amount the customer gave you. Hand the change to the customer in the order you took it from the cash drawer. Say again the amount of the sale and the amount the customer handed you. As you give change, say the amount you are handing the customer.

In this example, here is what you would say to the customer.

$8.68 out of $10.
$8.70, (give two pennies).
$8.75, (give a nickel).
$9, (give a quarter).
$10, (give a dollar).

Many new cash registers figure the amount of change due the customer. In this case, begin with the largest coin or bill. Suppose the cash register shows that the change due is $3.35. Count in your head "$3, $3.25, $3.35" as you take change from the cash drawer. The customer can see the change due is $3.35. So you can give change beginning with the largest bills and coins.

In this example, here is what you would say to the customer.

$3, (give three dollars).
$3.25, (give a quarter).
$3.35, (give a dime).

✔ **Check Up** ✔ ✔ ✔

1. What math skills are required when writing sales slips?
2. What is a discount?
3. How do you figure the price on a discounted item?
4. Are shipping charges added to a sale before or after taxes are added?
5. Where do you put a $20 bill when making change for a $9 sale?
6. When you give a customer change, do you count up or count down from the price?

O Expense
Accounts

You may have to travel on your job. If so, your company will *reimburse* you for travel expenses. To **reimburse** means to pay back. If your company reimburses you, it pays you back for the money you spent on company business. This includes what you spent for meals, lodging, and auto expenses. Sometimes there are other expenses, such as telephone calls and parking fees.

How will you keep track of all these expenses? Write them down. Your boss may give you an account book or expense forms. Either way, write down all of your expenses. Also, keep your receipts to show that you paid your bills. You will submit your receipts with your expense form.

Most companies limit the amount they will pay for meals and lodging. Suppose your company will pay up to $30 a day for meals. It also pays up to $60 a night for lodging. You may want to order expensive meals. You may want to stay in a fancy hotel. What if you spend more than the company allows? The company will still pay only $30 a day for meals and $60 a night for lodging. You will have to pay the rest.

Suppose you drive a company car. The company will pay you back for the gas. In fact, it will pay you back for all of your auto expenses.

Some people drive their own cars on the job. For this, most companies pay a rate per mile. For example, suppose your company pays you 30 cents per mile. You drive 425 miles one week. To find out how much the company will pay you for the use of your car, multiply the miles you drive by the rate per mile.

$$425 \times .30 = \$127.50$$

Look at Rosa Sanchez's expense report on page 33. Rosa drives a company car. So under the word *Auto,* she wrote in the amount she spent for gas and other car expenses. She also wrote in the amount she spent for meals, lodging, and other items. What if she must spend money for something that is not on the report? Then she would write it under the word *Misc.* (miscellaneous).

At the end of the week, Rosa added up the total for each day. She wrote the total at the end of each line, on the right. She also added the total for each expense. She wrote these totals along the bottom of the report.

Finally, she added the totals for each day to get the week's total. She wrote the week's total in the lower right corner. She also added the totals along the bottom for each expense. They were the same as the totals for

EXPENSE REPORT						

PRINT NAME		DEPT. OR SALES OFFICE	DATE OF TRIP	FROM	TO	
Rosa Sanchez		Dallas		9/2	9/6	

DATE	MEALS	LODGING	AUTO	POSTAGE, TELEPHONE	MISC.	TOTALS
9/2	$22.11	$46.02	$6.18	—	—	$74.31
9/3	26.92	51.81	8.21	9.45	3.00	99.39
9/4	34.16	54.92	7.16	—	6.00	102.24
9/5	32.11	51.10	6.14	7.31	—	96.66
9/6	30.01	51.10	—	4.34	2.00	87.45
TOTALS	$145.31	$254.95	$27.69	$21.10	$11.00	$460.05

▲ *Figure 2-3*
You fill out an expense report to get reimbursed for travel expenses.
How much did Rosa spend from 9/2 to 9/6 on meals?

each day. If they had not been the same, she would know that she had made a mistake.

Check Rosa's expense report. What were her total expenses for the week? Total expenses are in the lower right corner of the report.

Suppose her company pays up to $25 per day for food. How much of her own money will she pay for food for the week?

1. Multiply the number of days by the amount the company pays per day.

$$\$25 \times 5 \text{ days} = \$125$$

2. Subtract the amount her company will pay her from the amount Rosa spent.

$$\$145.31 - \$125 = \$20.31$$

Rosa will have to pay $20.31 for food.

▶ *You will submit your receipts with your expense report. Tell three types of receipts you might submit.*

Suppose her company pays $50 per night for lodging. How much of her own money will she pay for lodging for the week?

1. Multiply the number of nights by the amount the company pays per night.

$$\$50 \times 5 \text{ days} = \$250$$

2. Subtract the amount the company will pay for lodging from the total amount spent for lodging.

$$\$254.95 - \$250 = \$4.95$$

Rosa will have to pay $4.95 of her own money for lodging.

What percentage of her expenses were reimbursed? Total expenses were $460.05. Rosa paid $20.31 (for food) and $4.95 (for lodging).

1. Add the amount Rosa paid.

$$\$20.31 + \$4.95 = \$25.26$$

2. Subtract what Rosa paid from the total expenses.

$$\$460.05 - \$25.26 = \$434.79$$

The company paid $434.79.

3. Divide what the company paid by the total.

$$434.79 \div 460.05 = .945$$

4. Round the answer to two places. The company paid 95 percent of Rosa's expenses.

✓ Check Up ✓ ✓ ✓

1. What are three expenses that your company may pay?
2. Why must you keep your receipts for travel expenses?
3. How can you double check your totals on expense reports?

O Weighing and Measuring

You weigh and measure things almost daily. Have you ever baked a cake? If so, you measured milk, flour, and sugar. If you have ever hung wallpaper, you measured each strip.

Many jobs require weighing and measuring, too. If you work in shipping, for example, you will weigh the goods being shipped. Perhaps you will measure each box being shipped.

There is a way to describe things that are weighed and measured. In describing something weighed, you tell the number of units being weighed and the unit of measure. For example, suppose you buy five pounds of sugar.

Five is the number of units being weighed. *Pounds* is the unit of weight.

This same type of description applies to measuring things, too. For example, if you buy two yards of material, *two* is the number of units being measured. *Yard* is the unit of measure.

Units of weight include ounce and pound. Units of liquid weight include fluid ounce, pint, quart, and gallon. Units of measure include inch, foot, yard, and mile.

You will be able to work with measurements if you are familiar with these units of measure.

◀ *Many jobs require weighing and measuring. Do you think the person shown here is using quarts or pounds as a unit of measure?*

Units of Weight
16 ounces (oz) = 1 pound (lb)
2,000 pounds (lb) = 1 ton (T)

Units of Length
12 inches (in) = 1 foot (ft)
3 feet (ft) = 1 yard (yd)
5,280 feet (ft) = 1 mile (mi)

Units of Liquid Measure
16 ounces (oz) = 1 pint (pt)
2 pints (pt) = 1 quart (qt)
4 quarts (qt) = 1 gallon (gal)

▲ *Three common tools used to measure and weigh are the scale, the ruler, and the measuring cup. Which is used for liquid measure? Which measures units of length? Which measures weight?*

Did you notice that each unit has its own abbreviation? For example, *lb* is short for pound. *T* is short for ton. Often, the abbreviation is used more than the word for the unit.

▷ Unit Prices

Most products have a set price per unit. This is called the *unit price*. A load of sand may sell for $10 a ton. Fabric for a new dress may sell for $9 a yard. Gasoline may sell for $1.40 a gallon. You have probably seen the unit prices on the shelves at the market. You have also seen the price per gallon displayed at gas stations.

If you are a salesperson, you will sometimes sell smaller amounts than the priced unit. For example, you may sell only a third of a yard of fabric. To figure the amount to charge the customer, you must use *fractions*.

A **fraction** is part of a whole number. One-half is a fraction. It means one-half of the whole number 1. One-third is the fraction that means one-third of the number 1. One-fourth is the fraction that means one-fourth of the number 1.

Suppose you sell candy for $4 a pound. If your customer only wants one-half of a pound of candy, what will you charge?

You would charge half of the price per pound. To solve this problem, divide the price for one pound by two.

$$\$4 \text{ (per pound)} \div 2 = \$2$$

▲ *The per unit price labels at the supermarket tell you how much an item costs per unit. How might these labels be helpful when comparing two brands of the same product?*

The customer wants $2 worth of candy. Of course, you will have to add sales tax to get the final selling price.

Suppose you work in a fabric store. A customer picks out some ribbon. You measure it. It is 19 feet long. The price of ribbon is $3 per yard.

How do you know how much to charge your customer? First, see how many yards are in 19 feet. You know that there are three feet in every yard. So divide the number of feet in the length of ribbon (19 feet) by 3.

$$19 \text{ feet} \div 3 = 6\frac{1}{3}$$

The customer wants $6\frac{1}{3}$ yards of ribbon.

Next, multiply the number of yards the customer wants by the price per yard.

$$6\frac{1}{3} \times \$3 = \$19$$

You will charge the customer $19 for the ribbon.

✔ Check Up ✔ ✔ ✔

1. What are the two parts of every measurement?
2. What are three units of length?
3. What is a unit price?

A Desire to Succeed

Frank Woolworth

Frank Woolworth was born on a farm in New York state in 1845. His family was very poor. Frank was a frail boy. A hard day in the fields often left him too tired to eat.

Even as a young boy, Frank Woolworth dreamed of owning his own store. He believed he could have his dream if he worked hard enough.

Frank enjoyed school. At 16, he finished eighth grade. His father expected him to work on the farm, but Frank had other ideas. He asked his mother to send him to bookkeeping school. She agreed and gave him all her savings for tuition.

Frank finished bookkeeping school and looked for a job in one of the stores in town. No one wanted to hire a farm boy. Frank returned to the farm and worked for four unhappy years. But he kept looking for a store job. Finally, a store owner agreed to hire him if he would work three months for no pay. Frank jumped at the chance.

He worked 14 hours a day. He was not a good salesman, so he did stock work and cleaning. Frank spent many years working long hours for low pay. He learned as much as he could about running a store.

Finally, Frank felt ready to put his ideas to work in a store of his own. He wanted a store where nothing cost more than ten cents. His first store failed, but he did not give up. He learned from his mistakes and opened a second store. This store was a big success. Frank's dream grew. He opened many successful stores. Years later, he owned more than 100 stores. Frank Woolworth became a millionaire. His dreams and hard work paid off.

O Figuring Mileage

If you drive a car on your job, you will have to record your mileage. You must write down the number of miles you drive each day. You may need to find the number of miles you drive per gallon of gas.

Recording the miles you drive is easy. Before you start out, check your odometer. It measures the distance traveled. Write down the miles that show on the odometer. At the end of the day, check the odometer again. Subtract the beginning number from the miles that show at the end of the day.

Suppose your odometer shows 45,853 before you start out. At the end of the day, it shows 46,115. Subtract to find the number of miles driven.

$$46,115 - 45,853 = 262$$

The total number driven is 262 miles.

Finding the miles driven per gallon is easy, too. When you first fill your gas tank, write down the number of miles on your odometer. The next time you buy gas, write down the new number on your odometer. Subtract the beginning number from the new number. This will tell you how many miles you have gone. Then divide the number of miles you have driven by the number of gallons of gas.

For example, suppose your odometer showed 36,000 miles. The next time you stopped for gas, the odometer showed 36,262. To fill the tank, you bought 14.6 gallons of gas. Here is how you figure the miles driven per gallon.

$$36,262 - 36,000 = 262 \text{ (miles driven)}$$

$$262 \div 14.6 = 17.945 \text{ (miles per gallon)}$$

Round the answer to one place. You drove 17.9 miles per gallon.

▲ *This odometer shows 6,624 miles. How far must this car travel before it shows 7,500 miles?*

✔ **Check Up** ✔ ✔ ✔

1. Why do you need to write down the odometer mileage before you start out?
2. Why do you need to write down the number of gallons of gas you put in your car?

Chapter 2 Review

Chapter Summary

- Calculators can be used to solve all kinds of math problems.
- Calculators do not all work in the same way.
- Many jobs require working with percents.
- Good math skills are useful on the job and in everyday life.
- Figuring discounts and making change are common uses of math on the job.
- For some jobs, it is necessary to know how to weigh and measure, figure unit prices, and figure expenses.

Reviewing Vocabulary

Listed below are the new words that were used in this chapter. Next to each word is the page on which you will find the word. Turn to that page and read the paragraph in which the word is printed in **bold** type. Then use the words from this list to complete each of the sentences that follow. Write each completed sentence on your paper.

1. percent (27)
2. discount (29)
3. shipping charge (30)
4. cash drawer (30)
5. reimburse (32)
6. fraction (36)

1. When you must travel for your job, your employer may ////// you for your expenses.
2. If you have fifty cents, you have fifty /////// of one dollar.
3. A cashier must put the money from sales in the right compartments in the ///////.
4. Buyers who have goods sent out of town must usually pay for the ////////.
5. You receive a ////// when you buy goods at a sale price.
6. A //////// is a part of a whole number.

Looking at the Facts

1. Name four basic math functions that all calculators can perform.
2. When should you use the CE key on a calculator?
3. What does the C key on a calculator do?
4. How do you change a percent to a decimal?
5. What is a sales slip?
6. Describe the two steps you must follow to figure a discount.
7. How do you figure the cost for shipping?
8. What is a cash drawer?
9. Name three types of expenses that might be listed on an expense account.

10. Name three types of units of measurement.
11. What is a fraction?
12. How do you figure miles per gallon?

Thinking Critically

1. You are mailing a purchase to a customer. The goods being purchased are on sale for 25 percent off the regular price. Why must you figure the sales tax *after* you figure the sale price?
2. You are on a five-day business trip. Your company pays for all your business expenses. During those five days you meet with several business people and take them out to lunch. You also meet an old friend and take her out to dinner. You make several long distance phone calls to set up business appointments. Which of these expenses will you include on your expense account?
3. Your company pays you 30 cents for every mile you drive your car on the job. Do you think your company cares what kind of car you drive? Explain your answer.

Discussing Chapter Concepts

1. You will probably use calculators and cash registers on the job. Why is it still important to understand how to do math problems *without* these tools?

2. Some companies reimburse workers for all expenses. Other companies allow only a set amount for each type of expense. Which do you think is a better method? Why?
3. Name four times when you have measured something this week.

Using Basic Skills

Math
1. You are shopping for a new pair of jeans. One store has them on sale for $19.99. Another store is advertising them at 40 percent off the regular price of $31. Which store offers the best buy?

Communication
2. Read your local newspaper. Cut out two ads, articles, and/or charts that use math. Bring your clippings to school for a bulletin board display.

Human Relations
3. Your boss takes money from the cash drawer and asks you to run errands for her. The next day she tells you that the cash drawer was short at the end of the day. She expects you to be more accurate. What should you do? How might you help to keep this from happening again?

Activity for Enrichment

Make a collage of at least four careers that use math skills.

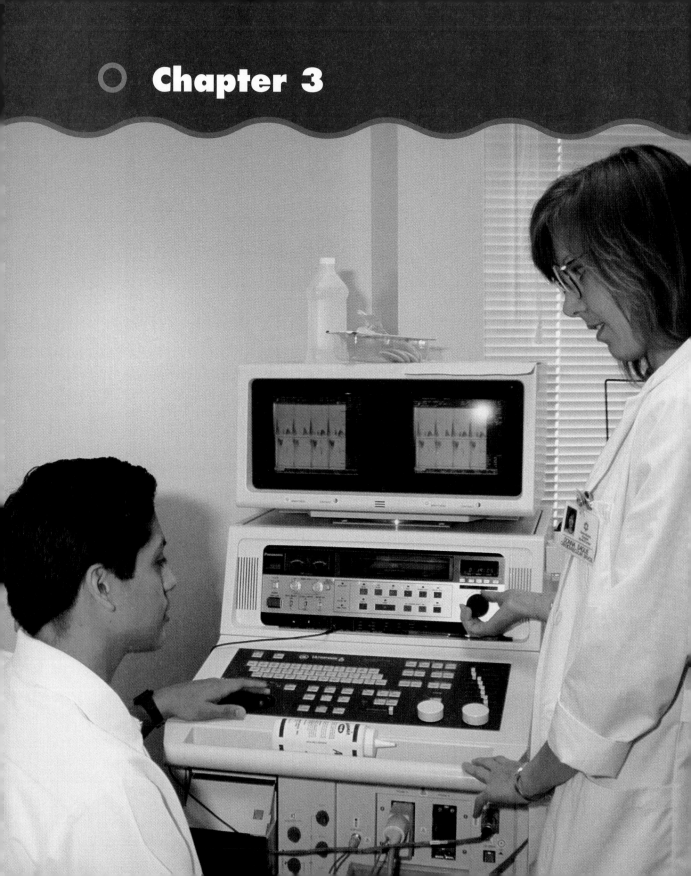

Introduction to Computers

Words to learn and use

Here are the new terms you will learn in this chapter. Challenge yourself. Read through the list to see if you know what they mean.

scanner
data
hardware
cursor
system unit
CPU
modem
plotter
mouse
software

Build on what you know

You already know...
- computers are a part of our everyday lives.
- computers can do many different jobs.
- computers must be given instructions.
- many people use a computer at home.

In this chapter you will learn...
- how computers affect our lives.
- what jobs are most often done on computers.
- the parts of a computer.
- how instructions are given to computers.
- how to buy a computer.

Your work will likely include using a computer. You may have already used one at school or on the job.

Computers are used in fast-food restaurants. They are used in clothing and video stores. They are used in auto parts stores. In fact, you see them just about everywhere.

In this chapter, you will learn how computers are changing our lives. You will learn the parts of a computer and what computers can do. You will learn the different uses for computers on the job. Finally, you will learn how to buy a computer.

O Computers in Our Lives

Computers affect our lives every day. At school, computers are used to help enroll you in classes. This helps shorten your wait in line. At the market, a computer reads the price codes on the items you buy. This ensures accuracy. At a retail store, a computer keeps track of the number of items in stock. In health care, computers can contain medical information. Many people use computers at home, too.

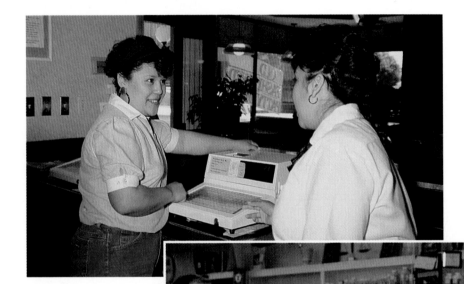

▲ *Computers are used in many types of businesses. Name three businesses in which you have seen computers used.*

▷ Business

Do you sometimes shop for food at a market? Do you buy hamburgers at a fast-food restaurant? Do you buy music tapes or CDs? Most businesses record these purchases on a computer. The computer keeps track of all sales. It also prints out your receipt.

Do you use a credit card? If not, you probably will in the future. What happens when you use a credit card? The sales clerk enters the card number into a computer. It checks to see if your credit card can be used for the purchase.

Many businesses use a *scanner* to read the numbers on credit cards. A **scanner** is a tool that reads *data* and saves it in a computer. **Data** is another word for facts.

▷ Health Care

Have you visited a doctor? If so, your name and health records are probably in the doctor's computer.

Computers are used in hospitals to check patients who are ill. A computer can check blood pressure and heart rate. It shows both on a screen. Doctors and nurses can watch the screen to see how the patient is doing.

Some computers use X-rays to see through the body. This helps doctors find the causes of illness.

Finally, computers are used in the study of diseases. They are helping to find the cause of many diseases.

▷ At Home

Computers have changed the way we live and work. For example, because of computers, some people do not travel to an office. Instead, they work at home on a computer. Some are able to use computers to communicate with a main computer at the workplace. Others send their work through the mail. They may go to work only once a week for a meeting. This helps cut down on problems such as traffic jams, smog, and crowded parking lots.

Many people start their own businesses at home. The computer makes it easy for them to do such work as bookkeeping and writing.

There are dozens of other uses for computers at home. Some people use them to write letters. Others use them to keep their bank account records. Whatever the use, computers are real time-savers.

✔ Check Up ✔ ✔ ✔

1. What are three ways computers are used in business?
2. Name three places you have seen computers used.
3. What is data?
4. How are computers used in health care?
5. How does a computer help people do their work at home?

O Today's Computers

The computers that scan prices at the market serve one purpose. Computers used in health care often serve only one purpose, too. Other computers, though, can be used for many purposes. They are used in every type of business. These all purpose computers are the ones we will study in this chapter.

Every year brings smaller and more powerful computers. The first computers were very big. They often filled up a large room. One made in the 1940s weighed 175 tons! It is in a museum in Boston.

Today, even the most powerful computers weigh only a few hundred pounds. They are used by some of the biggest companies. Most businesses, though, use smaller computers. The most popular size fits on a desktop. You may have seen them at school or on the job. These *desktop computers,* also called *personal computers*, are very powerful. They can do more work than the biggest computers of a few years ago. They work much faster, too.

An even smaller type of computer weighs less than 10 pounds. It fits on a person's lap. It is called a *laptop computer.* One model weighs just over a pound. It can run for up to 100 hours on two flashlight batteries!

▷ Computer Hardware

The parts of a computer system that you can touch are called **hardware**. The hardware includes three basic parts shown in Figure 3-1.

- The keyboard.
- The monitor.
- The system unit.

All of these parts work together. Here is a look at each part.

The Keyboard. You will use the keyboard to enter data into the computer. Keyboards are divided into at least four areas.

1. Typing keys.
2. Numeric key pad.
3. Cursor keys.
4. Function keys.

You use the typing keys just like typewriter keys. So if you can type on a typewriter, you can type on a computer.

Only the larger keyboards have a numeric key pad. If your keyboard has one, you can use it like a ten-key calculator.

The **cursor** shows where you are working on the screen. You can use the cursor keys to move the cursor around on the screen. You can move the cursor up, down, right, or left.

Many computers have function keys numbered F1 to F10 or higher. You can use them for functions like moving text.

The Monitor. The computer displays messages and data on a monitor screen. Many monitors have a white on black screen. (That is, the letters are white and the background is black.) Some monitors have a green, blue, or orange background. Some monitors display their messages in different colors.

Most screens have control knobs to make them brighter or darker. You can tilt some monitors up or down. Try moving your monitor around. This will help you work more comfortably.

The System Unit. The **system unit** is the main part of the computer. It houses the computer's "brain." The power cord plugs into the back of most system units. The monitor plugs into the back of the system unit, too. There are also places to plug in cables for printers and other equipment.

Many system units have spaces for options. Options can make the computer run faster or do different kinds of work. We will look further at options on page 49.

The system unit contains three parts.

1. The CPU.
2. The memory.
3. One or more disk drives.

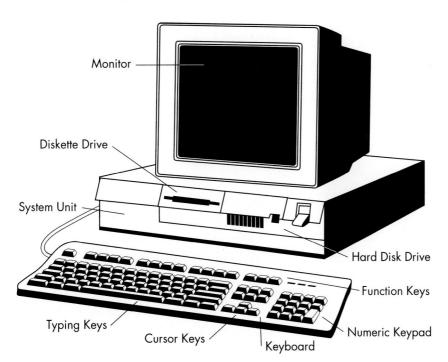

Monitor

Diskette Drive

System Unit

Typing Keys

Cursor Keys

Keyboard

Hard Disk Drive

Function Keys

Numeric Keypad

◀ *Figure 3-1*
Most computers are made up of a keyboard, a monitor, and a system unit. What is the purpose of each of these parts?

★ **Tricks of the Trade** ★

Booting Up

You start your computer by turning it on and inserting the operating system diskette. This is called "booting up." Think of this as giving your computer its morning cup of coffee to get its day started.

The Central Processing Unit (CPU) is the computer's control center. It carries out instructions. It processes data. It stores and gets data.

The system unit contains a *Random Access Memory* (RAM). RAM is the computer's workplace. This is where your programs and data for processing are stored. When you turn off your computer, RAM is erased. So you must store your data someplace else before you turn off your machine.

The system unit of most computers contains one or more disk drives. A disk drive saves and retrieves your programs and data. There are two types of disk drives.

1. Diskette drives.
2. Hard disk drives.

Diskette drives use small diskettes, often called *floppy disks.* Hard disk drives use a hard disk that is built in to the disk drive. You can save data on these diskettes and disks. You can also copy the data from a diskette or disk to

RAM. You can save more data on a hard disk than on a diskette. Hard disk drives also work faster.

▷ **Diskettes**

You can store your programs and data on diskettes. They provide safe and easy storage. You can take them out of the computer. You can put them in a file until you need them again. Write on a label what you are saving on the diskette. Stick the label on the diskette. Then you can always find the one you need.

You must buy the right size diskette for your disk drive. Two sizes are used today. One is 3½ inches, and the other is 5¼ inches. The 3½ inch diskette has a plastic cover to protect it from dust. The 5¼ inch diskette has only a paper cover. It can be damaged easily. Never place heavy objects on a diskette. Never touch the exposed part. Never place it next to a phone or tape recorder. Doing so could erase the data saved on the diskette.

Before you can use a diskette, you must *format* it. Formatting makes a disk ready for use. Read about how to format diskettes in the manual that comes with your computer.

After the diskette is formatted, put it into the diskette drive with the label side up. There is a light near the opening to the disk drive. When the light is on, the computer is reading or writing to the diskette. Never remove a diskette when the light is on. This may damage the diskette.

Some options include a *modem*, a *plotter*, and a *mouse,* like the ones in Figure 3-2 on page 51. A **modem** lets your computer talk to another computer over a phone line. A **plotter** makes graphs. A **mouse** moves a pointer around on the screen. You just move the mouse on your desk. It tells the computer what you want it to do, such as move text or draw pictures.

When you first buy a computer, you may not want any options. Later, you may decide to add one or two. You can add them yourself. Or you can have a computer service person do this for you.

Continued on page 51.

▲ *Two widely used diskettes are the 3½ inch and 5¼ inch sizes. What is the purpose of a diskette?*

▷ Options

You may want your computer to run faster. Or you may want it to do some special type of work. Most computers have a way of adding options. This is often done by adding special *cards* in the slots of the system unit. Some cards make your computer run much faster. Others will give it more memory.

▲ *To use a diskette, place it into the disk drive. A light on your computer will tell you when the computer is reading or writing to the diskette. Why should you never remove a diskette when the light is on?*

A Desire to Succeed

Bill Gates

Bill Gates was born in Seattle, Washington in 1955. He first tried using a computer when he was 13 years old. He was "hooked!" A few days later, he wrote a program to play tick-tack-toe on the computer.

Bill and his friends wanted to learn all they could about computers. They were so eager, they spent their spare time at a local computer company. They dug in trash cans to find programmers' notes. They studied the notes and tried to learn how the computer systems worked.

By the time he was 14, Bill and his friends had started their own company. They used computers to study traffic data for the city and county.

Bill continued to learn all he could about computers. The last half of his senior year, he worked full time as a computer programmer. At 17, he was earning $30,000 a year.

After high school, Bill went to Harvard. He and a friend from high school read about the creation of the first personal computer. They worked night and day to write a program for this first PC.

They succeeded. At 19, Bill started a company named Microsoft. It was the world's first microcomputer software company.

Bill worked seven days a week. He often worked 15 hours a day. He wrote the operating system for the IBM PC. Microsoft became the leader in software sales.

Bill still works hard at the business he loves. But he also tries to take some time to enjoy his new life-style. Through hard work and dedication, he has become the personal computer industry's first billionaire.

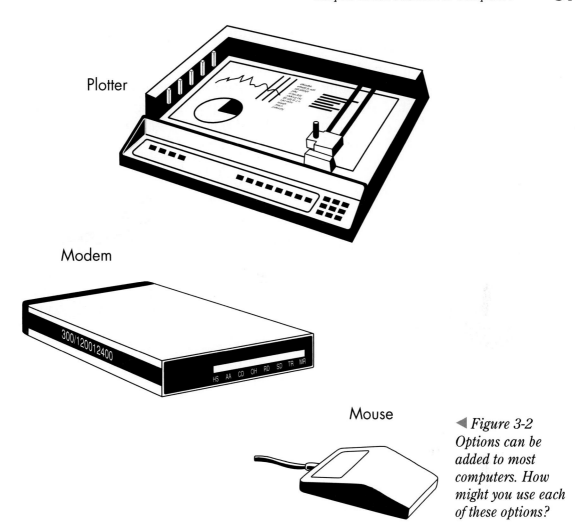

Plotter

Modem

300/120012400

HS AA CD OH RD SD TR MR

Mouse

◀ *Figure 3-2*
Options can be
added to most
computers. How
might you use each
of these options?

▷ Software

A computer cannot do anything by itself. It must be told exactly what to do. It needs instructions. **Software** is the name for a program that contains computer instructions. Software is soft compared to the hardware equipment. You cannot touch and feel it like you can hardware. That is why it is called *software*.

To run a computer, you must have software. All software is in code on diskettes. When you place the diskette in the disk drive, the computer can read its instructions.

There are many types of software. Those used most often are word processing, spreadsheet, database, and graphics programs. These are listed in Figure 3-3 on page 53.

Most programs are menu driven. After you load the program, a menu is shown on the screen. You can choose from the menu what to do next. Think of a food menu. You may choose from a long list of foods. You can use a program menu in the same way. A menu makes it easy to use many types of programs.

Word Processing Software. You can use a word processing program to type letters. You can also use it to type reports and memos. In fact, you can use it to type anything you want. The program will find and correct any words that are not spelled right. It is faster than using a typewriter. When your letter, report, or memo is perfect, you can print it on your printer.

Suppose you type a letter and print it out. Then you want to change some things. You can make the changes on your screen. Then you can print the letter with your changes.

Almost all companies use word processing programs. Many workers today wonder how people ever got along using only a typewriter.

Spreadsheet Software. A spreadsheet displays columns and rows of numbers. Rows go across the page. Columns go from top to bottom. A spreadsheet will add, subtract, multiply, or divide. It will do all the math you will need.

Companies use spreadsheets to keep records. Many use them to keep track of income and expenses.

Suppose you are in charge of buying supplies for your company. You could use a spreadsheet to keep track of how much money you spent. You would type in the name of what you bought, the price, and the number you bought. The computer would add up the total. Later, you may buy more. You would change the number you bought. The computer would quickly total the new amount.

A spreadsheet can use the data you enter to draw graphs. A graph might show how company sales have gone up or down in each state. In graphic form, the message gets across quickly.

Database Software. A *database* is made up of facts that are placed in groups. It allows you to find information quickly. The telephone book is a database that lists people's names and numbers. Companies use database programs to keep track of data. Some use these programs to keep track of their stock. Salespeople use database programs to keep track of their customers.

Suppose you work in an auto repair store that uses a database. You could type in a customer's name. The computer would show you all the auto repairs that customer had done on his or her car. It would show you when they were done. Suppose a customer needed a tire. You could type in the tire brand. The computer would tell you how many tires were in stock.

Continued on page 54.

Software Programs and Applications

Word Processing

Allows you to use a computer as a typewriter. However, it is much better than a typewriter. Words can easily be changed, moved, added, or removed. You may correct mistakes on screen and print out perfect copies.

Spreadsheet

Allows you to use a computer as a business ledger. Predicts future income or sales based on past numbers. All math is done by the computer. When you change a number, all math is done again. Prepares all types of graphs.

Database

Manages data. A database program works on data that has been stored. It can quickly look through all data and find what you want. Suppose you have stored data on cars. That is your database. Then you want to find a car with all the following:

1. Can reach 60 mph in less than 8 seconds.

2. Has a turning circle of less than 33 feet.

3. Can stop (60–0 mph) in less than 180 feet.

4. Is less than three years old.

5. Is priced less than $10,000.

Your database program can find the right car in seconds.

Graphics

Shows information using pictures, charts, and graphs. Graphic displays can be printed or made into slides. It is often used to make ads, videos, and movies.

▲ *Figure 3-3*
Software programs give the computer instructions to do certain things.
There are many types of software programs. Which of these four
programs do you think you might use?

► *This computer store offers many types of software. What are two types this couple might ask to see?*

Graphics Software. *Graphics* make messages more interesting. They show information in pictures, charts, and graphs. Graphics are often used to produce artwork. Graphics displays can be printed or made into slides. Graphics programs are often used to make ads, videos, and movies.

Other Software. Have you visited a computer store? If so, you know that there are thousands of software programs. Whatever you would like your computer to do, there is probably a program for it.

✓ Check Up ✓ ✓ ✓

1. What is the most popular size computer today?
2. What are the lightest weight computers called?
3. What are the three basic parts of a computer?
4. What are the three parts of the system unit?
5. What are two types of disk drives?
6. What are three popular types of software programs?

○ Buying a Computer

At the beginning of the 1990s, 25 million Americans owned computers. By the middle 1990s, more than 50 million people will own them. Most will use a computer for one of five reasons.

1. To run a business at home.
2. To do work brought home from their workplace.
3. To do school homework.
4. To do such personal work as writing checks or letters.
5. For entertainment.

It is easy for a first-time computer buyer to be confused by the types and prices. So what is the best way to buy your first computer? Follow these five steps.

1. Decide on the uses you need.
2. Set a budget.
3. Choose the software.
4. Choose the hardware.
5. Shop for service and support.

Here is a look at each step.

▷ Decide on Uses

What do you want your computer to do? You may think of many uses. Will you bring computer work home from the office? If so, you will need a computer that can run the programs you use at work.

Will you use it mainly for word processing or spreadsheets? Will you use it for homework? You will probably find that some uses are more important than others. Make a list of them.

▷ Set a Budget

Have an idea of how much you can afford or want to spend. You may have to adjust your budget when you go shopping.

▲ *Why should you set a budget before you shop for a computer?*

□ Case Study □ □ □ □ □ □

Mira is a college student. She is studying music. Her brother Luis has a new job working part time at a computer store. The store is planning a sale on some of its computers. Luis suggests to Mira that she should buy one of these computers. He thinks it will help her with her school work. Mira decides that this is a real bargain. She buys the computer for $1,500.

After Mira gets the computer, she begins to look for software that will help her with her music classes. But she learns that the best music software will not run on her computer. A different computer would have been better for her needs.

Mira made a costly mistake. If she had followed the five steps to buying a computer she would have avoided this mistake.

▷ Choose the Software

Find the software that will suit your needs. Read computer magazines. Visit your local computer store. But do not buy yet! Make a list of the software you think you will need.

▷ Choose the Hardware

Learn which computers will run the software on your list. There are three popular types of computers.

- IBM and IBM copies.
- Apple.
- Macintosh.

Computers that run the same programs as the IBM are called IBM copies or *clones*. IBM and IBM clones are used widely in business. Apple computers are widely used in schools. Macintosh computers are made by Apple. They are used mostly for graphic and design work.

There are many models of each type. New models come out every year. Look for models that will run your software. Then try them out at your local store.

Look for a computer that is fast enough to do the job. You will want more than just enough RAM. New software requires more and more RAM in order to work. Get a hard disk if you can afford it. It is much faster and easier to use.

You may want a color monitor if you are doing graphics and design work. You will not need a color monitor if you are only using word processing or database software.

You will need a printer, too. There are many types of printers. Laser printers make the best copies. But they are expensive. A dot matrix printer is fine for most work. Find one that works with your computer and software.

▷ Shop for Service and Support

Sometimes computers break down and need to be repaired. Ask local dealers about their repair service. Can you take your computer in for repair and get it back in a few days? If you have questions about setting up your computer, can you call the dealer? Will you get the answers right away?

When you buy your computer, you may need some help getting started. That is, you may need *support*. Support means there is someone to call for help. Support also means training. Many local stores give classes to get you started. They will teach you how to set up and use your computer. Ask local dealers if they have classes on the software you have chosen.

You may find the lowest prices on computers and software in magazine ads. If you order by mail, though, you may not be able to call a local repair person. So think about how much service and support you would like. Most software lists a number you can call for help. Still, it is easier to talk with someone directly.

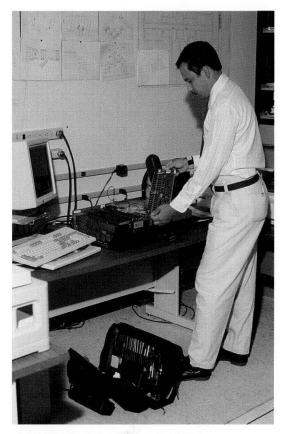

▲ *Local dealers offer computer repair services. What are two questions you should ask a dealer about their company's repair service?*

✓ Check Up ✓ ✓ ✓

1. What are five reasons for using a computer at home?
2. What are the five steps in buying a computer?
3. What are the three most popular types of computers?

Chapter 3 Review

Chapter Summary

- Computers affect our lives each day in many ways.
- Today's computers are small and powerful.
- The parts of a computer that you can touch are called hardware.
- The three basic parts of most computers are the keyboard, the monitor, and the system unit.
- The instructions that tell a computer what to do are called software.
- There are many types of software programs.
- It is important to know what you need before you buy a computer.

Reviewing Vocabulary

Listed below are the important new words that were used in this chapter. Next to each word is the page on which you will find the word. Turn to that page and read the paragraph in which the word is printed in **bold** type. Then read each question below. Notice the underlined word in each question. If the answer to the question is yes, write yes on a sheet of paper. If it is no, write no.

1. scanner (45)
2. data (45)
3. hardware (46)
4. cursor (46)
5. system unit (47)
6. CPU (48)
7. modem (49)
8. plotter (49)
9. mouse (49)
10. software (51)

1. Do <u>software</u> programs give a computer instructions?
2. Does the <u>CPU</u> carry out instructions?
3. Can <u>data</u> be stored in a computer?
4. Is a <u>modem</u> part of every computer?
5. Can a <u>mouse</u> be used to draw pictures?
6. Does a <u>plotter</u> allow one computer to talk to another computer?
7. Is a <u>scanner</u> a tool used to draw pictures and graphs on the computer monitor?
8. Is <u>cursor</u> another name for a keyboard?
9. Is the Random Access Memory part of the <u>system unit</u>?
10. Is <u>hardware</u> the part of the computer you can touch?

Looking at the Facts

1. Describe one use for a computer in business, in the health field, and at home.
2. What are the three basic parts of most computers?
3. What purpose does the keyboard serve?

4. Which part of the computer gives messages to you?
5. What are the three parts of the system unit?
6. Give three examples of computer options.
7. What is software?
8. What are the three most common types of software?
9. List five important steps to follow when you buy a computer.
10. What are the three most popular types of computers?

Thinking Critically

1. Sometimes people try to explain mistakes by saying the computer made an error. Do computers make mistakes? Explain your answer.
2. How can you save data you have put into a computer?
3. Why is it important to study prices when buying a computer?
4. In some ways, a computer is like a brain. It receives, processes, and stores data. What are some things computers can do that are difficult for people to do?

Discussing Chapter Concepts

1. List at least five jobs in which computers are used.
2. List at least five jobs in which computers probably are *not* used.
3. What three jobs do you think have been created in the computer support services?

Using Basic Skills

Math
1. Dana has a word processing program for her computer. She uses it to earn money. She types papers for people and charges them $.75 per page. How much would she charge to type an eight-page paper?

Communications
2. Use the Yellow Pages to find businesses that sell computers. Call two of them. Ask about the service and support they give their customers. List the services each business offers.

Human Relations
3. Your boss gives you a job that requires you to use a computer. The computer is different from the one you used on your last job. Should you ask for a manual? Should you try to figure it out on your own?

Activities for Enrichment

1. Keep a list for one week of the ways computers affect your life.
2. List four ways you might use a computer. Find out where you can get software for these uses.
3. Interview someone in the world of work. Ask him or her to list all the ways computers affect his or her work.
4. Visit a local computer store. Ask the clerk for a demonstration of two software packages.

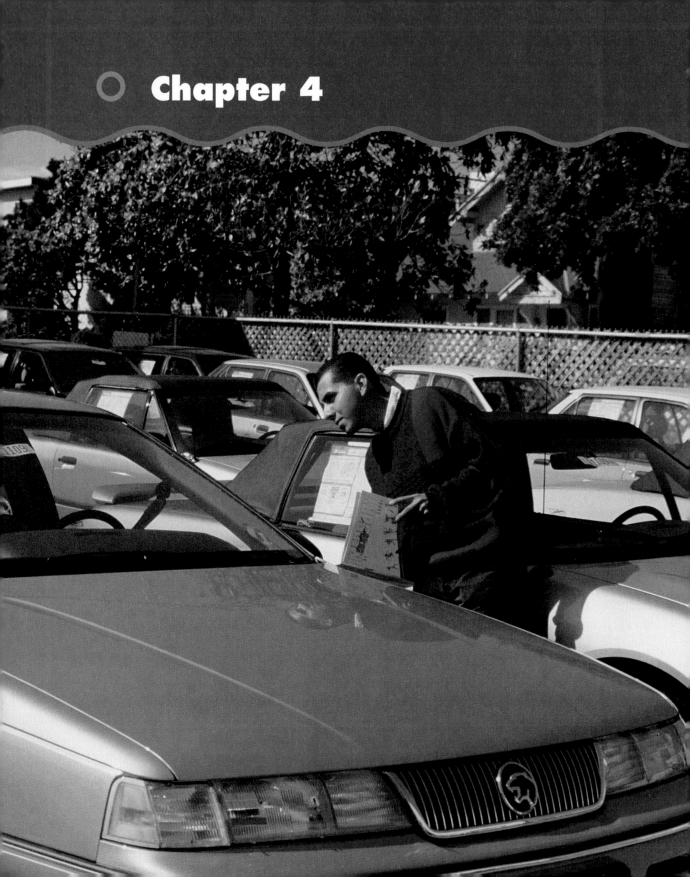

Decision Making

Words to learn and use

Here are the new terms you will learn in this chapter. Challenge yourself. Read through the list to see if you know what they mean.

labor union
labor contract
consumer
goods
services

Build on what you know

You already know...
- you make many decisions each day of your life.
- some decisions are easier to make than others.
- some of the decisions you make now will affect your life in the future.

In this chapter you will learn...
- how to improve your skills at decision making.
- the steps in decision making.
- how to apply your skills at decision making to the decisions in your life.

You make decisions every day. Some are simple and have little effect on your future. Choosing which clothes you will wear to school and what to eat for lunch are such decisions. Other decisions do affect your future. Decisions about school or your career will affect your life in many ways.

Making good decisions now will have a positive effect on your future. That is why it is important to learn the skill of decision making. This chapter will show you how to do just that with a decision-making model. Learn the steps in this model. Then you can apply them to the decisions in your life.

O A Model for Making Decisions

When you make a decision, you make a choice between two or more things. Think of the decisions you make every day. You may decide which clothes to wear. You may decide whether to go to a movie or a baseball game. You may decide what time to call a friend. These are small decisions. They do not really affect your life. Once you make them, you forget about them.

Other decisions, though, will greatly affect your life now and in the future. These decisions include choosing a career and how you will manage your money. You need to make such decisions carefully. Using the decision-making model shown in Figure 4-1 on page 63 will help you do this. Here are the seven steps you can use when making a decision that will affect your life.

1. Define your needs and wants.
2. Look at your resources.
3. Look at the choices.
4. Gather information on each choice.
5. Look at the value of each choice.
6. Make your decision.
7. Plan how to reach your goal.

Follow the steps in this model. They will help you learn how to make the best choice for you. Here is how one person used this model. It helped him decide what to do about his transportation problem.

▷ John's Challenge

John's car is wearing out. It is old. He has already fixed it many times. He is faced with a decision. He could repair it or replace it. He could carpool to work. Or he could ride the bus to work.

You may be faced with this decision some day. If you were John, what would you do? Here is how he used each step of the decision-making model.

Define Your Needs and Wants. John wants to get to work on time. He needs good transportation to do this.

He does not want to take the bus. His house is a long way from the bus line. Buses only run once every 45 minutes. He would waste a great deal of time waiting for the bus.

Look at Your Resources. John has saved some money the past two years from his co-op job. But he had planned to use it for further education.

John could borrow the money for a new car. But he does not want to make car payments. He could use some of

Decision-making Model

1. **Define your needs and wants.**
2. **Look at your resources.**
3. **Look at the choices.**
4. **Gather information on each choice.**
5. **Look at the value of each choice.**
6. **Make your decision.**
7. **Plan how to reach your goal.**

◀ *Figure 4-1*
Using the decision-making model will help you to make successful decisions. How does this model stop you from making hasty decisions?

his savings to repair the old car. But his car may need more repairs. This would use up more of his savings.

Look at the Choices. John thought about his problem. He listed four choices for solving it.

1. He could have his old car repaired.
2. He could buy a better car.
3. He could ride in a car pool to work.
4. He could ride the city bus.

Gather Information on Each Choice. John looked at the pros and cons of each choice.

- Repairing the old car would cost less than buying a new one. Of course, the old car may need more repairs in the future.

This would cost even more money than he planned to spend.

- Buying a better car would cost a great deal of money. But the new car probably would not need major repairs for a few years.
- In a car pool, John would drive only one day each week. He would still have to repair his car. But he would drive it less often. So he might get along fine with the old one.
- Riding the city bus would cost about $3 a day. This is cheaper than repairing his old car. And it is much cheaper than buying a new one. Still, riding the bus is not as easy as having a car.

Look at the Value of Each Choice. John learned that it would cost $2,000 to repair his old car. It would cost him at least $8,000 to buy a new one. He could drive in a car pool. But he would still have to pay $2,000 to repair his car. Driving his old car less would probably save him from buying a new car. Riding the bus would cost about $750 a year.

▲ *John decided to carpool to work. Would you have made the same decision as John? Why or why not?*

Make Your Decision. After looking at his choices, John decided to try carpooling. Taking the bus was cheaper than repairing his car. But it took too much time. He decided to spend $2,000 to repair his car. By carpooling, he would only drive his car once a week. He could then wait two or three years to buy a new car.

Plan How to Reach Your Goal. John's company helps its employees arrange car pools. He is sure it will not take long to get into one. He can join within a week. Later on, John may decide he does not want to be in the car pool. Then he can look at his choices again and make a different decision.

What would you have done if you were John? Your decision might have been very different. However, it would have been *your* decision. You would have looked at all the steps as they relate to *your* life. This is what is important about decision making. You do what is best for you.

> ✔ **Check Up** ✔ ✔ ✔
> 1. List the seven steps in the decision-making model.
> 2. What were John's resources?
> 3. What were John's choices?
> 4. What was John's decision on getting to work?
> 5. How did John plan to reach his goal?

⭕ Decisions About School

As you know, there are some high school courses everyone must take. These are called *required courses*. You cannot graduate without completing them.

You can also take *elective courses*. These are courses you can choose to take. They relate to your own career goals. Suppose you want to work as a secretary. Then you will probably take an elective course in keyboarding. If you want to work as an auto mechanic, you will probably take a course in auto repair.

Making successful decisions about your school work now will help you in your career. Here is how one student used the decision-making model in her school work.

▷ Ann's Challenge

Ann was finishing her sophomore year. It was time to enroll for her junior year. She had no choice about the courses she took in the first two years of high school. During her junior year, though, she could take two electives.

Ann was not sure what she wanted to do after high school. She liked to work with her hands. And she wanted to begin working full time right after high school. Here is her model for decision making.

Define Your Needs and Wants. Ann made good grades in courses where she worked with her hands. She liked art courses. She was also good at working with computers.

Ann needed to take some elective courses that would train her for a job. She thought that her school's vocational courses would help do this.

Ann's uncle was a printer. Her father was a carpenter. Her family encouraged her to train for a skilled career. Ann wanted to do this, too.

▲ *The decision-making model can help you to make decisions about your school courses. Why is it important for Ann to make wise decisions about her courses?*

Look at Your Resources. Everyone in Ann's family worked to help pay expenses. There was not much money for her education after high school. So Ann needed to get as much job training as she could in high school. She could not depend on her family for school expenses after she graduated.

She could depend on her own high school for help, though. It trained many students every year for work after high school.

Look at the Choices. Ann's high school offered a number of vocational courses. Among them were data processing, commercial art, computer aided design (CAD), and electronics. Any of these could train her for a job after high school.

Ann wanted to work part time while she finished high school. She thought it would be best to choose vocational electives in which she would learn skills she could use on a co-op job.

Gather Information on Each Choice. Ann's counselor gave her a copy of the *Occupational Outlook Handbook.* It tells about more than 200 occupations. It tells the education you need to do each job. It also lists the hours you will work and the money you can expect to earn. It even tells the outlook for each occupation.

Of the jobs Ann looked at, graphic design looked best. Her counselor told her she could enter the school's co-op program. Through it, she could work on a co-op job in an advertising agency.

Look at the Value of Each Choice. Ann looked at the pros and cons of data processing, commercial art, CAD, and electronics. Ann thought the commercial art and CAD courses would help her become a graphic designer.

Make Your Decision. Ann decided to take commercial art and CAD electives. There were two commercial art courses and three CAD courses open to juniors and seniors. Together, Ann and her counselor decided which ones Ann would take in her junior and senior years.

They also looked at some ad agencies that hired co-op students. They chose three agencies where Ann could interview.

Plan How to Reach Your Goal. Ann enrolled in two electives for her junior year. Before she started class, she visited each teacher. They gave her tips on how to prepare for her co-op interviews with local ad agencies. Ann's choice was much easier using the decision-making model.

✔ Check Up ✔ ✔ ✔

1. What was Ann's challenge?
2. How did Ann gather information about each choice?
3. What did Ann decide?

O Decisions About Career

Choosing a career is one of the most important things you will ever do. So making decisions about your career is a key to your future success.

Before you make a career decision, answer these questions. Can I do this type of work? Will I like it? Will the work meet my needs and wants? Is there room to grow in this job? Can I use the skills I learn on this job in other fields?

June is enrolled in her school's co-op program. This year she is working at Lion's Cafeteria. She is faced with making the decision about what to do after high school.

▷ June's Challenge

At Lion's, June has learned to make salads, bake, and cook. She has also served on the food line. Recently, she learned how to use the cash register.

June enjoys her work. She gets along well with co-workers and customers. Her manager has offered her a full time job after graduation.

June needs to make a decision. She can work at Lion's full time after she graduates. Or she can get further schooling. Most of her friends will attend the local community college or trade school. Here is how she used the decision-making model.

◀ *Before you can make a decision, you need to look at your choices. What are June's choices?*

Define Your Needs and Wants.
June's challenge is what to do after high school. She needs a job to support herself. But she wants a job with room for growth. She will probably need further schooling if she wants to become a food service manager. June is not sure that she will be able to go into management at Lion's. But the skills she learns there may help her advance to another job.

Look at Your Resources. June's parents could help her pay some of her tuition if she goes to school in town. June herself has saved some money. She also has income from her job. If she stays in town, she can work part time and go to community college. However, if she wants to go away to college, she needs to get a loan.

Look at the Choices. June has several choices open to her after graduation. She listed her choices.

1. She could work full time at Lion's after high school without attending community college.
2. She could work part time at Lion's and attend the local community college part time.
3. She could get a loan and attend college full time in another city.

Gather Information on Each Choice. June studied each of these choices. Working at Lion's would help her support herself. But it would take her longer to advance to a better job without more training.

She checked with the local community college. She could take classes in the morning and work at Lion's in the afternoon. The money she made at work would pay for her college fees.

She checked with a local bank about getting a school loan. She found out it would be possible to get one. It would take her several years, though, to pay it back.

Look at the Value of Each Choice. June thought about each choice. Working only at Lion's, it would take her longer to get a manager's job.

Working at Lion's and going to school, she could get job training and further schooling. She could also pay her school fees without taking out a loan.

Going to school out of town, she would get full-time schooling. But she would not have the job training at Lion's. Also, she would have to pay back her school loan over several years.

Make Your Decision. June decided on the second choice. She would work at Lion's and go to school at the same time. She liked her job and enjoyed what she learned there. She could use the money she earned to help her pay fees at the community college. The things she studied at the community college could help her grow on the job. And her job training would help her in her classes. She felt very happy with her choice.

☐ Case Study ☐ ☐ ☐ ☐ ☐ ☐

At the end of his junior year in high school, Nate had to make a decision about a summer job. He thought about his choices. He could paint houses. He would earn good money doing this. He would make enough to pay for next year's extra expenses.

He could work at the beach with his friends renting beach chairs. He knew he would have a great time with his friends at the beach. He would make some spending money. But he would not make as much money as he would painting houses.

Nate could also take an internship job at a local newspaper. He thought he would like to work as a writer when he finished school. The internship job would help him decide whether he liked writing as a career. It would also allow him to explore other types of jobs at the newspaper. But the internship job did not pay any money.

Nate chose the internship job because it could help his career. During the internship job, Nate helped design some ads for the newspaper. He found he liked doing design work more than writing. He was better at it, too.

The next year he took a graphic design course. He applied to a community college with a graphic design program. When he finished school he got a job in graphic design. Two years later he started his own graphic design firm. He was very happy with his work. As you can see, one good decision had a good effect on Nate's future.

Plan How to Reach Your Goal. June talked to her manager at Lion's Cafeteria about her decision. Her manager was happy that June would continue working at Lion's. He agreed to give June job duties that would help her advance and learn more about being a food service manager.

June applied to her local community college. She was enrolled in the food service management program.

✔ Check Up ✔ ✔ ✔

1. What was June's challenge?
2. What were June's needs and wants?
3. What were June's resources?
4. What were June's three choices about what to do after graduation?
5. What did June decide?

O Decisions on the Job

When taking any job, you will have many decisions to make. One of the most common decisions on a job is whether to join a *labor union*. A **labor union** is a group of workers who join together to get higher pay and better working conditions.

You may have to decide whether to join a union. If so, you will want to use the decision-making model to make this decision.

▷ Mark's Challenge

Mark was recently hired as a pipe welder at Ohio Welding. He enjoyed his new job. Every day he used the skills he already knew. He also learned many new ones.

After two weeks, Mark was invited to join the company's union. Mark had never been in a union. He knew that he would have to pay dues and attend meetings. He needed some time to think about his decision. Mark told his supervisor he would let her know by the next week.

Define Your Needs and Wants. Mark needed regular pay increases. He wanted a chance to advance when a higher level job became open. He wondered if union membership would help him with these two things.

Mark needed $250 for his union dues. He played basketball two nights a week. One other night he attended a class in auto repair. He knew he would need time to attend a weekly union meeting after work on Wednesday nights.

Look at Your Resources. Mark had enough money saved to pay the $250 union dues. But he played basketball on Wednesday nights.

He needed to have some questions answered about union membership. Would it help him get pay raises? Would it help him get a better job at his company? To answer these questions, he could check with his supervisor who was a union member.

Look at the Choices. Here are Mark's choices.

1. He could join the union now.
2. He could join at a later time.
3. He could not join the union at all.

Gather Information on Each Choice. Mark talked to his supervisor about the benefits of joining the union now. His supervisor told him that the union and the company management have a *labor contract*. A **labor contract** puts into writing everything that the union members and the company's management agree to.

Mark's supervisor said the labor contract states several things that benefit union workers. Union members get a set percent in regular pay raises. They must also be told about any job openings that occur. They can take their conflicts with managers to a committee. The committee is made up of company management and union members. Finally, the union works to keep communication open between workers and company management.

Mark could wait a while to join the union. But he might miss some of the benefits it would bring him now.

Mark could decide not to join the union at all. But he might not get the regular pay raises he hoped to get. And he might not hear of other job openings right away. He might not even have a chance to have his concerns heard by management.

Look at the Value of Each Choice. Mark's first choice—to join the union—would cost him $250. But there were many benefits to joining the union now.

His second choice—to wait a while before joining—would save him $250 now. But he would not enjoy the union benefits now.

His third choice—not to join the union at all—would save him $250 now. But it could cost him later. He might not receive the regular pay raises union members would get. He might not hear of other job openings in the company.

Make Your Decision. Mark looked at all his choices and made his decision. He decided to join the union right away.

Plan How to Reach Your Goal. Mark told his supervisor about his decision. His supervisor gave him all the forms to fill out. Mark moved his Wednesday night basketball game to Thursday night.

▲ *The information you gather on each choice will help you to make a decision. What kind of information did Mark's supervisor supply him with?*

✔ **Check Up** ✔ ✔ ✔
1. What was Mark's challenge?
2. What were Mark's choices?
3. How did Mark reach his goal?

A Desire to Succeed

Sandra Day O'Connor

Sandra Day O'Connor is the first woman to sit on the United States Supreme Court. Her decision-making ability brought her this honor.

Sandra Day O'Connor was raised in a four-room house. When she was only eight, she was riding horses and fixing fences. She learned early how to work hard. She learned to think for herself. She was never one to go along with the crowd.

O'Connor graduated from Stanford Law School in 1952. She found that no law firm in California would hire a woman. So she worked in the District Attorney's office in San Mateo County. In 1969, she became a member of the State Senate. While in the Senate, O'Connor voted for bills she thought were good for the state. She did not care which party had proposed them. Her decisions did not make her popular with those who often voted blindly with their party.

In 1973, she became the first woman majority leader in the United States. Later, O'Connor left office to become a superior court judge. She was often asked by the Republican Party to run for governor. But she decided to remain in law. She took her place on the Arizona Court of Appeals in 1979. Two years later, President Reagan chose her for the Supreme Court.

O'Connor has always been determined to succeed. She faced breast cancer in 1988. Within a few weeks, she was golfing, playing tennis, and working.

O'Connor focuses on issues. She does not allow politics to sway her. Her ability to make decisions makes her a strong influence on the law of the land.

O Consumer Decisions

As you may know, a **consumer** is a person who buys goods and services. **Goods** are products that you buy. They can be plants, clothing, stereos, or cars. **Services** are things that you pay other people to do for you. Dry cleaning is a service. Lawn mowing is a service, too.

As a consumer, you will want to get the most for your money. Kim used our simple decision-making model to decide what coat to buy.

▷ Kim's Challenge

Kim was a senior at North High School. She had worked all summer at an amusement park. She saved most of the money she made. For several months she had wanted to buy a leather coat. But there were other things she needed. The model for decision making helped her decide if she could afford to buy a leather coat.

Define Your Needs and Wants. Kim had saved $500. She listed the clothing she needed and wanted.

First, she needed a suit for job interviews. She also needed a pair of matching shoes.

Second, she needed a new pair of winter boots. Her old boots were very worn, and they no longer fit her.

Third, she needed a formal dress. Her senior prom would be held in June. And she did not have a formal dress to wear.

Finally, she wanted a leather coat. She had been looking at them for months. The price of one style she liked had been reduced from $250 to $200.

Look at Your Resources. Kim had $500 saved. She expected to get a co-op job this year. But she did not know how much it would pay. She did know, though, that most of what she earned would go toward school lunches and bus fare. She would also have to pay other expenses, like tickets to dances and athletic events. So she needed to watch how she spent her money.

✱ Tricks of the Trade ✱

Learn from Your Decisions

Do not think of a decision as good or bad. Think of it as a learning experience. After you make a decision, ask yourself, "What did I learn from this?" Always focus on the positive.

► *Your resources often determine the consumer decisions you make. If Kim had $1,000 to spend on clothing do you think her decision would have been different?*

Look at the Choices. Kim really wanted the $200 leather coat. But she needed a suit, shoes, boots, and a formal dress. Buying a wool coat would leave her more money to buy the things she needed.

So she listed her two choices.

1. Buy the leather coat and have less money for clothing she needed.
2. Buy a wool coat and have more money for the things she needed.

Gather Information on Each Choice. Kim compared the cost of a wool coat with that of a leather coat. If she bought a wool coat, she could save at least $100. The extra money would help her buy the other clothing she needed. She had to ask herself how important the leather coat was to her.

Look at the Value of Each Choice. Kim thought about how much she needed the leather coat. Then she thought about how much she needed the suit, shoes, boots, and formal dress.

Make Your Decision. Kim decided to buy a wool coat. This would allow her to afford the other items she needed to buy.

She also decided to save 10 dollars each week for a leather coat. She would save $40 dollars a month. ($10 × 4 weeks = $40). In five months, she would have enough for a leather coat. ($200 needed for the coat ÷ $40 per month = 5 months.)

Plan How to Reach Your Goal. To reach her goal, Kim went shopping. She bought a wool coat for $100. She bought a blue business suit for $150 and a pair of blue shoes for $80. She spent $330. ($100 + $150 + $80 = $330.)

Kim still had $170 left to buy a pair of winter boots and a formal dress. ($500 − $330 = $170.) If she *still* had money left over, she could save for a leather coat. She decided it was important to take care of her needs before taking care of her wants.

▲ *You will make important decisions throughout your life. Why is this person's method of making decisions not as effective as using the seven step decision-making model?*

✳ Tricks of the Trade ✳

Looking at the Choices

Whenever you are making a decision, write down your options on a piece of paper. This will make it easier for you to look at and review your choices.

✔ Check Up ✔ ✔ ✔

1. What is a consumer?
2. What are goods?
3. What are services?
4. How much money had Kim saved during the summer?
5. What were her two choices?
6. Which choice did she think was the best?

Chapter 4 Review

Chapter Summary

- Decision making involves making a choice between two or more things.
- Important decisions need to be made carefully.
- Using the decision-making model will help you make decisions.
- There are seven steps in the decision-making model.
- Your future depends on your decision-making skills.

Reviewing Vocabulary

Listed below are the important new words that were used in this chapter. Next to each word is the page on which you will find the word. Turn to that page and read the paragraph in which the word is printed in **bold** type. On a separate piece of paper, write the word and its meaning. Then write a sentence of your own using each word.

1. labor union (70)
2. labor contract (70)
3. consumer (73)
4. goods (73)
5. services (73)

Looking at the Facts

1. List the seven steps in the model for decision making.
2. Why is it important to learn the skill of decision making?

3. What is the difference between required courses and elective courses?
4. Why is it important to make wise decisions about your schoolwork?
5. What questions should you be able to answer before you make a career decision?
6. What is a labor union?
7. As a consumer, what is the benefit of making wise decisions?
8. What are goods?
9. What are services?

Thinking Critically

1. Suppose you are enrolling in classes for next year. You have selected all but one of your courses. For your last class, you want to take woodworking or printing. All your friends are taking the printing class. But the woodworking class might help you get a carpentry job this summer. How will you decide which class to take?
2. You and your counselor together have made a list of community colleges you think you want to apply to. How would you gather information on each choice?
3. General Hospital and County Hospital have offered you the same type of co-op job. You have to decide between the two

hospitals. You will learn more at General, but you will not make as much money as you will make at County. County will pay you $50 a week. What would you consider when looking at the value of each choice?

4. You want to buy new speakers for your stereo system. The more expensive speakers sound much better than the cheaper ones. But if you buy the cheaper speakers, you will have enough money to buy a tape deck, too. What will you consider when you look at the choices?

Discussing Chapter Concepts

1. Tell four important decisions you have made in the past month.
2. How would defining your needs and wants help you to make a decision?
3. Name three positive effects from decisions you have made about school courses.
4. Tell about a time when you made a hasty consumer decision in which you did not get the most for your money.
5. This chapter discusses four types of important decisions you may face. These are decisions about school, decisions about career, decisions on the job, and consumer decisions. What are two other types of important decisions you may face?

Using Basic Skills

Math

1. Suppose it cost you $6 per day to drive your own car to work. You could ride the bus for $2 per day. How much money would it cost you per week to ride the bus? How much would it cost you to drive your own car?

Communication

2. Look in a magazine or newspaper for two ads that show different brands of the same expensive product. (For example, consider two cars.) Use the model for decision making to decide which you would buy.

Human Relations

3. Your boss has asked you to stay late for a meeting on Wednesday night. You have a computer class that night. How will you decide what to do? What will you tell your boss?

Activities for Enrichment

1. Make a collage of pictures that shows decisions a teenager makes. Use magazine pictures, drawings, or photographs.
2. Keep a list of all the decisions you make in one day. Mark which decisions you think are important. Mark which decisions you think are not important. Circle the decisions for which you should use the model for decision making.

Part Two
Advancing in Your Career

Getting Along with People

Words to learn and use

Here are the new terms you will learn in this chapter. Challenge yourself. Read through the list to see if you know what they mean.

human relations skills
attitude
self-esteem
empathy
conflict
conflict resolution
negotiate
compromise

Build on what you know

You already know...
- your attitude can be positive or negative.
- you will have to solve conflict with others.
- some conflicts may not be resolved.

In this chapter you will learn...
- how a positive attitude helps to solve conflict.
- why you should know how to solve conflict.
- why some conflicts are not resolved right away.

Few of us know how to handle all types of conflict. But we all can become better at it by learning good *human relations skills*.

Human relations skills are the skills that help you get along with other people. They help you resolve conflict. They let others know that you respect them.

More people lose their jobs because of conflict than for any other reason. So success on the job depends on good human relations skills. It may take you a while to learn and practice them. But the effort will be worth it. It will help make you a success for the rest of your life.

O Your Attitude

The way you feel about yourself affects how you get along with others. If you like yourself, you will like others, too. If you do not like yourself, you will find fault in others. How you feel about yourself affects your *attitude*. Your **attitude** is the way you think and feel about things.

People carry their attitudes from home, to school, to work. So you have to feel good about yourself in daily life to feel good about yourself at school and at work.

For example, say that you doubt your ability to do a good job. This makes you feel badly about yourself. It makes you feel unsure. You may act negatively toward people around you.

People with negative attitudes often have a hard time at work. Others may not like working with them. So they often do not advance on the job.

You can find out some things about your own attitude by looking at what determines it: your *self-esteem*.

▷ Positive Attitude

Attitudes can be positive or negative. Having a *positive attitude* means that you look on the bright side. You enjoy others. You succeed at work because people like your attitude.

A positive attitude comes from believing in yourself and your skills. It gives you self-confidence. People with self-confidence are better at learning things. If they make mistakes, they do not dwell on them. They learn from them.

▷ Negative Attitude

Having a *negative attitude* means that you often see the worst in people and situations. A negative attitude comes from not believing in yourself.

▲ *A positive attitude helps you succeed on the job. How would a positive attitude help the people shown here succeed on the job?*

▷ Self-esteem

Self-esteem is the way you feel about yourself. It affects the way you think others see you.

Having good self-esteem helps you in many ways. You see yourself as able to do your job. You know you can get along with people. You feel that others see you this way, too.

If you have good self-esteem, you show that you feel good about yourself. Feeling good about yourself has a positive effect on your attitude. A positive attitude makes you a valuable member of any group. The group could be your family, your classmates, your friends, or your co-workers.

Of course, it is possible that people with good self-esteem may want to change some things. They might want to be better in math. They might want to improve job skills. But they still feel they have value. They do not need others' approval to feel good about themselves.

People with low self-esteem do not like themselves. They feel they must please people to be liked. They may feel they cannot do things "right."

▷ Empathy

By now you have met many people in your life. Some of the people have high self-esteem and good attitudes. Some may have low self-esteem and negative attitudes. You have found that some people are easier to get along with than others. Why is this so? What do you think the people who are hard to get along with are feeling?

Think about the people you know. Have you ever had people hurt your feelings? This probably upset you. You do not understand why you were not treated well. But did you ever think that the other person was being affected by things you did not know about?

Sometimes we need to understand how others are feeling. We need to have *empathy*. **Empathy** is being able to understand how someone else feels. To do this, you must imagine how you would feel in the same situation.

▲ *Having empathy will help you get along with other people. Is the person shown here showing empathy? How can you tell?*

☐ **Case Study** ☐ ☐ ☐ ☐ ☐ ☐

Terry was given free tickets to a baseball game. She was very excited. She called her best friend Nick. She asked him to go with her to the game. Nick was very short with Terry on the phone.

"Not today!" he growled. "I have a test tomorrow."

At first, Terry was hurt by Nick's response. She thought he would be excited. Instead, he seemed angry. Then Terry thought about what Nick said. She imagined how she would feel if she had a test the next day. She knew she would be frustrated if she could not go to the game. She began to understand why Nick was so short with her.

"Do not worry," she said. "Study for your test. I am sure I can get tickets for next week's game. We can go then."

"Really?" Nick said. "That's great!"

When Terry hung up the phone, she felt good. By having empathy, she could communicate better with Nick.

For example, suppose that your boss barely spoke to you when you came in to work. You would feel ignored. You may feel that you did something wrong. This probably would upset you. It could become a conflict if you let it.

But think about this for a moment. Perhaps your boss is worried. Maybe his child is sick. Maybe a customer upset him. Maybe he has to get out a rush order. How would *you* feel if these things happened to you? You can understand that he will be himself again when the problem has passed. You are being *empathetic*.

Empathy helps you to get along with people. It shows others that you respect them. When people know you respect them, it is easier to get along with them. They will communicate better with you. You will avoid conflicts. They will be more willing to help you solve problems.

✔ **Check Up** ✔ ✔ ✔

1. What is attitude?
2. What does it mean to have a positive attitude?
3. What does it mean to have a negative attitude?
4. What is self-esteem?
5. What is empathy?
6. How does empathy help you get along with people?

◯ Handling Conflict

Everybody sees things in different ways. What bothers some people may not bother you at all.

For example, you may like listening to a soft rock radio station at work. Your office mate, though, does not like rock music. It does not matter to him how softly you play it. He says it keeps him from doing his work. This could lead to *conflict.*

Conflict is the result of dispute. It can occur at home, at school, or on the job.

Your self-esteem affects how well you resolve conflict. If you have high self-esteem, you will work to solve the conflict. If you have low self-esteem, you may feel afraid of the other person. You may feel that the conflict is too hard to solve.

There will always be people with whom you disagree. So you must learn to resolve conflict with a positive attitude. Also, try to have empathy for the people with whom you have conflict.

◀ *To solve a conflict you must have a positive attitude. How does a positive attitude help these people to resolve a conflict?*

▷ Conflict Resolution Styles

The word *resolution* means agreement. So **conflict resolution** is bringing people who are in conflict with each other into agreement. Before you can resolve conflict, you must see who has the problem. Remember, a conflict may only be a problem for one person.

Think of the example of playing music at work. If you enjoy the music, this is not a conflict for you. It is only a problem for your office mate who does not like it.

If the conflict upsets only you, then *you* have the problem. Suppose your office mate does something you do not like. You are upset. But your office mate is not bothered by the problem. You have the problem with the conflict.

Sometimes both people feel there is a problem. For example, suppose your office mate does not like your music. But you do not like answering his phone calls and taking messages for him. In this case, both of you have a problem.

To solve a conflict, you have to *negotiate.* To **negotiate** means to try to reach an agreement through discussion. There are four styles people use when they are trying to resolve conflict. (See Figure 5-1.)

1. I win, and you lose.
2. You win, and I lose.
3. We both compromise.
4. You win, and I win.

Here is a closer look at each of these four styles. You may have used each at some point. See if you can choose a style you use most often.

I Win, and You Lose. With this style, you get what you want. But the other person loses. So if you have a conflict with your office mate over your music, how is this resolved? You keep playing the music. You are happy. But your office mate is unhappy. The music will affect how well he does his work.

You Win, and I Lose. With this style, you lose the conflict. The other person wins. So if you turn off your music in the office, what happens? Your office mate gets peace and quiet. He can do his job. But you do not get to listen to your music. You will be unhappy about the resolution.

If you use this approach, you might be trying to avoid conflict. This may not be the best solution to the problem.

We Both Compromise. In a **compromise**, both people give up something to resolve the conflict. What if your office mate says he can listen to jazz? What if you agree to play only jazz? This is a compromise.

With a compromise, sometimes neither person is happy. In this case, you get to listen to a type of music. But you might not like jazz. Your office mate does not get total peace and quiet. But he can put up with jazz.

▲ *Figure 5-1*
There are four conflict resolution styles. Which do you think is the best style? Why?

You Win, and I Win. This happens when both people get something they want. Suppose that you and your office mate have talked about your problem. He knows that you do not want to compromise. So he asks to be put with an office mate who also prefers a quiet office. You get to play music. He gets a quiet work space. You are both happy with the resolution.

✔ Check Up ✔ ✔ ✔

1. What is conflict?
2. What is conflict resolution?
3. What are four styles used to resolve conflict?
4. What is a compromise?
5. What happens in a "You win, and I win" situation?

A Desire to Succeed

Lech Walesa

When you think of a great leader, you do not think of an electrician. But that was before you heard of Lech Walesa. This electrician will be remembered as one of the great leaders of this century.

Lech Walesa worked as an electrician in the shipyards of Gdansk, Poland. In 1967 the workers in the shipyard and all over Poland started a movement. It was a movement to improve workers' rights. Walesa joined the movement.

In 1980, more than 50 Polish trade unions formed a group called Solidarity. Walesa was a part of Solidarity. That summer, Polish workers went on strike. They wanted higher pay, free trade unions, and political reform. The strike was a success. The government agreed to many of Solidarity's demands.

Walesa was named chairman of Solidarity in 1981. Later that year the government grew more opposed to Solidarity. It interfered with Solidarity's projects. The government put Walesa in prison.

When he was let out of jail in 1982, Walesa still was not free. The government tried to keep him from working for Solidarity. But its attempt to stop Walesa failed. Walesa's efforts had been noticed worldwide. In 1983 he was given the Nobel Peace Prize.

By 1990, Walesa had helped to create great political change all over Eastern Europe. On December 9, 1990, he was voted president of Poland.

The electrician from the shipyards of Gdansk was now the leader of his country. He had become one of the great leaders of his time.

O Positive Conflict Resolution

Conflicts can be unpleasant. But they always teach you something. So always try to resolve them in a positive way. See them as a way to grow.

When you are in conflict, take a positive approach. Be empathetic to the other person. Try to understand his or her feelings. Try to keep your emotions under control.

If you attack the other person, he or she will become defensive. The person will probably stop listening to you. He or she will only focus on planning a response. And you can bet that the response will be negative!

There are five steps you can follow to resolve conflict positively.

1. Focus on the problem.
2. Use clear messages.
3. Ask open-ended questions.
4. Be an active listener.
5. Build on common goals.

Here is a closer look at these steps.

▷ Focus on the Problem

Sometimes in a conflict, you may have a problem with the person and not the issue. You may dislike the other person. But that should not affect how you solve the problem. Try to focus your mind on the issue.

Look again at our example of playing music in the office. You may not like your office mate. But he has a right to want a quiet work space. The fact that you do not like him does not take away this right. So focus only on the conflict. Do not let your feelings for him affect how you resolve the issue.

▷ Use Clear Messages

When you are in conflict with someone, give clear messages about your feelings. Clear messages should do these things.

1. Tell what the conflict is.
2. Tell how the conflict is affecting you.
3. Describe your feelings.
4. Tell what solution you would like to see.

Here is an example of how to give a clear message.

You are often late coming home which makes me worried. (This tells the conflict and how it is affecting you.) I am afraid your car has broken down. (You describe your feelings.) I would like you to call me if you will be late. (This is the solution you would like to see.)

▷ Ask Open-ended Questions

Open-ended questions invite a person to give more than a yes or no answer. "What is the weather like today?" is an open-ended question. The person could tell you about the wind, the clouds, or the rain. "Is it raining outside?" is a closed question. It can be answered with a simple yes or no.

Open-ended questions let people tell their side of the story. They let people tell you their feelings.

How could you use open-ended questions in solving conflict? Here is an example.

Imagine that you know your roommate does not like the way you clean the apartment. In the past two weeks, you have cleaned twice. Each time, she has made nasty remarks about the poor job you have done. A conflict is forming. What open-ended questions could you ask her? Here are some examples.

- Why do I not clean the apartment well?
- What can I do to improve the way I clean?
- Why did you not tell me how you were feeling?

▷ Be an Active Listener

As you learned in Chapter 1, an active listener gets involved in the message. For example, when asking open-ended questions, listen for the answer. The person talking may be giving you a great deal of information. This may give you clues about how to resolve a conflict.

▷ Build on Common Goals

When you are in conflict with someone, try to find out if there is something you both can agree on. This is called *building on common goals.*

Building on common goals helps you resolve conflict. When both people can agree on *something*, it is easier to get to the "I Win, You Win" situation.

▲ *Being an active listener will help you solve a conflict. What is one way it can help?*

◀ *A conflict is resolved more quickly when you build on common goals. Why is this?*

★ Tricks of the Trade ★

Build on Common Goals

To build on common goals, start your conversation about the conflict with the word yes. Then state the truth. For example, "Yes, I have been absent four times during the past two weeks. Let me explain why." This positive approach will change the other person's attitude. He or she will be willing to listen.

✔ Check Up ✔ ✔ ✔

1. What are five things you can do to resolve a conflict positively?
2. What are four things clear messages should do?
3. What is an open-ended question?
4. How does being an active listener help to resolve a conflict?
5. How do you build on common goals?

○ Unresolved Conflict

Conflicts are not always resolved right away. Sometimes they are never resolved. In this case, you must learn to live with them.

Remember that some people are unwilling to make the changes it takes to resolve conflict. They may blame others for their problems. They may never accept their part in finding a solution. They will never see anything but "I win, and you lose."

On the other hand, some people blame only themselves. They do not know that others are also responsible for conflict. These people may be too quick to change. They may always feel

▶ *Not all conflicts can be resolved right away. If the people shown here are too upset to resolve the conflict, what should they do?*

☐ **Case Study** ☐ ☐ ☐ ☐ ☐ ☐

Jill is a manager at Jack's Grill. She has a conflict with one of her employees, Steve. He is a good worker. But every Tuesday night he leaves early. She has to finish his work.

Jill decides she must speak to Steve about this issue. She tells him she has a problem with his leaving early on Tuesdays. It bothers her very much. She feels that he is not being responsible.

Jill asks Steve why he must leave early on Tuesdays. Then she listens as Steve explains his side of the story.

Steve tells her he has to drive his mother to work on Tuesday nights. He did not tell Jill because he did not want to lose his shift.

They decide to rearrange his schedule so they can avoid this conflict. By following five important steps, Jill resolved her conflict.

that "You win, and I lose." You may be somewhere between these two types of people.

When conflict is unresolved, you may feel confused. This can hurt your self-esteem. It can make you feel less confident. You may feel that you have no control over the situation. So here are some things to remember about unresolved conflict.

First, the problem may work itself out. You will probably have the chance to come back to it again.

Second, stay positive about finding an agreement. It may happen someday.

Third, people can always change. Someone unwilling to resolve conflict now may change his or her mind.

Fourth, you may be too upset to resolve the conflict now. Come back to it another day when you feel calm.

Fifth, conflict resolution helps you grow. You learn to be responsible for the things you do. That is an important lesson. In fact, it is one of the best lessons you will ever learn.

✔ **Check Up** ✔ ✔ ✔

1. What are two types of people who prevent conflicts from being resolved?
2. What are five things to remember about unresolved conflict?
3. What should you do if you are too upset to resolve the conflict now?
4. What is an important lesson to learn about conflict resolution?

Chapter 5 Review

Chapter Summary

- A positive attitude helps you get along with people.
- Your self-esteem determines your attitude.
- Empathy helps you communicate with others.
- A conflict is a result of a disagreement.
- There are four conflict resolution styles.
- Try to resolve conflicts positively.
- There are five steps to follow to resolve conflicts positively.
- Conflicts are not always resolved right away.

Reviewing Vocabulary

Listed below are the important new words that were used in this chapter. Next to each word is the page on which you will find it. Turn to that page and read the paragraph in which the word is printed in **bold** type. Write the word and its meaning on a separate piece of paper.

1. human relations skills (81)
2. attitude (82)
3. self-esteem (83)
4. empathy (83)
5. conflict (85)
6. conflict resolution (86)
7. negotiate (86)
8. compromise (86)

Looking at the Facts

1. What are human relations skills?
2. What is the main reason most people lose their jobs?
3. What is attitude?
4. Why is it important to have a positive attitude?
5. Why is empathy the key to getting along with people?
6. How does self-esteem affect how well you resolve conflict?
7. What are four styles of conflict resolution?
8. What is the best negotiation style to use to resolve conflict?
9. List five things you can do to resolve a conflict positively.
10. What are four things that clear messages should do?
11. List five things to remember about unresolved conflict.

Thinking Critically

1. You and your roommate borrow each other's clothes. When you are done wearing your roommate's clothes, you wash them and put them away. But the clothes your roommate has borrowed from you are dirty and wrinkled. She tells you she will clean them, but she never does. You decide the time has come to tell your roommate about your concerns. What would you say?

2. A woman you share your office with at work has been upset lately. You wonder what might be wrong. What open-ended question could you ask this person?

3. You and a classmate are supposed to decide on and build a project for your science class. But you both cannot agree on what you will build. The project is due in a week. You still have not started it. You need to resolve your conflict right away. What three common goals can you build on?

Discussing Chapter Concepts

1. Discuss three ways your attitude might affect your life at home, at school, and at work.
2. Describe a time in which you were empathetic to someone.
3. Are there any jobs in which you would not have conflict? If so, what are they?
4. What conflicts might you deal with on your job?
5. List some conflicts that are not easy to resolve right away.

Using Basic Skills

Math

1. You and a friend earned $8 washing cars. You decide to spend your money at the bakery. Your friend wants to spend the money on a cake. You want to spend it on cookies. You resolve the conflict by agreeing to split the $8 evenly. Can your friend buy a $6 cake? Why or why not?

Communication

2. Suppose one of your co-workers takes a phone message for you. The message is not complete. The name of the caller is scribbled. You cannot read it. In clear language, tell your co-worker how you would like your messages to be written.

Human Relations

3. Your supervisor asks you to work an extra shift. You have made plans with your friends for the evening. The supervisor has never asked you to stay late before. You know that the extra help is needed. Use the "You win, and I win" style. Tell how you would handle this conflict.

Activities for Enrichment

1. For one week, write down any conflicts you have. How did you resolve each one? Was the conflict resolved positively?
2. Complete this sentence with as many words as you can think of. "I am valuable because…"
3. As a class, decide on a conflict that needs to be resolved. Pair up with a classmate. Negotiate to try to resolve the conflict. Once you have reached a resolution, determine what negotiation style you used.

Work Values

Words to learn and use

Here are the new terms you will learn in this chapter. Challenge yourself. Read through the list to see if you know what they mean.

values
initiative
responsible
self-control
loyalty
confidentiality
courtesy
respect
cooperation

Build on what you know

You already know...
- values help you set goals and make decisions.
- your values affect your work.
- employers want to hire people with work values.
- employees can develop work values.

In this chapter you will learn...
- how to develop values on the job.
- what work values employers are looking for.
- how to succeed by forming values.

Values are beliefs that are important to you. Other people can tell what your values are by the way you act. If you are truthful, for example, they know you value honesty. If you are willing to stay late at work, they know you value hard work.

It is important to show your values on the job. Employers look for people with work values. What are work values? How can they help you succeed? How can you develop them? These are the questions this chapter will answer.

O Work Values

Employers hire you to help make their business successful. So they look for people who will do a good job. This means they look for people with work values.

People who do a good job have these key work values.

- Initiative.
- Responsibility.
- Honesty.

We will take a close look at each of these work values. You will see how they make you valuable to your employer. You will also see how having these values will make you feel better about yourself.

▷ Initiative

Initiative means using your energy to make things happen. When you take the initiative, you act without waiting to be told what to do.

Employers want employees with initiative. Workers who have initiative do not need to be supervised as much as workers who do not have it. Workers with initiative do more work and do it better. They can work well on their own. They also work well as part of a team. Their positive attitude rubs off on others.

Employees who have initiative are self-starters. So employers often select them for further training. They give

▶ *Taking initiative is important on the job. How is the person shown here taking initiative?*

them more responsibility. And taking more responsibility often leads to promotions.

Showing initiative can help you on the job. These are some of the many ways you can show initiative at work.

- Improve the skills you have.
- Learn new skills.
- Ask for extra work.
- Show leadership.
- Help others.

Here is a closer look at each of these ways.

Improve the Skills You Have. You may reach a point in your job where your work does not challenge you. Do not say, "I am bored." Instead, think about how you can improve your skills. This will help you do your work better. You will save both yourself and the company time.

Learn New Skills. You may feel you know all of the skills you need to do your job. If so, ask to learn new skills.

Sometimes your employer will give you further training to teach you new skills. Perhaps you will learn to use different machines. Maybe you will add a new duty to your job.

Whatever new skills you learn, they will make your work more exciting. You will get more work done. You will feel better about yourself. You will enjoy your job more. You will do a better job overall.

Ask for Extra Work. Sometimes you may finish your work early. Or you may not have much work to do. In either case, find something to do! Ask for extra work. This will show your employer that you have initiative. You will also get a chance to learn new skills.

Show Leadership. Sometimes there are things that need to be done at work. But no one is doing them. You can show initiative by showing your leadership skills.

Suppose the company delivery truck needs to be cleaned. Tell your boss that you will be in charge of cleaning it. You can get other employees to help you. By doing this, you show that you are willing to help manage others. This shows that you value your own ability to guide others. It shows that you have leadership skills.

▷ Responsibility

Being **responsible** means you are reliable. If you are responsible, people know you will do what you say you will do. They can rely on you to get work done.

Wherever you work, you will be responsible for certain duties. Suppose you work at a fast-food restaurant. One of your duties might be cleaning the tables. If you are a secretary, you may have to order the office supplies.

☐ Case Study ☐ ☐ ☐ ☐ ☐ ☐

Pat has been late for work twice this week. Her boss thinks she may not be reliable.

Pat senses that she must change her behavior. She tells her boss she will be at work on time. She sets her alarm to wake up 15 minutes earlier.

This gives her time to do what she needs to do before she leaves the house.

Now Pat is at work on time every day. Her manager notices the change. She is pleased that Pat has become more reliable.

All employers want responsible workers. Here are some key traits of responsible workers.

- They are reliable.
- They help others.
- They have self-control.
- They admit their mistakes.

We will look closer at each of these traits. If you feel you do not have them now, try to develop them.

Being Reliable. There are things you can do to show that you are reliable. Your employer will see these things as very important.

Have a good attendance record. Do not call in sick unless you really are sick. Let your employer know well in advance when you plan to take your vacation.

Show up for work on time or a few minutes early. If you will be late, call your boss. Also, do not take long breaks and lunches.

Always finish every task. If you cannot finish a task, tell your boss. You may need further instructions.

Helping Others. There is always someone who can use your help at work. Do not wait to be asked. Ask yourself what you can do. Then take action.

If you are willing to help others, they will be more eager to help you. Sometimes you have to take the first step. Offer to help even if you are not asked. Never offer to do something and then fail to do it. The best teams are made up of people who help each other.

Having Self-control. Being able to control your actions means you have **self-control**. Having self-control means you can control your reactions in different situations. For example, suppose a customer blames you because the dress she bought at your store is torn. You have done nothing wrong. But she is blaming you anyway.

Instead of telling her that this is not your fault, keep your temper. Tell her you will exchange the torn dress for a new one. By using self-control, you have handled an angry customer.

Suppose your boss is considering promoting you. He or she will want to see how you show self-control. You can show your patience with customers and co-workers. You can be patient in learning your job duties.

Self-control is one of the most important traits you can have. Look for ways to develop self-control. It will help you get ahead in your work.

Admitting Mistakes. Everybody makes mistakes. It is one of the ways we learn. So when you make a mistake, admit it. Never let someone else take the blame for your mistake.

When you make a mistake at your job, try to fix it. Ask yourself how you can avoid making the mistake again.

Suppose that one of your job duties is to take phone messages. You take three messages in one hour. With two of them, though, you wrote the wrong numbers.

How can you avoid doing this again? As you learned in Chapter 1, make sure you repeat each phone number back to the caller. That way, you can be sure the number is correct.

▲ *Responsible people admit their mistakes. Why is it important for this employee to admit his mistake to his manager?*

✴ Tricks of the Trade ✴

Using Self-control

Speaking in a definite way lets others know what you will do and how you feel. This shows your self-control. So use words that show *you* are choosing a course of action. Say "I want to…" instead of "Maybe I should…." Say "I do not want to do that…" instead of "I probably should not…."

▷ Honesty

Honesty is a key work value. To keep their business successful, employers want to hire honest people. So they look for employees they can trust.

Can you think of some ways that people at work are not honest? Here are some of the most common ways.

- Cheating on time cards.
- Taking breaks when they should be working.
- Taking office supplies.
- Taking snacks they have not paid for.
- Leaving early without asking to do so.
- Calling in sick when they are well.

You may think that some of these examples are not serious. You may say, "I am not hurting anyone if I take a long break or leave early."

But you are really hurting yourself by doing any of these things. If your supervisor finds out what you have done, he or she will not trust you. Once you destroy that trust, it is hard to get it back.

So think about honesty on the job. Suppose you had to name three traits that show you are honest. What three traits would you name? There are three common traits of honesty.

- Confidentiality.
- Trust.
- Loyalty.

Here is a closer look at these traits.

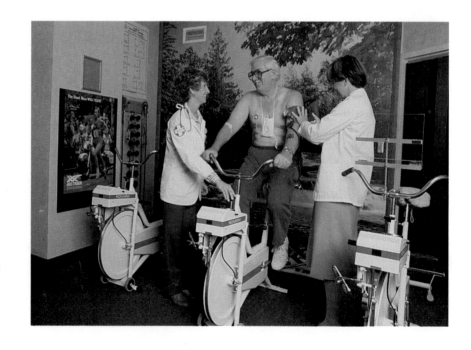

▶ *Many jobs require confidentiality. Why would this be important in the health care profession?*

Confidentiality. Protecting others' right to privacy is **confidentiality**. This is important in many fields. Think of some jobs in which confidentiality is important.

Health care workers, for example, work with those who are ill. But they should never talk to their friends about their patients. If they do, they are not protecting their patients' rights.

Bank tellers work with other people's money. They should not tell their friends how much a bank customer deposits in the bank. This is confidential information.

Think of the things you would not want your doctor, teacher, or boss to tell other people about you. Then remember that others want you to protect their rights to privacy, too.

Trust. Good relationships are built on trust. Dishonesty destroys trust. Your boss cannot and should not have to watch you at all times. So he or she needs to trust you.

If you handle money, your boss needs to know that you will not steal it. If you work with office supplies, your boss needs to know that you will not take any for yourself.

There will be times at work when you must make decisions on your own. Suppose your boss must leave early. She asks you to stay until closing time and answer the phones. You could leave early. No one would know. But the phones need to be answered. By staying, you show your honesty.

Loyalty. Being faithful is **loyalty**. What are you loyal to? You are probably loyal to your friends and family. This means that you support them in the things they choose to do.

It is also important to be loyal to your employer. This means that you support your company and your boss. You do not speak badly about your company or your boss to others. Your job depends on your employer's success. If you are not loyal to your employer, you may hurt the company.

When you leave a job, never say bad things about past employers. In job interviews, people sometimes blame past employers for problems they had on the job. Never do this. It will reflect poorly on you. The new employer may feel that you will say bad things about him or her, too. You may not get hired.

✔ Check Up ✔ ✔ ✔

1. What does having initiative mean?
2. What are four ways you can show initiative at work?
3. What are four key traits of responsible workers?
4. What are three common traits of honesty?
5. Why is trust important in the workplace?

A Desire to Succeed

Ben Cohen and Jerry Greenfield

Ben Cohen and Jerry Greenfield make ice cream. They call it Vermont's Finest All Natural Ice Cream. How did they start their business? They took a home study course. Then they opened their first shop in 1978 with only $12,000!

Today, Ben and Jerry drive around in a motorhome. They call it the Cowmobile. They give away samples of their products. *Time* magazine called their ice cream "the best in the world." President Reagan named them the U.S. Small Business Persons of the Year.

As you can see, Ben and Jerry are successful! But they care as much for their community as they care for their business. They have set up a non-profit foundation to give money to community service groups. They give 7.5 percent of their company's pre-tax earnings to this foundation each year. They also use part of their profits to help the environment. The money from their Rainforest Crunch ice cream goes to support the rainforest in South America.

Ben and Jerry also care about the people who work for them. They set up a Joy Committee in their company. The people on this committee create programs to put more joy in the workplace.

Ben and Jerry's business has had its setbacks along the way. The first Cowmobile burned on a trip across the country. Ben and Jerry said it looked like "the world's biggest baked Alaska."

All in all, though, Ben and Jerry's values have made them a success. Many people now enjoy Ben and Jerry's Ice Cream.

○ Work Values and Your Co-workers

You already know that more people lose their jobs because of conflict with co-workers than for any other reason. So employers look for employees who get along with other people. Getting along with people shows that you respect them. And your respect for others is an important work value.

When you respect people, it means you see their value. You see what skills each person has to offer. People who work well with others share these common behaviors.

- Courtesy.
- Respect.
- Acceptance.
- Cooperation.
- Humor.
- Friendship.

Here is more about why these are important work values.

▷ Courtesy

When you begin a new job, you meet many new people. You will not know each other very well. You hope they will be nice to you. They are expecting you to be nice to them, too. They will expect you to have *courtesy*. **Courtesy** is being considerate of others.

Think of ways you can show courtesy at work. You can hold the door for a co-worker. You can answer someone else's phone. You can be polite in talking to people. Showing courtesy will help you get along with your co-workers.

▷ Respect

Respect means you hold someone or something in high regard. He or she is worthy of your attention.

As you and your co-workers get to know each other better, you will grow to respect each other. Then you will be better able to work together.

Respect is important to any relationship. Think of reasons why you would *not* respect a person. For example, would you respect someone who was dishonest? Would you respect someone who is not loyal to your company? Your answer to both of these questions is probably no.

Think, then, how important respect is to your relationships at work. To work well together, people need to hold each other in high regard. They need to feel they are working with those who have work values. You will have to work to gain your co-workers' respect. You will have to show them you have work values.

Case Study

Ross joined the basketball team at work. He did it just for fun. Still, his team liked to win. Ross noticed that each team member seemed to be good at certain things. Some could shoot. Some could pass. Some were good at guarding. He could see the value of each team member. No team member was good at everything. But when they combined everyone's talents as a team, they all played together well.

The next day at work, Ross thought about the teamwork it takes to win games. "My co-workers are my team members," he thought. "When everyone works together, we help the company win."

▷ Acceptance

To work with others, you need to accept that they may be different from you. During your career, you will work with people who have different beliefs and backgrounds. You may not understand everyone you work with. But it is important to learn how to work with them.

Even when you have a lot in common with co-workers, you may approach tasks in different ways. You may have different strengths. You must see the value in your co-workers' skills.

▷ Cooperation

Cooperation means working together to achieve common goals. Accepting others leads to true cooperation.

▲ *Cooperation means working together to reach a common goal. Why is it important for this team to cooperate?*

In many companies today, employees must work in teams. This means that you may have to work with people you might not choose for friends. But you still must work together to achieve common goals.

Teamwork is only possible when people cooperate. All team members must look at the common goal.

For example, if your boss gives you and your co-workers a project, look at the common goal. It may be to write a report. It may be to figure out a better way to do something. Once you have a common goal, cooperate with your co-workers. See how you can all work together to reach that goal.

▷ Humor

Have you noticed how humor makes it easier to do any task? Have you noticed how much you like being around people with a sense of humor?

Humor in the workplace makes your day more pleasant. You enjoy your work more.

Never use humor to make fun of others. If you do, you will not get their cooperation. It will also show that you cannot accept their differences.

▷ Friendship

One of the nicest things that can happen on the job is forming friendships. Friendships grow out of respect, acceptance, and cooperation.

Friendships allow us to depend on each other. This is important on the job. We have to depend on each other to achieve company goals.

▲ *How can humor and friendship help you on the job?*

✔ Check Up ✔ ✔ ✔

1. What are five common behaviors that people who work well with others share?
2. What does *respect* mean?
3. Why do you need cooperation on the job?
4. When should you *not* use humor on the job?

Chapter 6 Review

Chapter Summary

- Values are beliefs that are important to you.
- Employers look for people with work values.
- Employers want workers who show initiative and responsibility.
- Honesty builds trust.
- Learning to work with other people on the job is important.
- You will get along better with people on the job if you respect them.
- People who work well with others share certain work values. These values include courtesy, respect, acceptance, cooperation, humor, and friendship.

Reviewing Vocabulary

Listed below are the important new words that were used in this chapter. Next to each word is the page on which you will find it. Turn to that page and read the paragraph in which the word is printed in **bold** type. Write the word and its meaning on a separate piece of paper.

1. values (97)
2. initiative (98)
3. responsible (99)
4. self-control (100)
5. loyalty (103)
6. confidentiality (103)
7. courtesy (105)
8. respect (105)
9. cooperation (106)

Looking at the Facts

1. List three work values.
2. Name three things you can do to show initiative at work.
3. What does being responsible mean?
4. What are four examples of people being dishonest at work?
5. Why is it important to get along with people at work?
6. What work value makes teamwork possible?
7. How will humor help you at work?

Thinking Critically

1. You are in a job interview. You are asked to talk about your three most important values. Write down what you will say.
2. At an interview, you are asked about the job you just left. The reason you left was because your boss was unhappy with your work. She did not like the way you did anything. What will you say to the interviewer?
3. You and a co-worker have been asked to use the company van to deliver packages. You deliver the first package. Then your

co-worker suggests you take a break for five minutes. What would you say to your co-worker?

Discussing Chapter Concepts

1. Can you think of a time when humor should *not* be used on the job?
2. How can dishonesty hurt your growth at your company?
3. You make a mistake at work that someone else could be blamed for. Nobody saw you make the mistake. Would you still admit it anyway? Why or why not?
4. Why is confidentiality so important in jobs such as health care?

Using Basic Skills

Math

1. You work at an ice cream store. Every day your co-worker sneaks eight spoonfuls of ice cream. He says it does not matter. Each spoonful only costs the owner a nickel. You want to prove to your co-worker that this adds up over a week. How much has the employee cost the owner in ice cream over seven days?

Communication

2. You are a bank teller. Your first customer comes in and deposits $5,000. After the customer leaves, the next customer in line says, "How much did she deposit? That looked like a lot of money!" Write one or two sentences telling what you would say to the second customer.

Human Relations

3. A new worker just came into your department. She seems nervous. What can you do to help her feel welcome?

Activities for Enrichment

1. Interview a business owner or manager. Ask the person to look at this list of work values. Then ask the person to rank them in their order of importance on a separate piece of paper.

List	Rank
initiative	
responsibility	
honesty	
trust	
loyalty	
confidentiality	

2. Pretend you have an interview for a bank teller's job. Write a brief sentence to tell how you would answer each of these questions.

   "Why do you want to work for this company?"

   "Why did you leave your last job?"

   "What are your career plans?"

   "What do you do to get along with others at work?"

   "What are some of your work values?"

Chapter 7

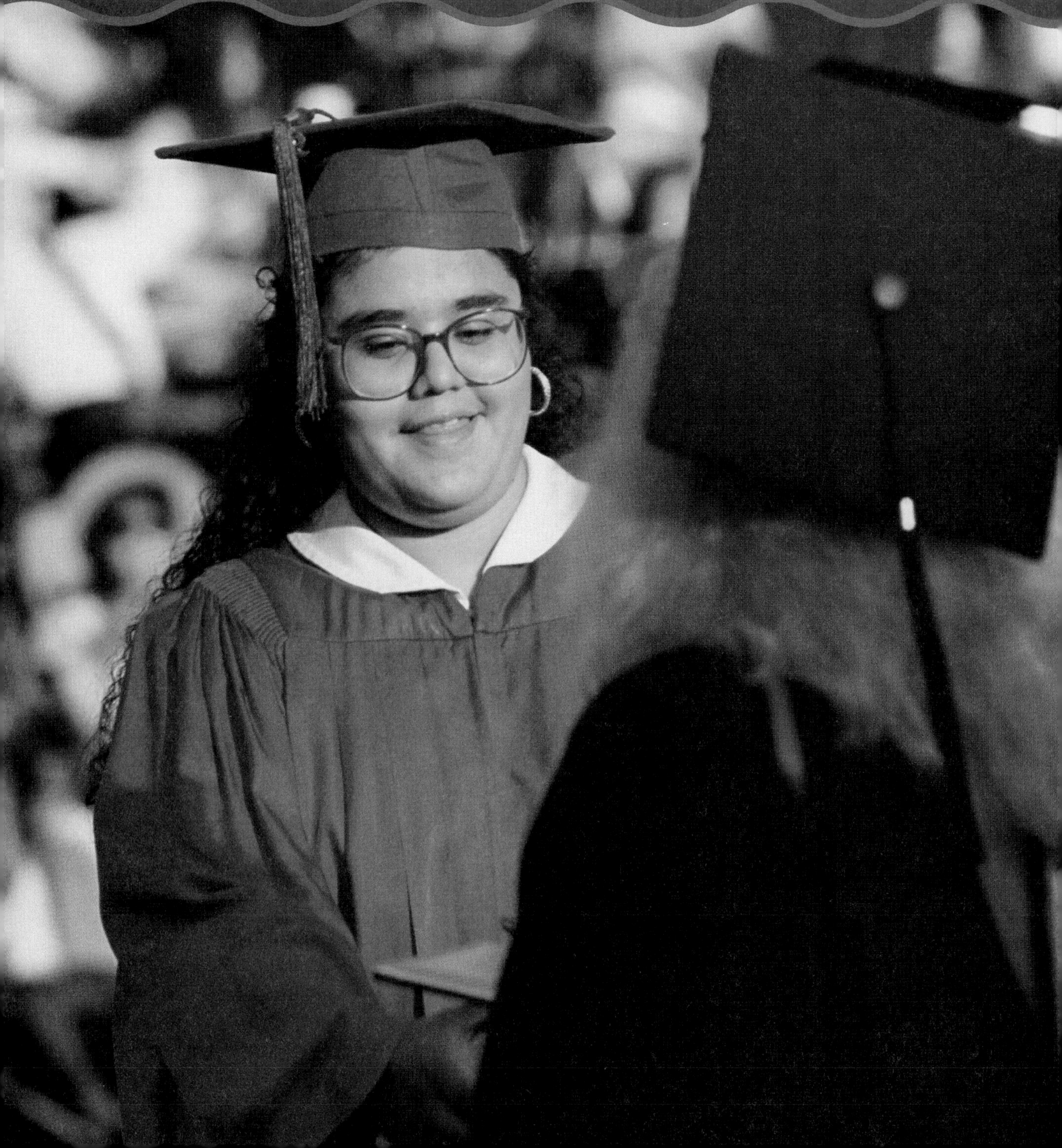

Further Education

Words to learn and use

Here are the new terms you will learn in this chapter. Challenge yourself. Read through the list to see if you know what they mean.

formal education
trade schools
apprenticeship
trade
home study programs
informal education
vocational student organizations
occupational organizations

Build on what you know

You already know...
- you go to school to learn skills.
- you can continue your education after high school.
- you can learn skills outside of school.
- you are in charge of your own learning.

In this chapter you will learn...
- how skills you learn now will help you on the job.
- how to continue your formal education.
- how to find opportunities for informal education.
- how to get the most out of your education.

Learning is a life-long process. You should always want to learn and grow. Some people find their place in life by trial and error. Others take time to plan and explore. Planning your life will help you reach your goals.

There are many ways you can plan and prepare for the life you want. The learning you do will help you to reach your goals. This chapter will show you the ways you can do so.

⭕ Formal Education

You have spent many years in *formal education*. **Formal education** is the learning that takes place in school. Soon you will graduate from high school. Then you must decide how you will further your learning. Will you go on to another school for more formal education? If so, what kind of school will you choose?

There are many types of schools to choose from. You could attend a trade school. You could study at a community college. You could enter an apprenticeship program. You could work and take classes through adult education programs. You might even enter the military.

Knowing which choice is best for you is important. Try to learn all you can about your choices.

▷ Your High School Years

Begin now to make the most of your high school years. Do you know what type of work you want to do? If not, see your counselor. He or she can help you explore careers.

▶ *School counselors can help you decide what type of work you want to do. Why is it important to decide on a career before choosing further education?*

☐ Case Study ☐ ☐ ☐ ☐ ☐ ☐

Tony was nearing the end of the tenth grade. He did not have much interest in school. He did not ask questions in class. He studied just enough to get by. He did not take part in any programs after school.

Tony's counselor called him in to help him plan next year's classes. The counselor asked about Tony's interests. But Tony did not want to talk. He thought it was too soon to be planning ahead. His courses were not that important to him.

Later, Tony asked his friends to help him pick his new classes. He looked for easy classes.

In his senior year, Tony became interested in opening a take-out food business after he graduated. He asked his counselor how he could do this. Tony learned that he had not taken the classes he needed to learn how to run a business. He needed to go to summer school to make up the classes. Tony realized he should have planned ahead.

Both counselors and teachers can help you learn about your abilities. They can help you think about the things you like to do. They can also help you learn about your values.

Knowing these things makes it easier to choose a career. After you make that choice, it is time to put your high school education to work.

Plan now how you will reach your career goal. Think about what you can do to get ready for a job. Most jobs require a high school diploma. Planning to finish your high school education is a big step toward your goal.

Different skills are needed for different jobs. Your counselors and teachers can help you find out what skills you will need. Then they can suggest classes that will help you learn those skills. They might also ask you to take a *career interest survey*. The survey will help show you what type of work you will like. It helps you find the direction you want to go in school and in work.

Think about the schools you could attend after high school. What type of schools will provide the training needed for your career? Are there any classes you must take in high school to enroll in those schools? Plan your high school schedule to include these classes. Planning ahead is a key to success. Let your teachers and counselor help you with your career plans.

▷ Trade Schools

Trade schools help people learn job skills. Sometimes they are called *technical schools.*

There are many trade schools you might choose to attend. Some are private schools. Some are public schools. Public schools often cost less. But private schools may train you faster.

What does it cost to attend a trade school? It depends on how many courses you take and how long you attend. Most programs will cost from several hundred to several thousand dollars.

Suppose you want to attend a trade school. But you do not know which one would be best for you. The first step is to decide what you want to learn. Then choose a school that offers courses in that skill. Choose a school that employers respect. Also, be sure the school is *accredited.* This means the school has met national standards of education. Ask your counselor for a list of all accredited schools.

Trade schools try to place you in a paying job while you are in school. The program at a trade school may take as long as two years to complete. In some cases, you may finish in a few weeks or a few months.

The length of your program depends on the skills you want to learn. For example, it may take up to two years to become a practical nurse.

It may take only a few months to become a food service worker.

Trade schools often start new courses every few weeks. So you do not have to wait until the end of the quarter or semester to enroll. You can graduate as soon as you finish your courses.

After you graduate, you are ready to look for a job. A good trade school will help you find a job through its *placement service.* Look for this service when you are choosing a trade school.

▷ Community Colleges

Most community colleges are public schools. They are low-cost colleges. Yearly costs are about half those of a four-year public college. In some parts of the country, they are called *junior colleges.* There are about 1,200 community colleges in the United States. So there is probably one close to you.

Community colleges offer several types of programs. If you attend a community college, you may want to enroll in a two-year program. Or you may want to enroll in a certificate program.

In a two-year program, you will graduate with an associate degree. This program prepares you to transfer to a four-year college. After you finish the program, the college transfer service will help you transfer to another school.

◀ *Community colleges offer programs at a lower cost than four-year public colleges. What type of jobs might this person be prepared for after attending this auto repair program?*

Most certificate programs can be finished in two years or less. You take classes that relate to the work you plan to do. When you complete the program, you will receive a certificate. This shows you are prepared to do a certain type of work. You can prepare for many types of jobs. These include auto repair, food service, and printing.

You can also combine a certificate program with an associate degree program. Your counselor can help you find out what choices are right for you.

Community colleges offer many services. They provide career counseling. They can help you decide what courses to take. Community colleges often help students figure out how to pay for college expenses. They offer financial aid and provide help for disabled students.

Community colleges provide many student activities. You may take part in student government. You can help publish the school newspaper. You can also choose activities such as drama, music, and sports.

Community colleges offer many choices. Does a community college near you have programs to help you reach your goal? Ask your counselor how you can find out.

▷ Apprenticeships

An **apprenticeship** is a training program that offers a way to earn while you learn. An *apprentice* is a person who learns by on-the-job training. Apprentices also do classroom work.

Apprenticeships are offered in more than 820 types of work. Most of these jobs are in the trades. A **trade** is a job that requires manual or mechanical skill. Having manual skill means you are good with your hands. Having mechanical skill means you understand and like subjects such as math and drafting.

You may be able to start your apprenticeship training while you are still in high school. But often you must have a high school diploma to be an apprentice.

Apprenticeships offer many benefits. You are paid while you take your training. You are paid less than a skilled worker. But you receive raises as you learn and become more skilled. You can register with the Bureau of Apprenticeship and Training (BAT).

You will be given credit for your apprenticeship hours. If you are registered with the BAT, your hours will be recognized all over the country.

The length of an apprenticeship is often about four years. Some programs are as short as one year. Others require up to six years. When you finish all the work, you receive a certificate of completion.

▷ Adult Education

Adult education is another way you can continue to learn new skills. These classes are sometimes called *continuing education*. Many community colleges and high schools offer adult education programs. Some private schools and groups offer these programs, too.

Often, these classes meet in the evening. So you can work while you go to school. Many adults use these classes to improve their job skills. This helps them to advance in their work. People also take these classes to learn new hobbies. New interests can sometimes lead to new jobs.

The cost of adult education classes offered by public schools is very low. You must be 18 to enroll in most of these classes.

Many skills are taught in adult education classes. Business skills, language skills, and craft skills are a few examples. Trade skills may also be taught in these programs.

★ Tricks of the Trade ★

Career Planning

Always have more than one plan for reaching your career goal. This will give you a better chance of reaching success.

Some adults choose to continue their education at home through **home study programs**. This is a good choice if you live far from a school.

With home study courses, you get written materials. You are also assigned a home study teacher whom you can write or call. Or, you may watch television programs or receive work on your home computer.

Do you study well on your own? If so, a home study course might be a way for you to further your education. Be sure the course is a good one.

▷ Military Service

You can continue your education through military service. The Army, Navy, Air Force, and Marine Corps are the branches of our military.

When you join, you agree to serve your country. You will be trained to defend your country in the event of a war. You will also have the chance to learn work skills. These skills may help you find a job after you are out of the military.

Continued on page 119.

◀ *Home study courses allow you to continue your education at home. What is an advantage of a home study course?*

A Desire to Succeed

Thomas Alva Edison

Thomas Alva Edison was born in 1847. As a young boy, he was always asking questions. When people gave him answers, he tested them to see if they were right.

Thomas began school when he was eight. His formal education did not last long. His teacher said that he was unteachable. He questioned everything the teacher said. So his mother took him out of school and taught him how to read.

Thomas never stopped reading and learning. He bought supplies to try all the science experiments he read about.

When he was 12, he took a job selling newspapers on a train. When he was not selling papers on the train, he worked on science experiments. He set up a laboratory in an empty boxcar. He believed there was too much to do to waste any time.

During those years on the train, Thomas began to lose his hearing. He said his poor hearing drove him to improve the telephone. Before his improvements, people had to shout to be heard over the phone. The parts he invented for the phone are still used today.

Thomas made 1,093 inventions. He credits his success to his hard work. Some of his best known inventions are the phonograph and the light bulb. It took him two years to find the right material for the light bulb. After more than 1,000 tries, he found a material that would work.

Edison worked until his death at the age of 84. He lived up to his saying that "to stop is to rust."

After you complete your basic training, you will attend classes to learn a job skill. The classes may last from a few weeks to a year. When you finish your classes, you will be given a job in the military. Some of the jobs for which you can train are fire fighter, welder, health care worker, and police officer.

▲ *You may continue your education through the military. What is one duty and one benefit of enlisting in the military?*

Serving in the military may help you get other benefits. After you have finished your service duty, you may get help in paying for more education.

Find out what the military has to offer you. One way you can learn more is to take a test. This is the Armed Services Vocational Aptitude Battery or ASVAB test. It will help you find out what careers you are suited for. Your high school counselor can tell you more about it. In fact, your school may offer it. Even if you have no interest in military service, you can take this test. It is a good way to learn more about your own talents and skills.

The results of the test will be sent to your school. They will also be sent to each branch of the military service. Recruiters will contact you. But taking the test does *not* mean you have to enlist in the military.

Some people like military life. Others do not. Talk to your counselor about it. Learn about the benefits and the duties before you enlist.

✔ Check Up ✔ ✔ ✔

1. What are four options for education after high school?
2. What type of school will train you fastest for a trade?
3. How long are apprenticeships?
4. What are home study courses?
5. What is an ASVAB test?

○ Informal Education

As you know, formal education is learning in a classroom. But there are many other ways to learn. You can join student clubs that meet to learn about jobs. You can learn while you work. You can read magazines about careers that interest you.

After you have a job, you can join groups that are just for members of your trade. You can learn from volunteer work and hobbies.

These ways of learning on your own are called **informal education.** The chances for informal learning are a part of daily life. Learn to look for them. Use them to help you reach your goal. As you pursue your learning, your goals may change. And you will need to keep on learning to achieve new goals.

▷ Vocational Student Organizations

You may have some **vocational student organizations** at your high school. They are also called VSOs. These are student clubs that allow students to learn about an occupation. There are many VSOs. FFA studies agri-business and science. DECA explores jobs in marketing. Business Professionals of America (BPA) studies office technologies. Health Occupations Students of America (HOSA) is for students with interest in health careers. Vocational Industrial Clubs of America (VICA) is for students with interest in the trades. What VSOs are at your school? Would you like to help start a new one?

There are many reasons to join VSOs. You will get to know other students who share your interests. You can learn from each other. You can work with other students on projects. You can develop leadership skills. You can learn about the occupation. You may even visit work sites.

Members of VSOs often get trade magazines, journals, special reports, and pamphlets. People from the community may talk to your group about the occupation.

★ Tricks of the Trade ★

Picture Yourself on the Job

Find a picture in a magazine of a person doing the job you want. Cut the picture out. Put it where you will see it every day. Next to it, put a list of the steps necessary to get this job. Then, work toward your goal daily. See yourself in the job.

VSOs are often formed on local, district, and state levels. Many have national groups. Special meetings are held to get people from these groups together. You can go to these meetings and learn from other people. Speakers will give you the latest news about occupations. Sometimes trade fairs are held at these meetings. This will give you a chance to see the newest products and tools.

Some VSOs help students get more training after high school. They do this by offering scholarships to deserving students.

Does a VSO sound like it could help you meet your goal? If so, check with your counselor for active VSOs at your school.

▷ On-the-job Training

A good way to learn a job is simply to do it. Some employers offer their workers on-the-job training. You will be taught skills by people on the job. They know how your boss wants the work to be done.

You do not need to wait until you have finished school to begin your on-the-job training. You could work part-time after school or on weekends. You could work in a local business through your school co-op program. You could also look for summer jobs.

Working part-time will give you a chance to find out if you like the work. It is a good idea to try a few types of

▲ *On-the-job training is a good way to learn while you work. What are four benefits of on-the-job training?*

part-time jobs. This will help you make career choices.

You may not find a part-time job in a career that interests you. But you can still learn good work skills from on-the-job training. These skills are useful in any work you do.

After high school, you may want to look for a job that offers on-the-job training. If so, find out what kind of training you will get. Will you learn more than one skill? Will these skills help you get the job you want? Be sure your choice will help you reach your career goal.

▷ Reading Trade Magazines

Many trades have their own magazines. For example, people in the automobile trades can read and learn from auto repair magazines. Health care workers can read trade magazines on health and fitness.

You can buy some trade magazines at stores. Others you must get through a trade group. (You may need to be a group member to buy the magazine.)

In trade magazines, you can read about ways to do your job better. You can find out about jobs in your field. This will help you advance in your work.

Ask the librarian in your school or public library about trade magazines. He or she can help you find magazines on trades that interest you.

▲ *Trade magazines can help you improve your skills and learn more about different trades. Which of these trade magazines would interest you?*

▷ Occupational Organizations

Occupational organizations are groups of people who do the same kind of work. These groups are sometimes called *trade associations.* They offer many of the same benefits as VSOs. They share the latest news in their fields. They hold fairs and meetings to exchange ideas. They support research on new products. They look for better ways of doing their work.

There are many trade groups in the country. There are trade groups that deal with clothing, cars, and roofing. These are just a few.

When you begin to work, find out what trade associations you can join. Your employer and co-workers can help. Make an effort to keep learning about your work. The more you know, the more choices you will have.

▷ Volunteer Activities

If you cannot find a part-time job, try volunteer activities. Hospitals often need volunteers. Museums and animal shelters need volunteers, too.

Many groups have large volunteer staffs. The American Red Cross and the American Lung Association are just two examples. Recycling centers and food service programs need volunteers. Youth sports programs always need volunteers.

▲ *Volunteering is a good way to learn more about different careers. What are some benefits of volunteering?*

Your high school may offer school credit for volunteer activities. Talk to your counselor about volunteer jobs in your area.

Volunteering has many benefits. You can learn new skills. The skills you learn depend on what you do. Office volunteers may do typing or filing. Hospital volunteers may help patients.

Volunteering will help you learn about jobs in new areas. It can help you choose the kind of work you want to do. Employers like to see volunteer experience. It shows that you have interest and initiative.

Volunteering also helps you feel good about yourself. And feeling good about yourself will help you succeed.

▷ **Hobby Groups**

Do you have a hobby that you enjoy? You may be able to turn a hobby into a job. Learn all you can about your hobby. The more you know about it, the better your chance of finding work in that field.

Even if you cannot combine your hobby and work, you can learn helpful skills. Are there hobby clubs at your school? Look for one that interests you.

Hobby groups often hold meetings to share ideas or to work on projects. Sometimes adults interested in the hobby serve as advisors. They can help you find out more about your hobby. They may know of clubs outside of school that you can join.

Look for work that interests you. You will be happier doing work that you like.

✔ **Check Up** ✔ ✔ ✔

1. What are VSOs?
2. What can you learn from trade magazines?
3. What can you learn from volunteer activities?
4. What do hobbies have to do with work?

Chapter 7 Review

Chapter Summary

- Formal education is learning in school.
- Plan your goals in high school.
- There are schools and programs for learning job skills.
- Informal education is learning on your own.
- Learning takes place through reading and working.

Reviewing Vocabulary

Listed below are the important new words that were used in this chapter. Next to each word is the page on which you will find the word. Turn to that page and read the paragraph where the word is printed in **bold** type. Write the word and its meaning. Then write a sentence of your own using each word.

1. formal education (112)
2. trade schools (114)
3. apprenticeship (116)
4. trade (116)
5. home study programs (117)
6. informal education (120)
7. vocational student organizations (120)
8. occupational organizations (122)

Looking at the Facts

1. List four types of formal education. Do not include high school.
2. Why should you finish high school?
3. Name two types of programs offered by community colleges. How are they different?
4. What are two of the benefits of apprenticeships?
5. What is your main duty if you join the military?
6. How can the military help you reach your career goal?
7. Describe three types of informal education.
8. On-the-job training and volunteer activities offer some of the same benefits. What is a special benefit you get from volunteering?
9. Why is combining a hobby with work a good idea?

Thinking Critically

1. How are trade schools and community colleges alike? How are they different?
2. How are apprenticeships and on-the-job training alike? How are they different?
3. Suppose you have a job you like. Is it still important to continue your education? Why or why not?
4. Suppose you have a job. You would like to learn skills for a different type of work. But if you quit working, you will not have enough money to go to school.

Name at least two ways you can continue your education.

5. What should you find out about a school before you choose to go there?

Discussing Chapter Concepts

1. You know that counselors and teachers can help you learn about careers. List other people and sources that can also help you learn about work.
2. Suppose you are thinking about two programs. One is a two-year program at a community college. The other is an apprenticeship for four years. How would you compare the costs of these programs?
3. Discuss the many ways you can learn informally. Make a list on the chalkboard of ways people learn.

Using Basic Skills

Math

1. You have decided to learn auto body repair. A local trade school offers a one-year program. The cost is $4,000. You can also learn this trade at the local community college. This program requires two years to complete. The cost of attending community college is $1,400 per year. What is the difference in the cost of the two programs? Which costs more?

Communication

2. Ask your counselor for the name of a VSO. Write to the district, state, or national office. Ask for information about the group. Share what you have learned with your class.

Human Relations

3. Getting along with others is an important job skill. Think about a time when you did not get along with a co-worker or student. Describe the problem. How did you handle it? What other way could you have used to deal with the problem?

Activities for Enrichment

1. Call your local adult education office. Ask for a class schedule. Read the current class schedule. Select a class that interests you. Find out the time and place where it is being taught.
2. Do some research to learn what hobby groups meet in your community. The public library is a good place to begin your research. Make a list of at least five groups you are able to locate.
3. As a class project, make a chart that compares trade schools, apprenticeships, community colleges, and military job training. Compare the length of each program, the cost, and the kinds of skills taught.

Changing Jobs and Careers

Words to learn and use

Here are the new terms you will learn in this chapter. Challenge yourself. Read through the list to see if you know what they mean.

career
field
job
career goals
promotion
lateral move
transfer skills
data

Build on what you know

You already know...
- you may change jobs and careers.
- your career goals may change.
- you like using some skills more than others.

In this chapter you will learn...
- why you may change jobs.
- how to transfer your skills from one job to another.
- how to get a job using the skills you enjoy.
- when to stay in the job you have.

Pretend you are standing at the edge of a forest. Think of this forest as your *career.* Your **career** is made up of the work you do during your life.

Now walk into the forest. Each tree represents a *career field.* A **field** is an area in which you have special skills or training. For example, you may work in the health care field.

Now imagine taking a leaf off a tree. The leaf represents a *job* within a field. A **job** is a collection of duties.

Most people today will probably work in about three fields during their lives. They may have more than one job in each field. This chapter will help you look at what you need to consider when changing career fields or jobs.

O Why Change?

As you know, you may change your job or career field one or many times. Many people change because they want to or have to. There are some common reasons why people change jobs or careers.

1. Their career goals change.
2. There is no room to grow in their present job.
3. They worry about their safety.
4. They have conflict with co-workers.
5. Their company closes.
6. They want a change.

Here is a closer look at each of these reasons for change.

▷ Career Goals

Your **career goals** are what you want to achieve during your working life. If you are a nurse, for example, you may want to try two or three types of nursing during your career. You may want to be an emergency room nurse. You may want to try working in an operating room, too.

But suppose you have been working in a doctor's office for five years. You may do only one type of nursing there. Your job will not help you meet all your career goals. So you may want to look for another job. You may look in a hospital. There you can do many types of nursing.

There are many career goals. If you work as a carpenter now, you might want to become a building contractor someday. If you work as a secretary now, you might want to become an office manager. Think about the career field that interests you. What are some career goals in that field?

▷ No Room to Grow

Some people like to think of jobs as ladders. You start at the bottom and work your way up. Every step of the ladder is a higher level at which you learn new skills. Getting promoted helps you climb to a higher level.

But sometimes there are no openings above you. Your climb up the ladder is blocked. Maybe you have learned all you can at this job. You have already reached the top of the ladder.

In either case, you need to find a new ladder. That is, you need to find a new job to advance in your career.

Sometimes you will leave a job to move to a higher level job. This is a **promotion** for you. Promotions are common reasons for changing jobs.

Sometimes, though, your new job may be at the same level as your old job. This is called a **lateral move**. Lateral means sideways. So making a lateral move means stepping sideways from one ladder to another.

◀ You may take a new job that is at the same level as your old job. What are three reasons you might do this?

A lateral move may not be a promotion for you. But you may see more room to grow at this new company. If so, you expect to climb higher on the new ladder.

▷ Your Safety

You may like your job. But you may feel that the work site is unsafe. If you feel your safety is at risk, you may want to find a new job.

Most jobs have some dangers. There may even be some risk at your co-op job. For example, if you work around machinery, you know that you must always be careful. With every job that involves any danger, you should receive safety training.

If you are unsure about the safety conditions where you work, you can contact OSHA. OSHA stands for the Occupational Safety and Health Administration. The people at OSHA can tell you about your safety rights.

▷ Conflict with Co-workers

You will probably have at least some conflict on every job. But if the conflict is never resolved, you will enjoy your work less. And it will be harder to work as part of a team.

Having constant conflicts on your job is draining, even if you are not part of the conflict. So, if there is an unresolved conflict, it may be time to find a new job.

⭐ **Tricks of the Trade** ⭐

Leaving on Your Terms

Never leave a job in a moment of anger. Give yourself a chance to calm down. Think the situation through. Leave a job on your terms, feeling good about the work you have done.

Before you leave a job, though, try to resolve the conflict. You may find a solution to the problem.

▷ Job Changes or Cuts

Companies sometimes have to change or cut jobs. Both can happen for two key reasons.

1. Changes in the economy that affect business.
2. Changes in equipment that affect the way the job will be done.

The first reason for job changes or cuts is a bad economy. People are not buying as much of a company's product. So the company does not need to make as many products.

In this case, the company must cut some jobs. Or it may change some jobs by combining the duties of two jobs into one.

The second major reason for job cuts or changes is a change in the equipment needed to get a job done.

Such modern advances as computers have changed the way many companies operate.

For example, suppose you are a graphic artist. For five years, you have been doing your work by hand. Now your company wants to do all its artwork on computer. This will change your job. You will need to learn new skills. You will need to learn how to use graphics software on the computer. If you do not want to learn new skills, you will have to look for another job.

Or maybe your company has six graphic artists. But using computers, only five of them will be needed. One of the artists will lose his or her job. If you have worked for the company fewer years than the other artists have, your job will probably be cut.

▷ The Company Closes

As you learned earlier, sometimes a bad economy forces changes in a company. Sometimes the company is doing so poorly, it has to close. If your company closes, you will be forced to change jobs.

If you think your company is in trouble, begin to look for a job before you are let go. How can you tell if your company is in trouble? Here are some things to look for.

- There are layoffs.
- There are plant closings.
- People above you within the company are leaving their jobs.

- People are leaving at your level.
- Competing companies are going out of business.
- There is a freeze on hiring.
- There is a freeze on pay increases.
- Employees are being urged to retire early.
- Your manager has hinted that changes are coming.
- Your company is bought out by another company.

You may notice these types of changes happening where you work. If you do, your company may be in trouble. You may need to start looking for a new job. You may even want to think about switching career fields.

> ★ **Tricks of the Trade** ★
>
> ### An Open Door
>
> Do not let a job loss get you down. Sometimes losing one job may mean an even better job is waiting for you. So think positively! Your job loss may be an open door!

Whether you switch jobs or fields, look for a field that is growing. For example, there will be many jobs in the health occupations field in the 1990s. Finding a job in a growing field will mean better opportunities for you.

◄ *Sometimes you have no choice but to change jobs. Give three clues that will let you know your company is in trouble.*

□ Case Study □ □ □ □ □ □

Michael has been in a job for four years. He is a receptionist at a busy lawyer's office.

Michael has to do a great deal during the day. He has to answer the phone. He has to order supplies. He has to do filing. He sometimes has to help out with the billing.

Michael is tired most of the time. Lately, he has not been pleasant with the people in the office. He does not look forward to going to work. He has begun making mistakes on phone messages. He finds that he is bored most of the day. He also knows there is no "next step" on the ladder at his job.

Michael likes the field of law. But he would like a job in which he could focus on only one or two things. He likes to work with legal papers. He also likes to do word processing. Lately, he has begun to look at job ads in the paper. If you were Michael, what types of jobs would you look for?

▷ You Want a Change

Sometimes you just need a change. You may feel that your skills are not fully used in your present job. Or you may want to learn new skills that you cannot learn in your present job.

Or you may simply feel *burned out.* This means that you are very tired of your work. Burnout usually happens when people have done a job too long. It can also happen when the job is very stressful. In either case, burnout will affect your work. You will not have as much to offer your employer.

Wanting a change is a good reason for leaving a job. It is also a good reason for changing career fields. A new job, or even a new career, makes you feel challenged. It helps you feel positive about your work.

If you feel you need to change, do so. Work to make your job and your life better.

✔ Check Up ✔ ✔ ✔

1. How is a career different from a job?
2. List six reasons why people change jobs.
3. What are career goals?
4. List six clues that will help you tell if a company is in trouble.
5. What is burnout?

⭕ Transfer Skills

Before you change jobs or fields, you have to look at your skills. Then you have to see how many of your skills you can use at a new job.

You could use some skills, like keyboarding, on many jobs. You will not have to learn how to keyboard again. But other skills, like running equipment in a factory, must be learned on the job.

The skills that you can use in any job or field are called **transfer skills.** Suppose that you learn how to supervise a team of people on one job. You begin a new job supervising a team of people. You know what it takes to get several people working together. You learned this skill on your last job. You have transferred your skills at supervising.

▷ Identify Your Skills

When you consider changing jobs, think about your transfer skills. You have more of them than you realize. You may have skills that qualify you for new jobs you might never have thought of applying for.

Think about what you did well at your last job. Here are some skills you may have.

- Computer skills.
- Communication skills.
- Decision-making skills.

- Human relation skills.
- Listening skills.
- Math skills.
- Organizing skills.
- Writing skills.

The more experiences you have, the more skills you learn. You learn skills throughout your life. You learn skills from three key places.

- On the job.
- In school.
- In daily life.

Here is a closer look at where you learn skills. Think about skills you have learned in these places.

Skills Learned on the Job. Skills that you learn on one job can be used in other jobs. Think about the work you do in one day. What skills do you use? Some common skills learned on the job include computer skills and skills needed to run office equipment. You may learn how to run a cash register. You may learn how to deal with customers. Or you may learn how to proofread.

Skills Learned in School. Skills that you learn in school can be used at work or in your daily life. Some skills that you learn in school are how to use a calculator and how to do math. You also learn how to make decisions and solve problems.

Of course, you could use these skills at work. But you could also use them at home. For example, you use all these skills in buying a car. You may need to calculate how much you can afford to pay for a car. For this you will use a calculator and do math. You may need to decide which type of car to buy. Here you will use decision making. You may also need to solve a problem about how to get enough money together for a down payment. Here you will use problem solving.

▲ *Communication skills are learned at school. What are three other skills you might learn at school?*

Skills Learned in Daily Life. You are born with many skills called *talents.* Talents make each person special.

Maybe you have a talent for singing. You could do many jobs with this skill. You could sing in a choir or deliver singing telegrams.

Maybe you are especially good at getting along with people. You could do such jobs as camp counselor or sales clerk.

▷ The Three Skill Groups

It is easier to find a new job if you look for jobs that use your skills. Each skill you have falls into one of three groups.

- Skills with *data.* (**Data** is information.)
- Skills with people.
- Skills with things.

Most jobs use a mix of skills from these groups. But a job often requires more skills from one group than the others.

You may not find a new job in the same field as your old job. But you should try to find a job in the skill group you prefer. For example, you may leave a job as a receptionist for a job as a flight attendant. These jobs are in different fields. But they both call on you to use mainly skills working with people. You have changed jobs but not skill groups.

◀ ▲ *Skills can be broken down into three groups: data, people, and things. Which skill group does each picture here reflect?*

Read about each skill group below. As you read, try to figure out which skill group you prefer. Then you can look for jobs that use the skills from your skill group.

Data. If you like working with data, you like working with information. This means that you are probably a good organizer. You like to analyze. Your math skills are good. You can gather information. You are a good record keeper. You can compare two things and tell how they are alike or different. You can figure out how things relate to each other.

If you feel you have good data skills, you might enjoy doing some of these jobs.

- Bookkeeper.
- Bank teller.
- Buyer.
- Cashier.
- Dental assistant.
- Librarian.
- Mail carrier.
- Newscaster.
- Nurse's aide.
- Proofreader.
- Secretary.

Continued on page 137.

A Desire to Succeed

Byron White

Have you ever known anyone to be successful in two different career fields? Byron White is such a person.

White sits on the United States Supreme Court. He is an Associate Justice in our country's highest court.

White went to the University of Colorado. He was an all-American running back on the football team.

While at Colorado, White earned a Rhodes Scholarship to Oxford University in England. These scholarships are given to college graduates who are both outstanding students and great athletes. Before he went to Oxford, though, White played a season of professional football with the Pittsburgh Steelers. Then he went to England. However, World War II broke out the next year. All Rhodes Scholars were sent home.

White entered Yale University Law School that fall. He also played professional football for the Detroit Lions!

White graduated from Yale with high honors. He then joined the navy where he served with John F. Kennedy.

After World War II ended, White returned to Colorado and practiced law for two years. Later he moved to Washington to clerk for the Chief Justice of the Supreme Court.

When Kennedy was elected president in 1960, he named White Deputy Attorney General. Two years later White was asked to fill an opening on the Supreme Court. White went from football star, to Navy man, to lawyer, to clerk, to Supreme Court Justice. Talk about successful career moves!

People. If you enjoy working with people, you like to help them. You are patient. You have empathy for others. You can express your feelings. People trust you. So you can motivate them. You are a good manager or leader. And you communicate well.

Do you like using skills from the people skill group? Then you might enjoy any of these jobs.

- Child care worker.
- Flight attendant.
- Food server.

- Nurse's aide.
- Receptionist.
- Salesperson.
- Teacher's aide.
- Tour guide.

Things. If you enjoy working with things, you are good at using your hands. You are good at gathering things. You can sort or separate things. You probably enjoy building and fixing things. You like jobs that allow you to move around. You are probably healthy and strong.

Do you prefer using skills from the things skill group? Then you might enjoy any of these jobs.

- Bus driver.
- Farmer.
- Food service worker.
- Furniture mover.
- Gardener.
- Hair cutter.
- Machinist.
- Mechanic.
- Plumber.
- Telephone repairer.
- Welder.

▲ *Most jobs use a mix of skills from the three skill groups. What are two skills that are needed for this job?*

✔ Check Up ✔ ✔ ✔

1. What are transfer skills?
2. List three places you can learn skills.
3. What are the three skill groups?

○ Think Before You Change Jobs

Before you change jobs, figure out which skills you like using the most. If you are not using these skills in your present job, it may be time to move on. But before you move, here are some things you can do.

1. Remember that no job is perfect.
2. Get an information interview.
3. Ask for more responsibility at your present job.
4. Look for other jobs in the same company.
5. Update your skills.

▷ No Job Is Perfect

Many people think there really is a perfect job. But this is not the case. All jobs have good and bad points. Sometimes there will be things you do not like to do. There will be tasks you do not enjoy. There will be people you do not want to deal with. There will be boring times.

But there are good points about every job, too. Remember that no job will fulfill all your needs.

If you are unsure about whether to look for a new job, do this exercise. Draw a line down the middle of a piece of paper. List all the things you like about your job on one side. List all the things you do not like on the other. Doing this helps you figure out the skills you like to use. It will probably also show you how many things you like about your present job.

You may not like every part of a job. That does not mean that it is wrong for you. But if you do not like *anything* about the job you have now, you are in the wrong job.

▷ Information Interviews

If you are thinking of applying for a particular job, find out as much as you can about it. You can do this with an *information interview*. That is, you interview someone already doing the job you want. This helps you find out more about it. Here is how to do it.

1. Decide what job you would like.
2. Pick out a company that hires people for that job.
3. Find out who at that company can tell you more about the job.
4. Make an appointment to see this person. When you ask for the interview, tell the person you are not looking for a job.
5. Interview the person. Take a list of questions with you.
6. Write a thank you note to the person you interviewed.

Information interviews help you make better choices. Sometimes you find that the job you thought you wanted is not right for you. At other times you find that you are over qualified for a job.

Finally, information interviews help you make contacts. The person you talk to may refer you to other people who can help you. He or she may also tell you how to learn more information about the job. Remember, the people you interview are giving you their time. Be polite. Limit your interview to about 30 minutes. And be sure to write a thank-you note to the person you interviewed.

▷ Ask for More Responsibility

If you are bored with your present job, ask for more responsibility. This shows you have initiative. It will help you advance in your job. It will also make your job more interesting.

Talk with your manager about doing new tasks. See if others need help. Find meaningful things to do with your time.

If your manager gives you more responsibility, be sure to do what you say you will do. If your manager refuses your request, it may be time to move on to a new job.

◁ *An information interview is a good way of finding out about different jobs. What questions would you ask if you were interviewing this travel agent?*

□ Case Study □ □ □ □ □ □

Jay is a buyer for a large company. He likes the company. But he is bored with his job. He talked to his personnel office about other jobs in the company.

Jay is good with data. He would make a good lab assistant.

Jay did an information interview with the head of the lab. He has decided he would like a job in the lab. Now he is watching the job board for openings in this area. He has also asked to be told about any job openings.

▷ Other Jobs in the Same Company

Sometimes there are other jobs you could do in your company. Perhaps someone is leaving a job you would like to have. Perhaps your company has a branch office in which you would like to work.

If you want to stay with your current company, do some research. Talk to people in the company. What openings do they know about? Check your job bulletin board. Often, jobs are posted there first.

Does your company have a personnel manager? If so, let him or her know the job change you would like to make. Ask to be told about any openings in this area.

▷ Update Your Skills

After you take a job, you must keep your skills up-to-date. This helps you do a better job where you work now.

▲ *Often jobs are posted on company bulletin boards. What is one other way to find out about jobs in your company?*

◀ *Taking classes that relate to your job will help you stay current in your field. What are two other activities that will help you stay up-to-date in your field?*

Most jobs today will require further training at some point. You will get some of your training on the job. You will also want to get some training through classes.

In addition to this, you should update your skills. For example, learn how to use new equipment. If your keyboarding skills need work, practice a little every day to improve them.

Employers want to hire people with current skills. So always keep your skills up-to-date. That way you will be prepared to take another job if the opportunity comes along.

Here are some things you can do to keep your skills current.

- Read trade magazines.
- Read books.
- Attend conferences.
- Take classes in your field.

Keeping your skills up-to-date will help you achieve success in your career.

✔ Check Up ✔ ✔ ✔

1. Why is there no such thing as a perfect job?
2. What is an information interview?
3. List four ways you can keep your skills up-to-date.

Chapter 8 Review

Chapter Summary

- Your career is made up of the work you do during your life.
- People change jobs for many reasons.
- Your career goals are the things you want to do during your working life.
- Transfer skills are those you can take from one job to another.
- Skills can be learned in many places.
- The three skill groups are data, people, and things.
- Before you change jobs, you should do information interviews.
- You should always keep your skills up-to-date.

Reviewing Vocabulary

Listed below are the important new words in this chapter. Next to each word is the page on which you will find the word. Turn to that page and read the paragraph where the word is printed in **bold** type. On a separate piece of paper, write a paragraph about your career goals. Include the list of terms.

1. career (127)
2. field (127)
3. job (127)
4. career goals (128)
5. promotion (128)
6. lateral move (128)
7. transfer skills (133)
8. data (134)

Looking at the Facts

1. What is a career field?
2. What are six reasons people change jobs?
3. List three examples of career goals.
4. What agency can you call if you have questions about workplace safety?
5. List five clues that may help you tell if your job might end.
6. What does feeling burned out on the job mean?
7. Give an example of a skill you could learn on the job.
8. What are three key places you learn skills?
9. Before you change jobs, what are five things you should do?
10. List the six steps you should follow in doing an information interview.

Thinking Critically

1. You have a job in a factory. You know that safety glasses are required in other factories like yours. But you are not required in your factory to wear glasses. How can you find out what your employer's responsibilities are?

2. Some of your co-workers are being laid off. Last week your manager quit. One of the companies that competes with yours has just gone out of business. Why are these events important?

3. Suppose you are a librarian. You decide you want to become a bank teller. Even though these jobs are in different fields, why might this be a good career choice?

4. You are applying for a job as a tour guide. At the interview, you are asked what skills you enjoy using. What will you say?

5. You are in an information interview. The person you are interviewing is a reporter. What types of questions will you ask?

Discussing Chapter Concepts

1. How can changes in equipment affect an industry?

2. Is being bored with your job a good reason for changing jobs? Why or why not?

3. Why would your career goals cause you to change jobs?

4. Tell one of your talents.

5. Why should you look at the things you like and do not like about your job?

6. Some people stay in a job for years. Others may change jobs every year. Discuss two reasons why this happens.

Using Basic Skills

Math

1. You have decided to take a class to update your skills. The tuition is $75. The books cost $25. The supplies you need cost $14. What is the total cost of this class?

Communication

2. You are going to an information interview for the job of your choice. Write out four questions you would like to ask.

Human Relations

3. You and one of your co-workers have not been getting along. She is very moody. This makes you feel tense. You decide to talk to her. What will you say?

Activities for Enrichment

1. List five jobs you most enjoy doing. What skills are you using? Do these skills involve mostly data, people, or things?

2. Pick a place that you would like to live. Pick a company where you would most like to work. Pick the types of people with whom you would most like to work. Draw a picture that shows the place, the company, and the people.

3. Interview three people. Ask them how many times they have changed jobs. Also, ask them the reason why they changed jobs. Share your information with the class.

Part Three
Independent Living

○ A Place to Live

Words to learn and use

Here are the new terms you will learn in this chapter. Challenge yourself. Read through the list to see if you know what they mean.

landlord
lease
tenant
security deposit
subleasing
utilities
eviction
condominium
mobile home

Build on what you know

You already know...
- many people move away from home when they get their first job.
- you will have to decide where you will live.
- living away from home means accepting responsibility.

In this chapter you will learn...
- how to find a place to live.
- the different types of leases.
- reasons for having a roommate.
- renter's rights and responsibilities.
- landlord's responsibilities.
- advantages and disadvantages of owning a home.

When you take your first job, you may be faced with the choice of where to live. You may want to live at home. There are good reasons to do so. Home offers safety and comfort. It costs less than living on your own. But it is not always possible to live at home.

Moving out on your own will change your life. You will have more freedom to make your own choices. You will also have more responsibility.

You can see, then, that this is a big decision. This chapter will help you decide whether living on your own is right for you.

Finding the Right Place to Live

Housing choices are limited by your income. For a beginning worker, housing is often the biggest expense. Even a small apartment may cost more than you can afford. You will need to plan carefully. Start by listing your needs and wants. Then compare your needs and wants to housing that you can afford.

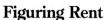 Locating Places to Live

How can you find an apartment? Start by asking family members, friends, and co-workers. They may know of places you could afford.

The most common way to find a place is to use the newspaper. Look in the daily classified section. It has listings of apartments for rent. Go through all the ads and mark the ones you like. You may also want to clip the ads.

You can also call real estate agencies. They are listed in the Yellow Pages of the phone book. They may have places to rent that are not advertised. Real estate agencies charge a fee for rental services. So find out if you or the owner must pay the fee.

Make a list of the places that are for rent. Begin with the ones you think would be best for you. Then call each apartment manager for details. After that, visit each apartment you want to see. You might visit two or three in the same area to save time.

When looking at an apartment, use a checklist to record details as in Figure 9-1. These are some of the things that you should look for.

1. Location.
2. Safety features.
3. Noise.
4. Pollution.
5. Type of residents.
6. Arrangements for the disabled.

Here is a closer look at these things.

Location. The location of the apartment is the first thing you should consider. Is it close to public

---

☀ Tricks of the Trade ❋

Figuring Rent

Try to spend no more than one-fourth of your total monthly income on rent. For example, suppose you earn $1,400 a month. You should try to find an apartment for about $350 a month.

transportation? Are there stores nearby? Is it close to your work? Is the apartment in a well-kept area of the city?

Safety. Consider safety factors both inside and outside. Is the outside of the building well-lighted? Is the apartment in a low crime area? Is the building secure? (A locked outside entrance is a good safety feature.) Are the steps and sidewalks in good condition and well-lighted? Is the parking area well-lighted and close to the apartment? Is there a fire escape?

Check the inside for safety features. Do the entrance doors have deadbolts and safety chains? Do the windows have locks? Do the ground floor windows have grills?

Each apartment should have smoke alarms. The kitchen should have a fire extinguisher. Each floor should be protected by fire doors.

In most cities, apartments are inspected. Inspection notices should be posted. Check to see that they have been inspected recently. Elevators must be inspected, too.

Apartment Inspection Checklist

Area	Condition	Area	Condition	Area	Condition
Entrance		**Kitchen**		**Bedroom**	
Door		Doors	*Doors*	Doors	
Light		Ceiling		Walls	
Doorbell		Walls		Windows	
Living Room		Windows		Floor/Carpet	
Doors		Floor		Light Fixtures	
Walls		Cabinets		Closet	
Windows		Counter		Furnishings	
Ceiling		Stove			
Floor/Carpet		Oven			
Light Fixtures		Refrigerator			
Closet		Furnishings			
Furnishings					
		Bathroom		**Heating**	
		Doors		**Air Conditioner**	
		Wall/Tile		Other	
		Medicine Chest			
		Tub & Shower			
		Sink			
		Toilet			
Date				Owner/Manager	

▲ *Figure 9-1*
Use a checklist like the one shown here when looking at an apartment.
Name one good reason for using a checklist.

Noise. The noise level is important. It is hard to sleep when the noise level is high.

Will noise from trains or a nearby subway be a problem? Is the apartment in a major traffic area? Is it near an airport? Is there a fire station or hospital in the area? Are there many children and pets in the building?

Visit the apartment at about five in the evening. That is when the noise level is often highest. This will give you a good idea of whether the noise will bother you.

Pollution. You need clean air for good health and comfort. But in a larger city, you may face air pollution. It comes from factories and cars.

How much pollution are you willing to live with? If pollution bothers you, you may want to live farther away from the city.

Type of Residents. Would you have much in common with those who live in your building? Are they people you would like to know? Are they old, young, or a mixed group? Will there be workers coming in from night shifts? Will this bother you? Talk to the people who live in the building. You will want to live around people you will enjoy.

Arrangements for the Disabled. Many newer apartments are equipped for disabled persons. They have wide door openings, ramps, or elevators.

▶ *When looking for an apartment, try to find the best location possible. What might be a disadvantage of this apartment's location?*

If you need this type of an apartment, call a social service agency, such as the United Way. It will have listings of apartments for disabled persons.

Other Factors. Here are some other things to look for. What is the condition of the apartment? Is the inside clean? Do the appliances work? Do the bathroom fixtures leak?

Is there a laundry room? Do the laundry machines work? Is the laundry room only for the use of people in the building?

▶ Meeting with the Landlord

When you decide on a place to rent, you will have to meet with the *landlord*. A **landlord** is a person who owns rental property.

This meeting is like a job interview. Landlords want good renters who are mature and trustworthy.

When you meet with the landlord, try to make a good impression. Dress neatly. Be polite. His or her first impression of you is important. If the landlord does not like you, he or she may refuse to rent to you.

You will probably be asked to fill out an application. Answer all the questions on the form. A landlord might decide to rent to you at once. Or he or she may want to check your credit record. The landlord should tell you within a week whether you have the apartment.

▲ *Dress appropriately when applying for an apartment. Why is this important?*

✓ Check Up ✓ ✓ ✓

1. What is an advantage of living at home?
2. What will most likely be your biggest expense when you are living on your own?
3. What two sources can you use to find an apartment?
4. What are three things you should consider when looking for an apartment?
5. How should you look when meeting with the landlord?

O Signing Leases

A **lease** is a legal contract between a landlord and a **tenant** (a renter). A lease, like the one shown in Figure 9-2, states the responsibilities of the landlord and the tenant.

Most leases are simple and easy to understand. Landlords often want a one-year lease. Some landlords may accept a lease for six months. Some may not require a lease at all. Tenants rent on a month-to-month basis. This means you can move out after giving one month's notice.

Read the lease carefully. If you do not understand the terms, ask someone to help you. You will be expected to know and follow the rules of the lease.

▷ Contents of a Lease

Some leases are longer than others. But most include this information.

- The name of the renter(s) and landlord.
- The address of the apartment and the apartment number.
- The amount of rent, date of payment, and where the money is to be sent.
- The amount of *security deposit* and terms for refund. (A **security deposit** is an amount the renter gives the landlord when the lease is signed. The landlord keeps this money as long as the renter leases the apartment. When the tenants are ready to move, the landlord will check for damage in the apartment. The money to repair damage caused by the tenant will come out of the security deposit. The renter will get back the rest of the deposit.)
- The rules on pets.
- The number of people who can live in the apartment.
- The renter's responsibility for the care of the apartment.
- The rules on *subleasing*. (**Subleasing** occurs when a tenant leases a place to someone else.)
- The renter's responsibility for paying for gas, heat, and water.
- Conditions under which the landlord can enter the apartment when the renter is away.
- The rules for ending or renewing the lease.
- The landlord and renter's responsibilities for damages to the apartment.
- The rules for changes the renter can make to the apartment, including painting and decorating.

Continued on page 154.

RENTAL AGREEMENT

THIS AGREEMENT, entered into this __3rd__ day of ____June____ , 19 _- -_ , by and between ____Henry Realty____ and ____Earl E. Lester____ , hereinafter called respectively "Owner" and "Resident."

It is agreed as follows:

1. **Rent.** Witnesseth that the Owner hereby leases to the Resident and the Resident does hereby lease from the Owner those premises described as Apartment number _8_ , address at ____850 Morega Drive____ , city ____Los Angeles____ , State ____California____ , to be occupied commencing on the __3rd__ day of June, 19 _- -_ , and at a monthly rental of ____four hundred and fifty ($450.00)____ dollars per month, payable monthly in advance on the __3rd__ day of each month.

2. **Occupancy.** Said premises shall be occupied only by _2_ adults and _0_ children.

3. **Pets.** Small pets, including dogs and cats, may be kept in the premises.
   Type of Pet _____Siamese Cat_____
   License Number _____1225-63-00_____

4. **Subleasing.** The Resident shall not sublease the demised premises, or any part thereof, or assign this agreement without the Owner's written agreement.

15. **Security deposit.** The resident has deposited the sum of ____$250.00____ as a security deposit (refundable within 30 days of moving).

Earl E. Lester _____ Resident   _J. Dumer, Mgr._ _____ Owner
(for Henry Realty)

▲ *Figure 9-2*
A lease is an important document. Why should you read it carefully before signing?

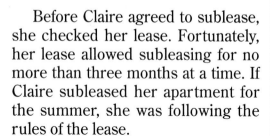

□ Case Study □ □ □ □ □ □

Claire is a teacher. Each summer she travels for three months. Her apartment is empty during this time. Last summer, Claire's friend wanted to sublease her apartment while Claire was away. By subleasing, Claire would have extra money.

Before Claire agreed to sublease, she checked her lease. Fortunately, her lease allowed subleasing for no more than three months at a time. If Claire subleased her apartment for the summer, she was following the rules of the lease.

▲ *What should this person do before signing the lease?*

▷ Special Conditions in a Lease

Some tenants make special agreements with the landlord. If you do this, write the conditions into the lease. This includes any promise to do repairs, replace carpets, paint walls, or change the decor.

Be sure you receive a copy of the lease. Keep your copy where you can easily read it over. When two or more people share an apartment, each person should sign the lease. This will protect both or all renters.

✔ Check Up ✔ ✔ ✔
1. What is a lease?
2. What is a tenant?
3. What is a security deposit?
4. What are ten items that are often in a lease?

○ Moving Expenses

Try to determine your moving expenses before you move. You will probably have to pay a security deposit of one or two months' rent in advance.

You will also have to pay for *utilities*. **Utilities** are services such as heat, gas, and water. You will need to budget for hook-up charges. Be sure you can afford the payments.

You will also need housewares, such as sheets, towels, and dishes. You will want furniture. You may need to rent a moving van.

Talk to parents or friends to make sure you have thought of every expense. Make a list like the one in Figure 9-3. Know what you can afford *before* you move out.

▲ *Moving is expensive. Be sure you know all the expenses involved. Besides housewares and furniture, what other expenses should you consider?*

	Moving Expenses	
1.	Month's Rent in Advance	$ 400.
2.	Utility Start-up	$ 200.
3.	Dishes, glasses, and flatware	$ 200.
4.	Furniture	
	bed frame	$ 150.
	mattress	$ 250.
	sheets and pillow cases	$ 55.

▲ *Figure 9-3*
Listing your moving expenses is a good way to determine what you can afford. What are some things you might add to this list?

✔ Check Up ✔ ✔ ✔

1. What are utilities?
2. What are four expenses you should consider before moving?

○ Getting Along with a Landlord

You need to get along with your landlord. You will expect certain things from each other. Know the renter's and the landlord's rights and responsibilities. This will help you avoid conflicts.

▷ Renter's Responsibilities

When a renter signs a lease, he or she legally agrees to follow these rules.

- Pay the rent on time at the place named in the lease.
- Take care of the landlord's property.
- Keep the property clean.
- Follow the rules on keeping pets.
- Get permission to sublease.
- Give notice before moving. (Usually, you must give 30 days' notice.)

Renters have other responsibilities that may not be listed in the lease. But they are important to apartment living. So, as a renter, remember these responsibilities.

- Respect your neighbors' rights by keeping your noise level low.
- Do not fight with your neighbors.

- Be careful not to cause a fire.
- Watch for any crime in the apartment complex.
- Park your car in its assigned spot.
- Report any housing problems to the landlord.

Remember, a lease is a legal contract. By signing it, you agree to follow the rules it contains.

▷ Renter's Rights

As a renter, you have certain legal rights. You can expect the apartment you rent to be clean and safe. You can also expect the landlord to do upkeep and repairs. For example, if your ceiling leaks, the landlord should fix it.

The renter can also expect the landlord to follow the terms of the lease. Rent increases can only be made when the lease is renewed.

You cannot be refused a rental because of your race, religion, sex, or age. If you *are* refused because of any of these things, this is called *discrimination*.

If you think a landlord has discriminated against you, file a complaint with your local housing office. It may be difficult to prove that the landlord is not renting to you because of your race, religion, gender, or age. Be sure you have the facts before filing a complaint.

▷ Landlord's Responsibilities

Like a renter, a landlord must follow the terms of the lease. He or she must also follow all city codes dealing with health, safety, and building maintenance. Here are the landlord's main responsibilities.

- Maintain a quiet, peaceful environment.
- Make repairs as needed.

- Keep the area safe.
- Maintain each renter's privacy.
- Follow local, state, and federal laws dealing with discrimination.
- Follow the law when evicting (forcing out) tenants. (We will look closer at eviction on page 158.)
- Return of security deposit (or part of deposit if repairs have been made).
- Follow legal rules when increasing the rent.
- Carry insurance to cover any accident caused by landlord's neglect.

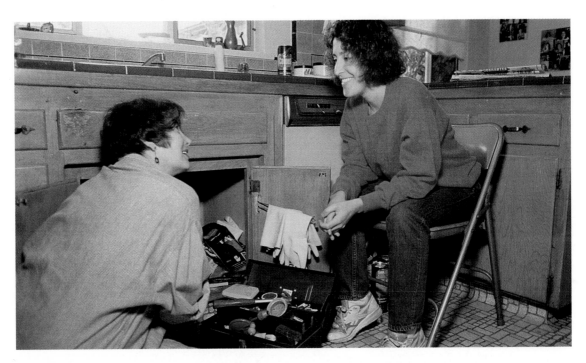

▲ *The landlord has certain responsibilities. Besides repairs, what are some of the landlord's other responsibilities?*

☐ **Case Study** ☐ ☐ ☐ ☐ ☐ ☐

The ceiling in Jake's apartment leaked. He spoke to his landlord. His landlord said he would fix the problem right away.

After two weeks the ceiling still had not been fixed. Jake put his complaint in writing and sent it to the landlord. The next day the landlord called a repairman. The repairman came and fixed the ceiling in Jake's apartment. By following the proper procedure, Jake was able to resolve his problem peacefully with his landlord.

▷ Renter and Landlord Conflicts

Conflicts can occur between the renter and landlord. How can you resolve these conflicts? It depends on the problem. If you think a fire code is being broken, file a complaint with the fire department. Health complaints, such as garbage problems, should be filed with the city health department.

Be sure you complain to the landlord first. If nothing is done, file a second complaint in writing to the landlord. Keep a copy of your complaint. If the landlord still takes no action, write a letter to the city landlord or tenant office.

▷ Eviction

Eviction is forcing a renter from the landlord's property. Eviction may occur when the renter does not follow the lease agreement.

The landlord may serve an *eviction notice*. It tells the renter when he or she must leave the property. If the renter does not leave, the landlord may remove the renter's things from the property.

Some states publish a renter's handbook. It explains the rights and responsibilities of both the renter and the landlord.

You should avoid being evicted. It will hurt your credit rating if you are evicted for not paying rent.

✔ Check Up ✔ ✔ ✔

1. What are four renter's responsibilities?
2. What are two renter's rights?
3. What are three landlord's responsibilities?
4. What does eviction mean?

O Living with a Roommate

You may find that living alone is too expensive. So you may want or need to share a living space with others.

Sharing an apartment has advantages and disadvantages. The main advantage is that it is less expensive. Two or more people can share the cost of renting a better apartment. There is also an advantage in having a companion.

When you share living space, you must be patient. And you must respect the rights of others. It is a business relationship. It is also a social relationship that may cause conflict.

Roommates often become good friends. Sometimes, though, they develop a dislike for each other. Before choosing a roommate, check his or her interests and habits. Discuss the duties and responsibilities you expect of each other.

Make a written agreement on such things as cleaning and grocery shopping. Each roommate should sign the agreement. Post a copy for daily review. The written agreement should include this information.

- Length of notice required before moving out of the apartment.
- How the security deposit will be divided if one person moves.
- How the cost of food and supplies will be divided.
- How the housework will be divided.
- Rules on overnight guests.
- Rules on keeping pets.
- Rules on smoking, use of a stereo, and musical instruments.
- Use of telephone.
- Who will keep records and pay bills.

Sharing living quarters can be stressful. So set rules from the start. Before making an agreement, discuss with your roommates their interests, habits, and behavior. Many times, you can see problems in advance. It is better not to enter into an agreement when problems are likely to develop.

Continued on page 161.

★ Tricks of the Trade ★

Roommate Relationships

Make a point to have a weekly meeting with your roommates. Discuss any problems you may be having. Use this time to talk about ways to improve your relationship.

A Desire to Succeed

Frank Lloyd Wright

Frank Lloyd Wright was one of the great architects of the twentieth century. He was born in 1867 in Wisconsin. From the moment he was born, his mother decided that Wright should become an architect. She encouraged him by giving him blocks to make buildings.

Wright never finished his formal education. He dropped out of high school in his teens. He studied engineering in the 1880s at the University of Wisconsin. But he never finished school. At the same time, Wright continued to pursue informal education. He painted, read, and drew all the time.

At 19, Wright left the University of Wisconsin and moved to Chicago. There he became a draftsman for an architect firm.

In 1893, Wright opened a firm of his own. His buildings were unique. They contained large open spaces and high ceilings. They were often designed to fit in with the landscape. One of his houses was actually built right over a waterfall!

In the 1950s, Wright designed some of his most striking buildings. Among these was the Guggenheim Museum in New York City. This building had a ramp that spiraled up to the top of the building. The Guggenheim is one of Wright's most famous buildings.

Wright's buildings are very modern and creative, even by today's standards. During his lifetime, he designed over 1,000 buildings. Six hundred of these were built in his lifetime. Wright's impressive work has changed the way we look at housing today.

☐ Case Study ☐ ☐ ☐ ☐ ☐ ☐

Megan and Tina shared an apartment. Their arrangement worked well for ten months. Then Tina told Megan she was moving out in a week. She wanted her share of the security deposit back.

Megan did not know what to do. She was left with the full rent to pay. She did not have money to pay for Tina's share of the security deposit.

Megan was fortunate. Her friend Reba needed a place to live. She moved in with Megan. But this time Megan was smart. She and Reba signed an agreement. It included an agreement on the amount of notice required before moving out of the apartment. The agreement helped Reba and Megan's relationship as roommates.

▲ *People who are roommates should sign a written agreement. What things should the unhappy person shown here have put into a written agreement?*

★ Tricks of the Trade ★

Roommate Responsibilities

With your roommates, draw up a list of weekly duties. Write down who is responsible for each duty. A written list will help you avoid conflicts.

✓ Check Up ✓ ✓ ✓

1. What is an advantage of having a roommate?
2. What should you do before choosing a roommate?
3. List four things that you should include in a written agreement.

O Saving for a Home

Many people start saving to buy a home when they begin their first job. Buying a home is one of the biggest purchases you will ever make.

How much of your earnings should you save for a home? You could save as much as 20 percent of your earnings. Saving this much requires cutting back spending on such items as clothing and vacations. For most people, it requires saving in every way possible.

To save money for a home, you need a good savings plan. Talk to your bank about savings accounts. A good savings plan will reduce the time it takes to save money for a down payment.

What type of home do you want? Many people's goal is to own a single family home. However, this may not be possible until you make more money.

▷ Single Family Homes

Prices vary widely on single family homes. Older homes are often less expensive. New homes may be in a more popular area. Plan well before buying a single family home. Talk to your bank to find out how much of a down payment you need for the home you want.

▷ Condominiums

Condominiums (often called *condos*) are privately owned units. They are joined together like apartments. They often cost less than single family houses.

Condo owners most often form a group. The group elects officers and makes the rules. There is a monthly membership fee. The fee covers the cost of maintenance and repairs on the whole condo building.

▷ Mobile Homes

Many people live in *mobile homes*. **Mobile homes** are homes that can be moved from one place to another. They are less expensive than single family homes. So a mobile home could well be your first home purchase.

Many mobile home owners rent some space in a mobile home park. In fact, some cities restrict placement of mobile homes to mobile home parks. These may be farther out from the city.

Some people, however, place mobile homes on their own land. The city or county restrictions on mobile home placement vary from state to state. If you are planning to buy a mobile home, check the regulations in your area.

▲ *There are several housing options available today. Among them are apartments, condos, and mobile homes. Which of those pictured here would you choose?*

★ Tricks of the Trade ★

Saving for a Home

Have a specific dollar amount of your paycheck sent directly to a savings account each month. It is much easier to save for a home when a part of your check goes directly into a savings account.

✓ Check Up ✓ ✓ ✓

1. What are three types of homes you might consider buying?
2. What are two ways you can save money for a home?
3. What are condominiums?
4. What is one advantage of a mobile home?

Chapter 9 Review

Chapter Summary

- Many young workers choose apartment living when they first leave home.
- A rental agency and classified ads can help you find an apartment.
- The location of an apartment is important.
- You should check safety features of an apartment before renting.
- A lease is a legal contract between the renter and landlord.
- A written agreement should be used when sharing an apartment with others.
- Buying a home requires a good investment plan.

Reviewing Vocabulary

Listed below are the important new words that were used in this chapter. Next to each word is the page on which you will find the word. Turn to that page and read the paragraph in which the word is printed in **bold** type. Then use the words from this list to complete each of the sentences that follow. Write each completed sentence on a separate piece of paper.

1. landlord (151)
2. lease (152)
3. tenant (152)
4. security deposit (152)
5. subleasing (152)
6. utilities (155)
7. eviction (158)
8. condominium (162)
9. mobile home (162)

1. A //////// //////// is a home that can be moved.
2. A ///////// ///////// is the money the landlord holds to pay for any damage.
3. The person who rents an apartment is a ////////.
4. A /////// is a type of apartment that is privately owned.
5. Services such as gas, heat, and water are called ////////.
6. The person who owns the rental property is called a ////////.
7. A //////// is a legal contract between the renter and the landlord.
8. Forcing a tenant from the landlord's property is called ///////.
9. //////// is when a tenant leases a place to someone else.

Looking at the Facts

1. What are two sources for locating apartments?
2. What are three questions you should ask yourself about the location of an apartment?
3. List five safety features you should check when looking for an apartment.

4. Why should you read a lease carefully before signing it?
5. Name three moving expenses you should consider.
6. What are two advantages of having a roommate?
7. How can you prevent conflicts when sharing living space?
8. Name an advantage of buying a condo over a single family home.

Thinking Critically

1. You plan to move into an apartment with two roommates. Before you do so, you decide to write up an agreement. What things will you include?
2. When you move into an apartment, you find cockroaches. You complain to the landlord. Two weeks later nothing has been done. What will you do?
3. You have just moved into an apartment. You are thinking of buying a dog. What should you check before you buy the dog?

Discussing Chapter Concepts

1. What things would be important for you to consider when looking for an apartment?
2. Why is it important not to be evicted?
3. Discuss the different options when buying family housing. Which would you consider? Why?

Using Basic Skills

Math

1. You and a roommate share an apartment that costs $600 per month for rent. How much more per year would it cost you if you did not have a roommate?

Communication

2. Your apartment roof leaks. You have told the landlord two times on the telephone. The roof has still not been repaired. Write a short letter to the landlord telling why immediate repairs should be made.

Human Relations

3. The people living on the second floor play their stereo late every night. You need to get up early. You need more sleep. How will you solve your problem? Write what you will say to your neighbors.

Activities for Enrichment

1. Suppose you and three friends want to rent an apartment big enough for four people. List what you will want and need in your apartment.
2. Suppose you make $1,300 a month. Look through the rental section of the newspaper. Clip the ads for apartments you can afford to rent. The rent should be no more than one-fourth of your income.

Transportation

Words to learn and use

Here are the new terms you will learn in this chapter. Challenge yourself. Read through the list to see if you know what they mean.

public transportation
mass transit
light-rail vehicles
private transportation
installment
liability insurance
collision insurance
comprehensive insurance
deductible
uninsured motorists insurance
medical insurance
defensive driver

Build on what you know

You already know...
- most people drive cars.
- many people ride bicycles.
- many people ride buses.
- there are other forms of transportation.

In this chapter you will learn...
- how to buy a car.
- the benefits of riding a bicycle to work.
- how to use buses and other public transportation.
- the benefits of other forms of transportation.

Passenger transportation is carrying people from one place to another. This is very important in today's world of work. People must have a quick and sure way to get to their jobs.

Most Americans use cars for transportation. But there are many other ways to get where you want to go! This chapter shows you your transportation choices.

✸ Transportation Needs

Every day, millions of people *commute* to work. That is, they travel to and from their workplace. The average commute in the United States is ten miles each way.

When you get a job, you must decide how you will get to work. Will you walk? Will you take a bus? Will you ride a bicycle? Will you drive a car, or will you carpool?

▲ *Millions of people commute to work each day. Which of these forms of transportation appeals to you?*

Your answer depends on several things. How far is it to your job? Is there any public transportation you could use? Could you carpool with a co-worker? Could you afford to buy a car yourself? Is the weather in your area suitable for riding a bike or motorcycle?

As you can see, you have many transportation choices. The type you choose will depend on your own needs. You will also want to think about the environment when planning your transportation. Air pollution is a big problem in major cities. Car exhaust creates air pollution. Carpooling and using public transportation help reduce air pollution.

▷ Transportation for the Disabled

There are about 35 million disabled people in the United States. Many of them cannot drive a car. But they still must work, shop, and live their lives as we all must do.

Many cities have special vans for the disabled. Some companies buy and operate their own buses or vans.

Cities also provide special parking for disabled people who can drive. For convenience, these parking spaces are located near the entrances of buildings. Finally, many buses and trains have special lifts for people in wheelchairs. These lifts help people get on and off the vehicle.

▲ *Many cities have special vans for the disabled. What are two other arrangements cities make for disabled people?*

✔ Check Up ✔ ✔ ✔

1. What does it mean to commute?
2. What are three ways you might get to work?
3. What questions should you ask yourself when deciding on transportation?

⭕ Public Transportation

Most cities have what we call *public transportation*. **Public transportation** is owned and run by private companies or by the government. It includes buses, subways, and trains. People pay a fee to ride public transportation.

▷ Local Service

In a large city, thousands of workers must commute to and from work every day. Many do not have a car. Some who do have cars prefer public transportation.

Public transportation that carries many people is called **mass transit**. Most towns and cities have buses, trains, or subways for mass transit.

Some cities today use **light-rail vehicles** for mass transit. These are electric railroad cars. They run on tracks along major traffic routes. Light-rail vehicles are ideal for people who commute many miles to work. They commonly run from the suburbs where people live to large cities where they work.

▷ Inter-city Service

Some people live in one city and work in another. They may have to commute more than 100 miles a day!

In these cases, many people travel on high-speed trains.

High-speed trains are common in Europe. They are becoming more common in the United States. Florida, for example, is building a high-speed train that will connect the cities of Tampa, Orlando, and Miami. This inter-city train will travel at 150 miles per hour! It will be completed in 1995.

Amtrak plans to run a high-speed train between New York City and Boston. In the future, many other American cities will have high-speed trains, too.

▷ Improvements in Public Transportation

The number of people who need to use public transportation grows each year. But many cities cannot afford to build new mass transit facilities. So they are trying to improve the systems they have. For example, some cities reserve a lane on the major highways for buses only.

A new type of mass transit service is the *people mover*. People movers are electric cars that move people quickly from one place to another. They are usually used in smaller areas for traveling short distances.

☐ **Case Study** ☐ ☐ ☐ ☐ ☐ ☐

Eric had a job interview downtown on Saturday at 11 a.m. Eric had ridden the #32 bus to school many times. He knew it stopped near where he was going to interview. So, he decided to take the bus.

Eric knew that the #32 bus came every 15 minutes during the week. He arrived at the bus stop in time to catch the 10:15 bus. But the 10:15 bus did not show up. At 10:30 the #11 bus arrived. Eric asked the bus driver whether the #11 bus went downtown. The driver told him that it did not. He also told him that the #32 bus only came every hour on weekends.

Eric knew he was going to miss the interview. He went to the nearest phone and rescheduled it. He realized he should have been more careful about planning his transportation.

▶ Options in Your Area

Many people like to use public transportation to get to work. It is cheaper than driving a car. It can be more relaxing than driving in busy traffic. Not having to park a car saves time and money. By avoiding traffic jams, you can get to work faster. Public transportation is safer than driving a car, too. And when you do not drive a car, you help cut down on air pollution.

Find out what types of public transportation your city has to offer. Are there buses? Are there subways? Are there trains? Get local time schedules and learn to read them. See what their daily and weekend schedules are. (They might be different.)

Find out how much it will cost to ride public transportation before you use it. You may need to have exact change. Often, you can buy a monthly pass to ride public transportation. This can save you money and the trouble of having exact change. Find the method of transportation that is best for you.

✔ **Check Up** ✔ ✔ ✔

1. Who owns and runs public transportation?
2. What are three kinds of mass transit?
3. What are two advantages to public transportation?

O Private Transportation

When people use **private transportation**, it means they travel in their own vehicles. Private transportation includes cars, bicycles, and motorcycles. Many people prefer private transportation. It is often more convenient than public transportation. It may also be the only form of transportation available.

▷ Bicycles

Millions of people ride bicycles for fun and exercise. More and more people are riding bikes to work, too. In 1991, millions of Americans rode bicycles to work.

Many companies urge their workers to ride bikes to work. Some companies have employee cycling clubs and give out commuter maps for bicycle riders. Some companies even loan bikes to their workers.

Here are six benefits of riding bicycles.

1. Riding a bike can save money. If you use your bike for all trips within three miles of home, you could save about $400 a year.
2. Riding a bike saves fuel. The average commuter who rides a bike to work saves about 400 gallons of gas a year.
3. Riding a bike helps reduce air pollution.
4. Riding a bike is good exercise.
5. Riding a bike relaxes you, improves your mood, and helps you think.
6. Riding a bike saves the trouble and cost of parking. Many companies do not have enough parking spaces for their workers. So workers must find and pay for their own parking. This can be costly. Finding a parking space can take a lot of time.

Many cities are urging people to ride bikes to work. So more businesses are supporting bike commuting by providing safe bike racks and employee lockers.

Before you decide to commute by bicycle, however, consider how far you must ride to work each day. Also consider the weather where you live. Does the distance seem reasonable? Will you have the energy? Will it be too cold or too hot to ride? Thinking about these questions will help you decide whether biking is a good choice for you.

Bicycle Safety. If you choose to commute by bicycle, learn to ride safely. You will probably have to ride in traffic. If so, you will have to obey traffic rules as cars do.

Always ride in the same direction as the cars, on the right-hand edge of the road. Ride in bike lanes whenever they are provided.

Learn to use the hand signals shown in Figure 10-1. Hand signals let others know when you are stopping or turning. Putting your left hand straight out to your left means you are turning left. Bending your left elbow up in a right angle means you are turning right. Pointing your left hand to the ground means you are stopping.

Make certain your bike has reflectors. Wear light colored clothing, especially if you are riding at night. These things will make you more visible. Consider using a small sideview mirror. This can help you see oncoming cars. And wear a helmet. This may save your life if you are hit by a car.

If the weather is bad, think about using other forms of transportation. Rain and snow can make it dangerous to ride a bike.

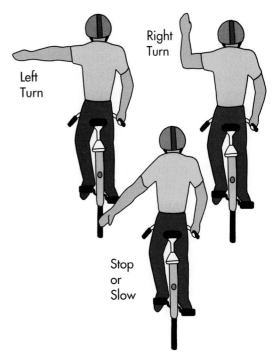

Left Turn

Right Turn

Stop or Slow

▲ *Figure 10-1*
Using hand signals will let others know when you are stopping or turning. What are two other things you should do when riding a bicycle?

▷ **Motorcycles**

A motorcycle is a vehicle with two or three wheels and a gasoline engine. Motorcycles come in many sizes, types, and weights. People use them for transportation, recreation, and sport.

If you are considering buying a motorcycle, check with your local Department of Motor Vehicles. There are specific laws in each state on motorcycle licensing and safety. (We will look at motorcycle safety on page 174.)

Consider your climate and the number of miles you must commute. A motorcycle is cheaper to buy and operate than a car. But if you must ride it daily in all types of weather, it may affect your health. Commuting even ten miles on cold, snowy winter days is uncomfortable at best. It may put you on the road to increased doctor bills!

Mopeds. Mopeds are small motorcycles. They look like bicycles with a motor. They can go up to 40 miles per hour. Mopeds are good for short commutes. They do not cost much. They use very little fuel. And they are easy to repair.

Does a moped sound like a good way to get around? If so, consider how far you will ride, the climate, parking, and where you live.

- **Distance.** The best distance for moped commuting is about five miles. At that distance, the moped is faster than a bicycle, a bus, or a train.
- **Climate.** Riding a moped when it is warm outside is very comfortable. But riding it in rain and snow can be dangerous. The moped is too small to "hold the road" like a car or motorcycle can.
- **Parking.** Does your employer provide parking? If not, you will have to pay to park a moped. It may not fit in a bike rack.
- **Location.** If you live within a few miles of your work, a moped could be good transportation! But mopeds are not allowed on major highways, on bridges, or in tunnels.

Motorcycle and Moped Regulations. In most states, you must have a motorcycle license. You must pass a test to show that you can drive a motorcycle safely. Many states also require riders to wear safety helmets.

With a moped, many states do not require you to have a special license. You must have a regular driver's license, though.

Motorcycle and Moped Safety. When riding a motorcycle or moped, you have very little protection. In an accident, there is a high risk of injury or even death. If your motorcycle is hit by a vehicle, you will probably be thrown from the bike. So you must learn to drive well and wear protective clothing.

The Motorcycle Safety Foundation has developed courses on motorcycle safety. You may take them at your high school, community college, or police department.

On a motorcycle or moped, you must always be visible to other drivers. Keep the headlight on at all times. Be careful at intersections. This is where most accidents happen. Be extra careful in bad weather.

Wear protective clothing, especially when riding a motorcycle. It can help you in an accident or a fall. A helmet is most important. It can reduce injuries and even help save your life. Thick denim or leather jackets and pants give some protection. Nonslip gloves help you keep a firm grip on the handlebars. Protect your feet with leather boots or sturdy shoes that

▲ *If you ride a motorcycle, you should wear protective clothing. What protective clothing is the person here wearing?*

come up above the ankles. Eye protection is important, too. Always use the face shield on your helmet. At the very least, wear eye goggles.

▷ Cars

Most people in the United States travel by car. The car is a big part of American life. In fact, the United States is often called a "nation on wheels." You are probably looking forward to owning a car.

Buying a New Car. Before you buy a new car, think about your needs and wants. What is important to you? Is it style, economy, performance, or safety?

Your library will have books on how to buy cars. Some consumer guides compare models. Use these guides to check the car you think you might want to buy. You can see how often it needs repair and how well owners like the particular model. You can also see how well it performed on road tests.

Decide how much you can afford to pay for a car before you shop. Include the cost of insurance, gasoline, and maintenance. The selling price of a car does not include tax, license, or registration fees. You will need to include these in the total cost.

Find out the *dealer invoice price.* That is the price the dealer paid for the car. The price on the window sticker is the *retail price.* The price you should pay is somewhere in between. You will need to negotiate with the dealer to get the best price. To *negotiate* means to talk back and forth until you agree.

You may decide to trade in your old car. The money you get from a trade-in will help you put a down payment on your new car. Check the library for books that tell how much your old car is worth. Do this before you talk to the dealer about trading in your car. You may want to sell your old car yourself. It may take longer, but you might get more money for it.

Check the car before you buy it. Take a test drive. Does everything work? If not, have it fixed before you sign any papers.

Do not rush into buying a car. It is a big investment. So take your time. Never let the salesperson pressure you into buying. Speak to friends and relatives to find out more information about buying cars. Research several types of cars. You may find that the car you want is not the best car for your needs.

Buying a Used Car. A used car costs less to buy and insure than a new car. But a used car can cause you problems if you do not buy wisely.

Where do you buy a used car? The classified ads in the newspaper list cars for sale. You can go to used car dealers and to new car dealers. You also can look at local gas stations and car rental companies. Ask your relatives if their companies sell used company cars.

When looking at a used car, inspect it thoroughly. Use a checklist as in Figure 10-2. The best time to do this is during the day. Sunlight will make any defects more visible. You may want to bring a friend along with you to help with the inspection.

Test drive the car, too. Note how it handles. Note how well the brakes work. Does it hold the road well?

Take the car to a mechanic to check it over. The mechanic will charge you for his or her time. But it is worth the cost to know what you are getting.

Know how much the car is worth. Go to the library and look at the "Blue Book" of wholesale car prices. The asking price should be around the wholesale price. Is the car in good shape for its age? Does it need repair? Think about these questions when you consider what price to offer for the car.

Negotiate the price with the owner. You may be able to pay less than the owner is asking for the car.

Used Car Checklist

Check the Outside
- ☐ Is the paint in good condition? (Check it in daylight.)
- ☐ Is the body free of rust and dents?
- ☐ Are the windows and headlights free of cracks?
- ☐ Are the shock absorbers OK?
- ☐ Are the tires in good condition?

Check Under the Car and Under the Hood
- ☐ Is the car free of oil and water leaks?
- ☐ Is the engine fairly clean?
- ☐ Are the hoses free of cracks?
- ☐ Is the battery clean?

Check the Trunk
- ☐ Is the trunk clean?
- ☐ Is the spare tire in good condition?
- ☐ Is there a jack for the tire?

Get Inside the Car
- ☐ Is the mileage low enough to allow you good service?
- ☐ Are the seats, safety belts, and carpet in good condition?
- ☐ Are the gas and brake pedals in good condition?
- ☐ Do the headlights, turn signals, and all accessories work?

Take the Car for a Test Drive
- ☐ Do the brakes stop the car quickly and evenly?
- ☐ Does the transmission shift smoothly?
- ☐ Does the car have good power going uphill?
- ☐ Is the exhaust clean? (Step on the gas and look in the rearview mirror.)

Take the Car to a Mechanic
- ☐ Does the mechanic think the car is a good buy?

▲ *Figure 10-2*
You should use a checklist such as this one when you consider buying a used car. Why do you think this is important?

Financing a Car. How will you pay for your car? Do you have money in the bank? Or will you borrow the money and pay it back over a certain period of time?

It is cheaper to pay with cash than to borrow money. You must pay interest on a loan. Even if you have the cash, you may prefer to use credit.

When you use credit, you get a loan to buy now. You must pay the money back in installments. An **installment** is a regular monthly payment made over a period of time.

Where do you borrow money? You may get a loan from a bank, a finance company, or a credit union. You may also get a loan from the car dealer.

Finance companies charge higher interest rates than banks. Credit unions charge less than banks do.

The interest rates at car dealers can be high or low, depending on the type of car. Sometimes dealers offer very low interest rates on new cars. But when they do this, they may raise the asking price of the car.

When you get a loan to buy a car, the lender will keep the title to the car. This means that the bank or credit union owns the car until you make your last payment.

When you apply for credit, you will fill out an application. You must prove that you have a job and can make monthly payments.

Car Insurance. You will need car insurance. In some states, it is illegal to drive without it. Insurance is expensive for young drivers. You may get a lower price if you are a good driver, do not smoke, and get good grades in school. Shop around. Call several insurance companies. Find out how much your policy would cost.

Most policies give you five kinds of insurance.

1. Liability.
2. Collision.
3. Comprehensive.
4. Uninsured motorists.
5. Medical.

Liability insurance covers you if you cause an accident. It is the most important type of insurance. The insurance company will pay if someone is hurt or if the cars need repair.

Liability may be written as 10/20/5. This means the company will pay $10,000 for injuries to one person, and up to $20,000 if more than one person is injured. The company also will pay $5,000 for property damage. You also can get liability insurance at 50/100/5 or 100/300/25.

Collision insurance pays for damage to your car if you hit something. With collision insurance, you will probably have a *deductible amount* of $50, $100, $250 or more. The **deductible** is the amount you pay.

For example, say you have a deductible of $250. This means that you would pay $250 toward repairing the damage. Your insurance company would pay the rest.

Comprehensive insurance pays if your car is damaged by fire, hail, or flood. It also pays if someone breaks into your car.

Uninsured motorists insurance covers you if you are injured by a driver who does not have insurance.

Medical insurance pays your medical bills if you are injured in your car.

Another type of insurance, called *no-fault*, is available in some states. It pays for damage no matter who caused the accident.

Car Safety. Most car accidents happen because drivers break traffic laws. Obey the laws and learn to drive safely. One of the most important things you can do is wear a seatbelt.

The federal government is doing its part to make cars safer. It requires safety belts and shatterproof windows

---

★ **Tricks of the Trade** ★

The Right Time to Buy

You may be able to save money when you buy a car near the end of the month. Salespeople are eager to meet monthly sales goals. So you may be able to negotiate a better deal.

on all new cars. It also requires cars to have a steering column that collapses and special bumpers. Carmakers hope to put air bags and antilock brakes in every new car before the year 2000.

More than 11,000 lives each year could be saved if people wore seatbelts. In many cars made today, the driver must use the seatbelt. If he or she does not, the car will not start.

A proper attitude is the most important part of safe driving. This attitude is *social responsibility*. It means respecting the safety of others. You practice social responsibility by obeying traffic laws. Be considerate of others. Learn to *concentrate*. Think about your driving, and keep your eyes on the road. Do not drive if you are angry or worried.

Learn to be a **defensive driver.** This means being alert and thinking ahead. Be prepared for anything. A car ahead of you may stop suddenly. A car may run a stop sign. A child might run out in front of your car. Pay attention, and be ready. Do not speed. And never follow another car too closely. At 40 mph, leave about four car lengths between you and the car ahead of you. At 50 mph, leave five car lengths.

Finally, do not drink if you are going to drive. Drinking slows down your reaction time. You are not as alert. One study showed that out of 1,000 traffic deaths, 650 drivers had been drinking. This means that 65 percent of the deaths were caused by drunk driving.

Continued on page 181.

◄ *Seatbelts are one safety feature that new cars are required to have. What are three others?*

A Desire to Succeed

Henry Ford

Henry Ford grew up on a farm in Michigan in the 1860s. Farm life was hard work. Henry and his six brothers and sisters chopped wood and milked cows. They also plowed the fields and harvested crops. They went to school in a one-room schoolhouse.

Henry's father wanted him to stay at home and help out on the farm. But Henry's interests were in other things—mechanical things. When Henry was seven, he saw the inside of a watch for the first time. He quickly learned to take a watch apart, repair it, and put it back together! In fact, Henry liked to take everything apart.

When Henry was 16, he left the farm. He worked as a machine-shop apprentice. Later, he traveled across the country fixing machines.

His dream, though, was to build a "horseless carriage." It was difficult to get the money for this project. Many people thought he was crazy. But Henry was determined and built his first car when he was 33.

He then built his first racing car. In 1909 he produced the first "Model T" Ford. The Ford Motor Company became one of the most successful companies in America.

Henry Ford came up with many new ideas. He was the first to make cars on an assembly line. He improved working conditions for laborers and raised wages. He used new manufacturing methods. He was a pioneer. His new ideas created the car industry!

Henry Ford had dreams. He was determined and he worked hard to see his dreams come true.

Improvements in Cars. Cars are a popular form of transportation. But they do cause problems.

The fuel used in most cars is gasoline. And gasoline comes from oil. Cars use about half of the energy used for all transportation in the United States. At the current rate of use, the world's supply of oil will be gone in 50 years.

Cars are also the main cause of air pollution. Smog from cars causes about $40 billion worth of health problems a year.

Traffic in many cities has become very bad. Freeways and highways have become clogged with cars. Heavy traffic forces people to spend much more time on the road.

Steps are being taken to find ways to solve these problems. The Environmental Protection Agency (EPA) works to control car pollution. It requires that new cars put out less pollution than old cars. So car makers are now building cars that are smaller, cleaner, and use less fuel.

Today, many commuters drive to work alone. These people could help solve some of the air pollution and traffic problems by carpooling. This also saves gasoline.

Many highways have car pool lanes. Sometimes car poolers pay less for road tolls. Many companies have car pools for their workers. Other companies offer rewards to workers who carpool. Some companies give the best parking spots to those who carpool. Some companies pay for their workers' bus, train, or subway passes. Other companies give workers extra money each month if they carpool, bicycle, or use mass transit. Certain cities now require companies to have a percentage of their employees carpool. You may find carpooling a good choice for transportation.

Car companies are now developing electric cars. General Motors brought out its first electric car, the Impact, in 1990. Electric cars run on batteries rather than gasoline. Electric cars and other future developments may help to solve our car problems.

✔ Check Up ✔ ✔ ✔

1. What are three forms of private transportation?
2. What are three good reasons to ride a bicycle to work?
3. What are two ways you can make riding a motorcycle safer?
4. Why do you need to negotiate when you buy a car?
5. What are four kinds of car insurance?
6. What two things could prevent most car accidents?
7. Name two ways of improving car transportation.

○ Reading Maps

A map is a picture that represents an area. Maps help people find their way from one place to another.

A road map shows roads, highways, cities, and state parks. People use them to travel long distances. (See Figure 10-3.)

A street map shows a smaller area than a road map. It shows all the streets in a town or a city. People use a street map to find an address.

A transit map shows the routes of a mass transit system. It could show where buses, subways, or trains go. It will often show a time schedule, like the one shown in Figure 10-4. This tells you the time of day mass transit will be leaving and arriving at certain stations.

Using a map can be a challenge. To read a map, you need to understand map legends, scales, and indexes.

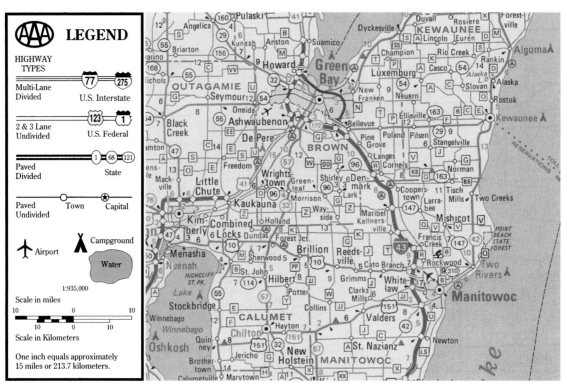

▲ *Figure 10-3*   © *AAA reproduced by permission.*
It is important to know how to use a map when you travel. What four symbols can you identify on this map?

Brooksville ... Newton ... Windam ... York						Train Services
Train Number		228	123	126	401	☕ Sandwiches and snacks
Train Service		C ☕	E	☕	D ☕	E Express Train
Brooksville	Depart	515 AM	700 AM	850 AM	1115 AM	
Hill Valley		545 AM		920 AM	1145 AM	
Newton		615 AM	750 AM	950 AM	1215 PM	C Commuter Train
Jackson		640 AM	810 AM		1240 PM	
Sargentville		700 AM	825 AM	1035 AM	100 PM	
Windam		720 AM		1055 AM	120 PM	
Lewiston		757 AM	915 AM	1132 AM	157 PM	D Deluxe Class
Swains Cove		820 AM		1155 AM	220 PM	
San Juan	Arrive	845 AM	945 AM	1220 PM	245 PM	

(Northbound Trains)

▲ *Figure 10-4*
This transit map shows the times that trains depart from different stations. For example, the #228 train leaves Brooksville at 5:15 and arrives in San Juan at 8:45. What time does the #123 leave Brooksville?

A map legend explains the symbols and colors on a map. You may see circles, tree shapes, and other pictures on a map. A circle may mean a city. A tree shape may mean a campground or a park. A blue line may mean a river. A green line may mean the edge of a forest. You have to look at the legend to know what the shapes and colors mean.

A map's scale tells you about distance. You can use the scale to look at the map and find out how far something is. For example, the scale might say "1 inch: 15 miles." This means 1 inch on the map equals 15 actual miles.

Map indexes help you find places on the map. Maps often have lines across them and lines up and down. A letter marks each line across the map, and a number marks each up and down line. The index is a list of cities or streets. Next to each one is a letter and a number. Find the line with that letter. Then find the line with that number. Find where those two lines cross. The place you are looking for is near that point on the map.

✔ Check Up ✔ ✔ ✔

1. What is a map?
2. What are three types of maps?
3. What does a map legend show you?
4. What does "1 inch: 10 miles" mean?

Chapter 10 Review

Chapter Summary

- Getting to work is the most common need for transportation.
- The best choice of transportation depends on your own needs.
- Government and private companies provide public transportation. It may be used for a fee.
- Buses, trains, and subways are common forms of public transportation.
- Public transportation is cheaper than private transportation.
- Private transportation is traveling in your own vehicle.
- Cars, bicycles, motorcycles, and mopeds are forms of private transportation.
- Using a vehicle safely is your responsibility as a driver.
- The costs of owning a car include the purchase price, fees, fuel, upkeep, and insurance.
- Reading a map is a skill you will need for traveling.

Reviewing Vocabulary

Listed below are the important new words that were used in this chapter. Next to each word is the page on which you will find the word. Turn to that page and read the paragraph in which the word is printed in **bold** type. Write the word and its meaning. Then write a sentence of your own using each word.

1. public transportation (170)
2. mass transit (170)
3. light-rail vehicles (170)
4. private transportation (172)
5. installment (177)
6. liability insurance (178)
7. collision insurance (178)
8. comprehensive insurance (178)
9. deductible (178)
10. uninsured motorists insurance (178)
11. medical insurance (178)
12. defensive driver (179)

Looking at the Facts

1. What is transportation?
2. List four factors to think about when deciding how to commute to work.
3. Name four forms of public transportation.
4. Name three types of mass transit used in a city.
5. What form of public transportation can be used to travel between cities?
6. What are three advantages of public transportation?
7. What is private transportation?
8. What are four advantages of riding a bike for transportation?
9. What are two things you should consider before deciding to commute by motorcycle?

10. What is one way of financing a car?
11. List the four kinds of insurance provided by most car insurance policies.
12. Name and describe three types of maps.
13. What information can be learned from a map legend, a map scale, and a map index?

Thinking Critically

1. You work for a company that urges employees to use public transportation. What are the pros and cons of using public transportation?
2. The chapter describes many benefits of using a bike. What are some problems a bike commuter might have? What are some solutions?
3. Describe a safe driver.
4. List three questions you would consider when you are thinking about buying a car.

Discussing Chapter Concepts

1. Safety is a very important responsibility. Some states pass laws against riding in a car without using a seatbelt. Is safety a personal responsibility? Or should laws require people to practice safety?
2. What do you think is the most important thing to consider when buying a car?

Using Basic Skills

Math
1. After driving to work for one week, you have used nine gallons of gas. If the gas costs $1.09 per gallon, how much did the gas cost for one week of commuting?

Communication
2. Plan some role-playing with a partner to present to your class. Assume you are buying a car from a car dealer. One person should be the customer and the other the car dealer. Assume a car dealer is trying to sell a customer a more expensive car than he or she can afford.

Human Relations
3. Your school board is considering a rule that would not allow students to drive cars to school. Write a letter to your school board telling reasons you do or do not like the idea.

Activities for Enrichment

1. Read consumer magazines from the library or home. Find out which three cars get the best gas mileage. Also find out which three cars have the best safety records.
2. Make a table of the types of transportation used by members of the class for getting to school. Discuss the reasons why people use the transportation they do.

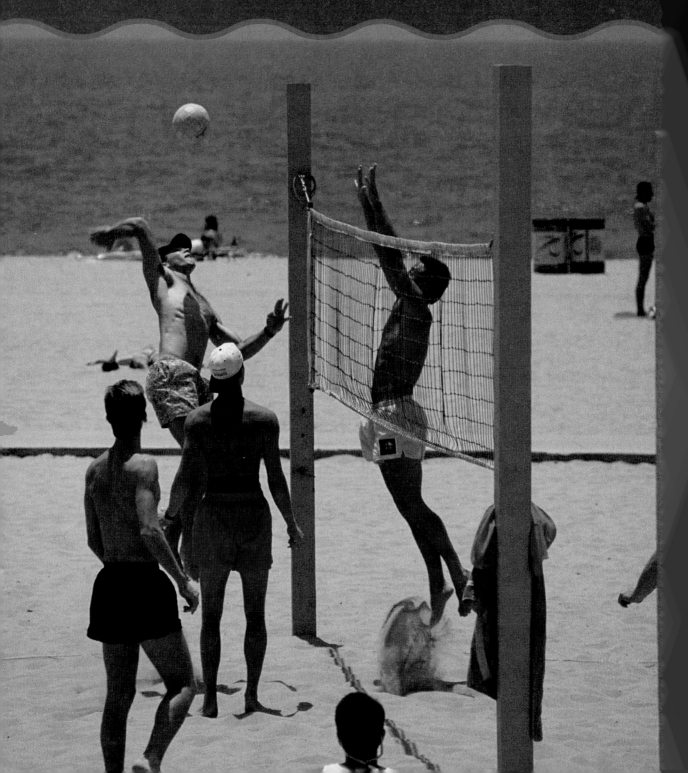

Leisure and Recreation

Words to learn and use

Here are the new terms you will learn in this chapter. Challenge yourself. Read through the list to see if you know what they mean.

leisure time
recreation
aptitude
ability
spectator sports
visa
passport
youth hostel
atlas

Build on what you know

You already know...
- you must work hard to achieve success.
- leisure time is for recreation.
- you enjoy certain kinds of recreation.
- going on a vacation can be fun.

In this chapter you will learn...
- how to balance hard work with recreation.
- why recreation is good for you.
- how to find new kinds of recreation you enjoy.
- how to plan a vacation.

Your work will be an important part of your life. You will plan your life around your work. You will buy clothes for your work. Your work will affect every part of your life-style.

Does this mean that you will only have time for work in your life? No. Most people take time in their lives for *leisure* and *recreation* as well as work. It takes practice to balance work and play. Working long and hard hours on a regular basis can create stress and health problems. Leisure and recreation are important for keeping healthy.

O Balancing Your Life-style

Most people work eight hours a day, five days a week. What do they do with the rest of their time? They do important chores, like shopping, cooking, and cleaning, of course. But most people have time left over after work and chores are done. This free time is called **leisure time**.

How you spend your leisure time is your choice. If you do something you enjoy in your leisure time, you will feel happier about your life. It is important to balance your work hours with play hours. Young children in school have recess during the day. Their work is balanced with play. Working adults do not have recess. But they can balance their work with play during leisure time. They have leisure time during the weekends and after work. Holidays and vacations also provide leisure time. It is important to make use of leisure time.

▷ Benefits of Recreation

The activities you choose to do during leisure time are called **recreation**. Sports are a kind of recreation. So are movies, walks in the park, playing cards with friends, and vacation trips. There are many kinds of recreation.

Recreation should be an important part of your life. It is fun. But it does more for your life than provide fun. These are some of the benefits of recreation.

- Controls stress.
- Helps you become aware of your interests, aptitudes, and abilities.
- Helps you to meet new people.
- Builds self-confidence and self-esteem, and gives your life balance.

Here is a closer look at these benefits.

Controlling Stress. Everyone's life is stressful at times. Work can be demanding and tiring. Shopping, cooking, and cleaning can become boring. Problems with family and friends can be upsetting. Recreation will not solve your problems. But it can make you feel happier. You can face your problems more clearly if you have some fun in your life. A healthy life has a good balance of work and fun.

Many people feel better after playing hard. A good run, a soccer game, or a tennis match will tire your muscles. Yet you will feel happy and refreshed. A hike in the hills or a long walk in the park can put you in a good mood.

189

8

XI

"hbk" sm - y
"r" ru - c
"sc" sa - s
"b "hm" h] -k
"hah" oh] -s
"mp" ch - m
r "mm" s -

◀ *Hiking can help to reduce stress. What are three other benefits hiking might provide?*

hbk "hbk" sm
r" ru

Exercise is not the only kind of recreation that relieves stress. Many people feel relaxed after playing cards with friends, going to the movies, or reading a book. What is fun for one person will not always be fun for another. People relax in different ways. Some people enjoy stamp collecting. Some enjoy painting. Some like working on cars. Others enjoy talking with friends. Choose the kind of recreation that *you* enjoy.

Everyone needs a break now and then from the daily routine of his or her life. You will like your work more if you enjoy yourself on the weekend or after work. Recreation is a good source of enjoyment.

Self-awareness. Think for a minute about the many kinds of recreation. Here is a list of just a few.

- Team sports.
- Movies.
- Picnics and parties.
- Hobbies.
- Spectator sports.
- Travel.
- Dancing.
- Gardening.
- Volunteering.
- Reading.

There are probably some kinds of recreation that you would like to try. But you do not know if you would be good at them. You do not know if you would like them. By trying new activities, you will find out more about yourself.

You may not know what kind of recreation would interest you. Daydream for a while about what you would like to try. Would you like team sports or bicycle riding? Does stamp collecting interest you? Would you like your life to be more active or creative? Would you like to see more of nature or different cities?

Think of what you want to do. Then try out some new kinds of recreation that interest you. Later in this chapter, you will read about some new kinds of recreation that you might enjoy.

Recreation can help you discover your *aptitudes*. An **aptitude** means that you have a knack or potential for learning certain skills. Perhaps you

▲ *You may discover your creative talents through leisure activities. What creative talents do you think you may have?*

have an aptitude for art. You may want to enroll in an art class. You may find out you do not have an aptitude for a certain activity. If so, you may be happier trying something else.

Recreation gives you a chance to develop your *abilities*. An **ability** is a skill that has already been developed. You may have the ability to dance well. Taking some dance classes will develop your ability. Or perhaps you already know how to play tennis. You might enjoy learning another racket sport.

A Way to Meet New Friends. Recreation is a good way to make new friends. Sometimes it is hard to talk to people you do not know very well. You might feel shy. You might not know what to talk about. But you could talk to a person in your dance class about dancing. You can talk to a person at your tennis lesson about tennis or other sports. You might decide to go to a tennis match together. You can talk to the people in a hiking club about your love of the outdoors. They will understand because they like hiking, too. You will have something in common.

Recreation is often social. That is, part of the enjoyment of the activity is in being with other people. You would not be the only person there interested in making new friends.

When people are having fun, they are more relaxed. This is a good time to make new friends. People like to talk about their hobbies and their favorite activities. You will, too.

Other Benefits. Recreation will help you to build self-confidence and self-esteem. It makes you feel good about yourself. Playing your hardest as part of a team makes you feel proud. Learning a new skill, like dancing or making pottery, makes you feel successful. Helping people through volunteer work makes you feel needed. Going on a tough hike in the hills makes you feel strong and confident.

Recreation also gives your life balance. People need equal time for work and play to have a healthy life. People work better if they also have some fun. Work will sometimes make you tense and nervous. Physical activity is a great way to relieve tension. Some large companies even have gyms or racquetball courts for their employees. Hobbies can also relieve tension. Focusing your mind on doing something you enjoy can be very relaxing. It can take your mind off of the things that are worrying you.

Everyone has the need to be creative in some way. Some people like to paint. Some like to build furniture or make toys. A hobby gives you a way to be creative.

Recreation also helps us meet our social needs. We all have social needs that are as important as our work needs. We need friends. We need to learn social skills. We need to trust and enjoy other people. Recreation helps us do that.

✔ Check Up ✔ ✔ ✔

1. What are four benefits of recreation?
2. What are six kinds of recreation that can relieve stress?
3. Why is recreation a good way to meet new friends?

A Desire to Succeed

Mikko Mayeda

Born in 1960, Mikko Mayeda was a gifted student and a fine athlete. At age 11, she began taking riding lessons. She practiced jumping and riding horses. She also played on an all-star softball team. Recreation was a big part of her life.

Suddenly, Mikko's life changed. At 15, she became severely depressed. Her doctors could not find out what was wrong. During the next five years, she was in and out of mental hospitals. Nothing helped. Then she began to lose her vision. Several times she tried to commit suicide. Finally, the doctors learned that she had multiple sclerosis (MS). The disease left her blind. She also lost the use of her legs.

Mikko's mother used Mikko's love of riding to help her gain a desire to live. Mikko became the only blind rider to jump horses over two feet. She created a walkie-talkie system. She and her trainer used it to guide her through the jumps.

She has competed in many riding events. In 1984, she entered the International Games for the Disabled. She won both a gold and a silver medal.

Riding is not Mikko's only skill. She has written the story of her life and sold the movie rights. She also paints and writes poetry. And she does public service announcements for the National MS Society.

Not all of Mikko's days are good. Sometimes the disease makes her very ill. Then she must receive special treatment at a hospital. Even with all her losses, Mikko has kept a special vision. She wants to "teach other people with disabilities not to give up."

O Recreation Choices

There are many types of recreation. Some are very active, like sports and dancing. Some are quiet and do not involve physical activity. You might be a member of the team and play hard. Or you might be a spectator and enjoy yourself by watching the game. You might be alone, working on your hobby. Or you might be with a group of people. Here are some of the choices for recreation.

▷ Recreation at Home

Many people like to relax and unwind at home. There are many creative and satisfying projects that you can do at home. You can do them alone, with your family, or with a few friends. And they usually cost less than other types of recreation. Many people enjoy cooking, sewing, and knitting. They enjoy shopping for the materials and equipment they need. They take great pride in their creations.

Model-making, woodworking, and furniture repair can be done at home. Setting up a shop or workplace in the garage or basement can be fun.

Many people enjoy working in their gardens and yards. Growing flowers or vegetables is an important type of recreation for them.

Artistic activities are often done at home. Some people set up art studios in their homes. People who like taking pictures sometimes set up a darkroom in a basement or garage. You can even set up a temporary darkroom in a closet or a bathroom.

Playing a musical instrument can be enjoyed at home. You can practice to improve your skills. You can write your own music and songs. You might have friends who would like to bring their instruments to your house and play with you.

Learning new uses for their home computers is a relaxing hobby for some people. Playing computer games and making up your own computer games might be a fun hobby for you.

▷ Hobbies

In Chapter 10, you read about hobbies as a way to learn something new. Hobbies are also a good way to relax. You do a hobby because it interests you. Some hobbies are creative. You can paint, make pottery, take photographs, or learn to play a musical instrument. Some hobbies involve collecting things, like stamps or coins. Some hobbies are more physical, like scuba diving or fishing.

How do you choose a hobby? First, you must know your interests. Make a list of activities you like and activities you dislike. Then check out hobbies that match your interests.

You will enjoy your hobbies for years to come. A hobby that is right for you will be fun and will challenge you to learn. You can always improve your skills.

▷ Spectator Sports

Spectator sports are sports that you enjoy by watching them. Football, baseball, and hockey are examples of spectator sports. Many people have fun going to watch them. Tickets for the World Series or other major league playoffs sell out fast. These tickets are expensive. But tickets for the other games are usually less expensive. You can buy tickets from a ticket office. The number is usually listed in the phone book.

You can even watch spectator sports at home. Invite some friends over to watch the game on TV. This is a good way to enjoy both the game and your friends.

Your community probably has its own sports teams, such as softball leagues. These games are also fun to watch. And they are usually free.

▲ *Spectator sports are a type of recreation. Can you name two other spectator sports?*

▷ Team Sports

Millions of people play team sports. Team sports have many benefits. They keep you physically fit. They help you develop your skills. They provide a sense of pride and achievement. They are fun and relaxing. They help to meet social needs, too. You may make friends with your teammates. You will learn how to be a team player. You will have fun laughing, joking, and practicing with them.

How do you get on a team? There are many ways. Some people play softball, football, basketball, or soccer on weekends. They get together with a group of friends. This is an informal team. You can get a group of friends together and start your own team.

Most communities have organized team sports. There are men's teams, women's teams, and mixed teams. Often, these teams are sponsored by local businesses. The businesses provide uniforms with the company name on them. The teams may be organized into leagues with playoff games, championships, and trophies. Sometimes the teams are organized by ability. This makes the teams more even. Everyone has a chance to play.

You do not have to be a champion player to get on a team. You can try out for a team and see if you have the ability and interest to play. Call your city recreation department to find out about team sports in your community.

Your parents might work for a company that has a company team. You might be able to join that team. Or you might get a job with a company that has a team. People play hard on these teams. They do their best. Yet the main reason for these teams is to have fun and relax.

▷ Recreational Groups

Your community probably has several organizations that offer different kinds of recreation. Call them for information. Here is a list of a few organizations that may have recreation groups you can join.

- Churches.
- Sierra Club.
- YMCA or YWCA.
- City Recreation Departments.
- Boy Scouts or Girl Scouts.
- Special Olympics.

Many churches have youth groups that meet for discussions, social events, field trips, or summer camp. Many churches have groups that meet for suppers, games, or dances.

The Sierra Club helps build and maintain trails in national parks and wilderness areas. It can always use volunteers in its fight to preserve the wilderness. You might enjoy a Sierra Club hike. The hikes are rated to the experience level of the hikers. If you are new to hiking, for example, you can go on a slower-paced hike.

The YMCA and YWCA have many classes, activities, and camps that do not cost much. Many Y's have swimming pools and gyms. They also need young people to work as counselors and teachers for children's classes.

City park and recreation departments offer many classes and team sports. They may have language clubs, sports teams, dance classes, and lifeguarding classes. They also look for people to coach children's teams.

Most communities have volunteer programs. Many people get great pleasure from helping others. Youth sports programs, Special Olympics, programs for the elderly, and scouting programs all need volunteers.

▷ Dance and Theater Groups

Dancing is a recreational activity many people enjoy. Different styles of dance appeal to different people. Some towns have clubs that teach the dances of other countries. These are called folk dances. There are square dance clubs in many towns. Some people enjoy taking classes in modern dance and ballet. The classes keep them physically fit and develop their skill. Dancing to rock music at clubs is a popular type of recreation.

Many towns have theater groups. They put on plays. If you like acting, you may want to try out for a part in a play. Or you might like doing makeup or building sets.

▷ Outdoor Recreation

There are many forms of outdoor recreation. Some require special equipment, like skiing and bicycling. Before you buy a new bike or skis, rent what you need and try it out a few times. See if you really enjoy the activity before you spend a lot of money. A new bike or skis may cost several hundred dollars.

Camping and backpacking require some special equipment, like tents, packs, and boots. You can rent this equipment from backpacking stores. See if you enjoy these activities before you buy the equipment for them.

▲ *Rent the equipment you need and try it out before you decide to buy. Why is this a good idea?*

You might like to try horseback riding. Most communities have stables where you can rent a horse for a few hours.

Some outdoor activities require very little equipment. So you can enjoy them without spending a lot of money. Gardening, nature study, bird watching, and hiking are such activities. They can be done alone or with a group of friends. Many communities have classes that teach outdoor recreation skills. You can learn about nature walks and bird walks, hiking, and other outdoor skills. Look in your local newspaper to find out what is offered. You can also find out about day walks and hikes that may be going on.

▷ Outward Bound

Outdoor adventures can be very challenging and exciting. Would you like to learn wilderness skills and mountaineering skills? You might like to take a course from Outward Bound. This and other outdoor schools teach climbing, camping, and outdoor skills. They have courses in sailing, river rafting, and kayaking.

These courses teach leadership skills. They also boost self-esteem. You learn to trust in yourself. This type of school often has scholarships to help you pay for the courses. Ask your reference librarian for information on Outward Bound.

▲ *Outdoor schools such as Outward Bound teach leadership and wilderness skills. What are two other benefits these schools provide?*

✔ Check Up ✔ ✔ ✔

1. How can you enjoy spectator sports for very little money?
2. How can you go about choosing a hobby?
3. What are six forms of outdoor recreation?
4. What are six kinds of recreation you can do at home?
5. What are three skills you can learn from an outdoor school?
6. What are three benefits of team sports?

⃝ Opportunities for Travel

Traveling and taking vacations are fun. On vacation, you often go somewhere new. You do new and exciting things. There are many kinds of vacations. Some are long, some are short. Some are expensive, some are very affordable.

There are many different ways to travel. You can go by car, bus, train, or plane. You can go on a hiking or biking vacation. You must decide what you want to do. You also must decide where to go and when to go. And you need to decide how much money you can spend.

▷ Benefits of Travel

Millions of people travel in the United States every year. They look forward to their vacations. Why is travel so important to people?

You see new places when you travel. You meet new people. You can learn more about your own country. If you live in a city, you might see how people in rural areas live.

If you travel to a different country, you will see other ways of living. You will learn about other cultures. Travel makes you understand more about the world.

▶ *Traveling can be exciting. What are three things you should do when you decide you would like to travel somewhere?*

☐ Case Study ☐ ☐ ☐ ☐ ☐ ☐

Liz is a manager at a clothing store. She manages several employees. She works very long hours. She has a great deal of responsibility.

Lately, her work has begun to make her feel tense. She has little patience for her employees' problems. She feels nervous and overworked. Her employees have asked her if she is feeling well.

Her boss notices the change in Liz's attitude. She suggests that Liz take a vacation. It has been two years since Liz has taken time off.

Liz realizes she needs to take a break from work. With help from a travel agent, she plans a two-week vacation to Canada. She sees many new things on her trip. When she returns to work two weeks later, she feels relaxed and ready to work.

Travel takes you away from your daily routine. It refreshes you. Sometimes tension and stress build up in our daily lives. Travel relieves stress. You may return from your vacation happy and ready to work.

Travel is good for self-esteem. Taking a trip might seem scary at first. Going to new places might make you nervous. Yet, when you find out you can do it, you feel good about yourself.

Traveling takes planning. There are many details to think about, such as tickets, hotels, and being on time. Taking care of these details gives you self-confidence.

Most of all, travel is fun. You will remember your trips all your life. Traveling will make you better understand different cultures and life-styles.

▷ Overcoming Anxiety About Travel

Does the idea of traveling make you nervous? Traveling is like anything else new. Most people feel anxious until they learn how to do it. You can learn how to overcome travel anxiety.

There are two important things you can do to make your first trip easier.

1. You can get help from a travel agent.
2. You can travel with a group.

Travel agents help people plan their trips. They do not charge you a fee. You probably know what you want to do on your vacation. Do you want to ski? Do you want to lie on a beach? Or would you like to travel through foreign countries?

Travel agents will suggest places for you to go. They will tell you how much it will cost. They can help you find ways to travel inexpensively. They will make plane reservations. They will make hotel reservations if you want. Some travel agents can give you information about unusual vacations. They can tell you about river rafting trips or mountain bike tours.

Many people travel with an organized group. This is a good way to get used to traveling. You will not have to worry about where to stay and what to do every day. Usually, the hotel and travel arrangements are made for you. You will be with other people who are seeing new sights for the first time. You might make good friends in your group. A travel agent can help you find organized tours.

Maybe you would like to be more independent. You can join a group of friends who want to travel. Together, your group can plan the trip and share the work.

▲ *Getting help from a travel agent is one way to ease anxiety about travel. What is another way?*

> ## ▷ Choosing Your Destination

Where would you like to go on your vacation? Do you have a place picked out? If so, you need to learn how to get there and where to stay. What if you do not know where to go? First, you must decide what you want to do. Do any of these things sound interesting?

- Visiting new cities and going to museums.
- Riding a mountain bike through beautiful mountains.
- Seeing how people live in a foreign country.
- Going scuba diving.

★ Tricks of the Trade ★

When to Travel

Traveling to popular vacation places in the off season can save you money. Ask a travel agent to find out when the off season begins.

Look through some travel magazines. Talk to a travel agent. Decide on a few places. Then go to the library and read about them. You can write to the tourist office of the state you want to visit. Or you can call the Chamber of Commerce of any city. They will send you information.

If you want to go to a foreign country, you can write to the country's tourist office nearest you. They will send you information. Some countries make you get special travel permits, called **visas**, before you can travel there. The tourist office will tell you if you need a visa and how to get one. You will also need a *passport*. A **passport** is a document that identifies you as a citizen of a country. It allows you to travel to other countries.

▷ Places to Stay

You will need a place to stay when you travel. The place you choose will depend on how much money you can spend. It also will depend on where you go. You may stay in a hotel, motel, or *youth hostel.*

A **youth hostel** is a place where traveling students can stay overnight. Meals are often provided there.

Call the motel or hotel before you go. They will reserve a room for you. Ask them how much the room costs. Ask if they have any special rates. Call other hotels and motels to compare prices. A travel agent can help you.

▲ *Youth hostels provide an inexpensive place to stay while traveling. What is another inexpensive place you could stay?*

Youth hostels are much less expensive than hotels. There are hostels in most countries. You must join the American Youth Hostels Association before you can stay in a hostel. They can send you the addresses of hostels in 46 countries.

The cheapest way to travel is to camp. Most campgrounds charge a small fee. When you know where you are going, buy a guide to the local campgrounds. Reserve a campsight ahead of time. If you are camping for the first time, rent your equipment. If you find out that you love camping, you might want to buy your own gear. Many sporting goods stores sell camping equipment. Some of them also rent camping gear.

▷ Planning Transportation

Most people travel by car, bus, train, or plane. Your choice of transportation will depend on these three things.

1. The amount you can spend.
2. Where you are going.
3. How much time you have.

Cars. Traveling by car usually costs less than flying or going by train. If friends travel with you, they can share the costs. Driving is not usually the fastest way to travel. Yet it can be fun. You can stop when you want. Or you can take interesting side trips. You have more freedom.

Make sure your car is safe and reliable before you go on your trip. You will not want to waste vacation time waiting for car repairs. Make sure you have car insurance, too.

Buses. Some people like to travel by bus. Someone else does all the driving. You can relax and look at the scenery. Bus fares are cheaper than train or airplane fares. Call the bus station for schedules. You may need to make a reservation. Some bus companies sell passes. A pass allows you to ride the bus as much as you want for a certain period of time.

Trains. Trains are usually more expensive than buses but cheaper than flying. You can buy meals on the train. Amtrak operates trains all over the United States.

If you are going to Europe, you can buy a Eurail Pass. This allows unlimited travel for a period of time. Rates are lower for students.

Train travel is slower than flying. But you can see the countryside from a train as you go by. Many people like train travel better than flying.

Planes. Planes are the fastest way to travel. They are also the most expensive. But you will probably want to fly if you have a long way to go in a short length of time.

Make your reservations as soon as you can. Look in the paper for special prices on plane tickets. A travel agent can make arrangements for you. He or she will help you find the cheapest tickets. A travel agent will also find the best routes to travel. You will also need to find out how to get from the airport to your hotel. Travel agents can help you do that, too.

▷ Using Maps to Plan Your Trip

Use an *atlas* to plan your vacation. An **atlas** is a large book of maps. The index will tell you what map your vacation spot is on. Find the map, and find your destination. Is your home town on the same map? Can you find a map with both your home town and your destination on it? If not, you will have to use two or more maps to plan your trip.

If you plan to drive, find the shortest way to get from your home town to your destination. Will you go on major highways or small back roads? How far is it? How many days will it take you to drive there? Where will you stop overnight?

Use a map to make sure you are not planning to drive too far in one day. Some experts say you should drive no more than about 300 miles per day. If you drive farther than that, you may become too tired to drive safely. Many road maps have a simple chart that tells you the distances between cities.

The map may show you places you would like to see along the way. Study the map carefully. Maybe there is another way you would like to go.

Study the maps around your destination. You may see places to go on short trips. Could you take a bus to a nearby lake or beach? Maybe there is a park or a monument you could visit. Some maps show historical sites. If your atlas has one of these maps, you will know how to find interesting historical places.

If you are going to a new city, study the map of that city. Try to find the location of your hotel. Put a mark on the map there. Find other places on the map you would like to go. Mark them and draw the way to get there from your hotel. You can plan each day's activities using the map.

A map can give you a great deal of information. Using a map will make your vacation more fun.

▲ *An atlas is a book of maps. What are three ways an atlas can help you plan your vacation?*

✔ Check Up ✔ ✔ ✔

1. What are four benefits of travel?
2. What are two things you can do to overcome travel anxiety?
3. What are three things you can do to help choose a destination?
4. What are two inexpensive places to stay while on vacation?
5. What are four ways to travel? Which way is often cheapest for two people?

Chapter 11 Review

Chapter Summary

- It is important to balance work with leisure time.
- Recreation provides many benefits in your life.
- Exercise helps relieve stress.
- Recreation is a way to learn about yourself.
- Recreation expands your social life.
- Recreation may be active or quiet.
- Recreation can take place indoors or outdoors.
- Your community will have groups that provide recreation.
- Travel is a form of recreation.

Reviewing Vocabulary

Listed below are the important new words that were used in this chapter. Next to each word is the page on which you will find the word. Turn to that page and read the paragraph in which the word is printed in **bold** type. Write the word and its meaning. Then write a sentence using each word.

1. leisure time (188)
2. recreation (188)
3. aptitude (190)
4. ability (190)
5. spectator sports (194)
6. visa (201)
7. passport (201)
8. youth hostels (201)
9. atlas (202)

Looking at the Facts

1. What are four benefits of recreation?
2. How can recreation help you learn about yourself?
3. Give three examples of how recreation can be social.
4. What are two benefits of having a hobby?
5. Name six organizations that might offer recreation in a community.
6. How does the cost of recreation at home compare to the cost of other kinds of recreation?
7. What are three benefits of outdoor education?
8. What special benefits can be gained from playing a team sport?
9. How can travel improve your self-esteem?
10. What two things can you do to make your first trip easier?

Thinking Critically

1. Employees who work long hours do not always get more done than those who work normal hours. How would you explain this?
2. You read that recreation can develop self-awareness. How would knowing yourself better affect your life?

3. Some people think about recreation interests when they decide where they want to live. How can where you live affect the recreation you choose?
4. You read that it is important to plan your travels. How detailed do you think your plans should be? Give some examples.
5. Assume traveling is an important life-style goal for you. How might this affect the kind of work you choose?

Discussing Chapter Concepts

1. Recreation is one way to relieve stress. Can recreation create stress? How?
2. Some people enjoy work so much that they pursue it as a hobby. What are the advantages and disadvantages of this?
3. Some kinds of recreation require you to have expensive clothing and equipment. Name five kinds of recreation that do not require you to have expensive clothing or equipment.

Using Basic Skills

Math
1. You are planning a trip. You can choose to either fly or drive to your destination. Round trip air fare is $300. The car rental is $50 per day, including gas. You will need the car for two days. You will also need to spend $125 for food and lodging while you are traveling by car. How much will you save by driving?

Communication
2. Assume you are a travel agent. Collect pictures and information on a trip that interests you. Use the things you collect to create a travel brochure. Include a written description about the trip that will sell the travel package.

Human Relations
3. Your co-worker tells you he feels very stressed on the job. He says he does not know many people in his town. He spends all of his time working. What would you suggest that your co-worker do? What are four benefits of recreation that you could tell your co-worker about?

Activities for Enrichment

1. Get recreation schedules from as many local organizations as you can. Then choose an activity you might enjoy. Write a brief paragraph about the activity. Tell why you chose it.
2. Learn what air, bus, and train service is available in your area. Select a place that you can reach by all the services. Compare the costs and travel times.
3. Contact an auto club such as the American Automobile Association (AAA). Find out what services it offers to people traveling by car.

Affording Your Life-style

Words to learn and use

Here are the new terms you will learn in this chapter. Challenge yourself. Read through the list to see if you know what they mean.

life-style
personal values
equity
convenience foods
balanced life-style
budget

Build on what you know

You already know...
- your likes and dislikes.
- your life-style will depend on your income.
- you will make changes in your life-style.

In this chapter you will learn...
- how your values will affect your future life-style.
- how to plan the costs of your life-style.
- how to include changes in your living costs.

Your **life-style** is the way you live. Your future life-style will depend on your values and your income. Your future life-style will include some of the ways you live now. It will also include many changes as you work toward the way you would like to live. Looking at your values and planning are the first steps in achieving your future life-style.

Everyone needs to plan for the costs of his or her life-style. The more you know about costs, the more likely you will be able to afford the life-style you want. This chapter will help you think about the life-style you would like. You will plan for the living costs you will face. You will learn about choices you can make to keep your living costs within your income.

O Your Desired Life-style

The first step in planning your life-style is to determine what type of life you want. What things will you want to include as a part of your life? Examining your *personal values* will help you determine your desired life-style.

▷ Your Personal Values

Personal values are ideas about your life that are important to you. These ideas may include having money, raising a family, having good health, and having friends.

▲ *Personal values are ideas about your life that are important to you. What are two personal values that are important to the people shown here?*

Your personal values will influence the decisions you make about your life-style. For example, do you value good health? If so, having health insurance will be important to you. Do you value raising a family? If so, you will want to get married and have children. Affording a home for your children will be important to you.

Some of the things you value are things you need. Other things that you value are things you want. Separating your needs from your wants will help you make wise life-style choices.

Rank your values according to your needs and wants. You will want to include your needs before your wants as you make choices about your life-style. For instance, you may *want* to have a new car. But you do not *need* a new car. However, you do *need* to have food. It will be easier to plan your life-style if you can determine what you need and what you want.

Of course, your plans will change as your values change. The things you value today may not be as important in a couple of years. For example, today you may value your career most. You may feel you *need* new business clothes. Later on, you may value having a family more than having a career. You may *need* to have a home more than new clothes.

Your Dream Life-style. Do you ever daydream about your future life? Daydreaming helps you to plan the life-style you want.

When you daydream about your future, think about your own family's life-style. That is, think about where you and your family live. Think about other parts of your life-style, too. What are your family's choices in clothing and food? What type of transportation do you and your family use most often? Do you have a family car? Or does your family ride the bus most of the time? Do both your parents work outside the home? What do you and your family do in your leisure time?

Answer these questions in your mind. Then think about the changes you would like to make in your life-style. Ask yourself what you like best about your life-style now. And think about what things from your current life-style you will want to include in your future life-style. Decide which things you *need* and which things you *want*.

Even in your dream life-style, be realistic. Your dream life-style should become a goal. It describes who you want to become. If you set a dream life-style that is far beyond your reach, you set yourself up for failure. Think of what you can achieve in life if you work hard. As you daydream about the life-style you want, write it all down. Your life-style description will help you work toward your desired life-style.

▲ *Daydreams help you determine your desired life-style. Why is it important to keep your daydreams realistic?*

✔ Check Up ✔ ✔ ✔

1. What are personal values?
2. Why is it important to know the difference between your needs and wants?
3. Why will your needs and wants change?
4. How can thinking about your own family's life-style help you plan your future?
5. Why should you keep your dream life-style realistic?

A Desire to Succeed

Chris Burke

Chris Burke is the young actor who plays Corky in the TV series *Life Goes On.* Chris was born with Down's syndrome. The doctor said he would never learn to read. He thought Chris might not even be able to feed himself.

Chris and his family proved the doctor was wrong. Like others with this disability, he was slower to learn. His speech was slow and hard to understand. But he kept on learning.

When Chris was eight, he said he wanted to be on TV. His family did not want to discourage him. But they did not want him to hope for something impossible.

Chris did not give up. He got a part in a school play. He kept dreaming about being an actor.

Chris worked his way up to reading at the fifth grade level. He finished his special schooling when he was 21. His sister helped him get a volunteer job. He worked with students who had disabilities more severe than his own. Chris liked his work. Yet he still wanted to be an actor.

Chris saw a young actor, Jason Kingsley, on TV. Jason had Down's syndrome. Chris wrote to him. Jason's mother helped him get a tryout for a movie part. Chris got the part. He was in a TV movie!

This was just the beginning of his success. A whole TV series was written for him. The series, *Life Goes On,* shows what it is like for a family and a child with Down's syndrome.

Chris tells people that he has "Up" syndrome. He thinks it is important to believe in what you *can* do. Because he kept his eyes on the goal, his desired life-style has become a reality.

O Life-style Costs

Many people do not spend much time planning the cost of their life-style. Some spend time planning what they want but not how to afford it. By planning the cost of your desired life-style, you will get more of what you want out of life. You will spend your money for things that are important to you. The more time you plan, the closer you will come to reaching your desired life-style. Once you have determined the life-style you desire, follow these three steps.

1. Estimate the cost. What will each part of your desired life-style cost?
2. Estimate your income. Your work provides the earnings for everything you do. Your income will be your guide to what you can afford. How much do you expect to earn in the next five to ten years?
3. Change your plan. Your desired life-style may cost more than you expect to earn. If so, change your life-style plan. You could spend less on things you *want* and spend only on the things you *need*.

As you know, there are many parts to a person's life-style. Here are the parts you should consider when you estimate costs.

- Will you live alone or with others?
- Will you be single or married?
- Will you have children?
- Where will you live?
- What do you prefer in clothing?
- What are your tastes in food?
- What transportation will you use?
- How will you use your leisure time?
- How important is health care?
- What type of vacations do you prefer?
- Will there be other life-style costs?
- How important is saving money?

Here is a closer look at the things you should consider.

▷ Married, Single, or Roommate

When you think about your future life-style, consider whether you would *prefer* to be married or single. Estimate your life-style costs according to what you prefer.

Will you be married? If so, you can share expenses.

If you are single, you will have to pay all of your expenses by yourself. How can a single person save money on housing? One way is to get a roommate. If you live with a roommate, you will be able to split the rent and other living costs.

☐ Case Study ☐ ☐ ☐ ☐ ☐ ☐

Diane was very excited about her first full-time job. She wanted to use her first paycheck for a down payment on a new car. She had been dreaming about owning her own car since high school.

Diane went to a car dealership. She wanted a car with style. After an hour, she found the perfect car. It had a great stereo system and a sunroof. Diane decided she would come back the next day and buy the car.

On the way home from the car dealership, Diane thought about the car. She thought about other things she would need money for in the next five years. She wanted to get an apartment. She also wanted to go back to school to advance in her career.

When she got home, Diane wrote down all the things she needed for her future life-style. She added up the car payments for five years. She realized much of her money would have to go toward car payments.

Diane discovered the car was not as important to her as she had thought. She realized she would need to be careful about planning to afford her desired life-style.

▷ Children

If you have children, you must plan how you will pay for their expenses. Many people do not consider the costs of having a child. But having children is very expensive.

You will have to consider clothing, health care, and food costs for your child. The total cost for one child for the first 18 years is about $100,000. The cost of attending a four-year state college is about $5,000 to $10,000 dollars per year. This cost is increasing every year. You will need to plan for these costs.

Who will take care of the children? Will you or your spouse have to leave your job and stay home? If so, this will cut your income in half.

Maybe you have other family members who can take care of your children. If so, this will save you money.

Maybe you will choose to use child care. Child care services take care of your children while you are working. However, they can cost about $100 a week. Sometimes companies provide child care for their employees. You may be able to use this option. But you will still need to plan for the expense of any child care you need after work.

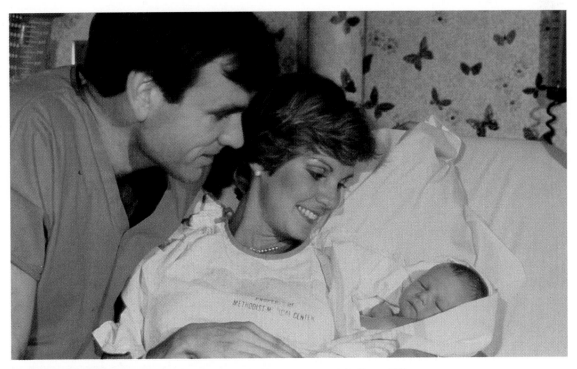

▲ *Having children is an important part of many people's lives. What are three child expenses this family will have to consider?*

▷ A Place to Live

You may live with your parents after you begin full-time work. By living with your parents, you can save some money. But you will probably want to move out within a year or two after high school. The cost of housing will depend on whether you rent or buy a home.

Buying. After you have worked and saved for a few years, you may want to buy a home. More than half of the families in the country own their homes.

There are some good reasons to buy a home. You may want to live close to where you work. You may want to live near the best schools for your children. What if there are no rentals where you want to live? What if the rentals are not large enough for your family? Then the only way you can live there is to buy a home.

Very few people pay all cash when they buy a home. Most get a home loan and make monthly payments. Part of each payment is for interest on the loan. The home loan interest you pay helps lower your income tax.

Part of each payment lowers the amount you owe on the loan. This increases your home equity. Your **equity** is the share of your home that you really own.

Home values in most parts of the country have increased greatly over the past 30 years. Most people make down payments of 10 to 30 percent on their homes. And many have sold them after a few years and made big profits. Why? It is because they get the increase in value for the full price of the home. So building equity or ownership in a home is a good way to earn income.

Some people buy older homes and fix them up. After a few years, they sell them. This is also a good way to make a profit.

There are also some reasons for not buying a home. Homes are expensive. Even buying a condo or a mobile home costs more than renting. It may take you a few years to save up money for a down payment. Monthly payments on a home are often higher than paying rent, too. And when you buy a home, you must take care of all repairs. Sometimes it is hard to sell a home. This can be a problem if you are transferred and need to move to another city.

Renting. Even when you can afford to buy, there are some good reasons to rent. When you rent, you do not have to tie up your savings for a down payment. Your monthly costs are often less when you rent, too. Monthly payments on home loans can be very high. Renting does not tie you down. Suppose you are transferred to a job in another city. It will be much easier to move if you are renting a place. Renting is also less work. All homes need repair work from time to time.

What will it cost to rent? It depends on the size of the apartment or house you want. It also depends on the location. Look in the *For Rent* ads in your local newspaper. Most rentals require at least two months' rent in advance. You will probably have to pay for some utilities. They will add to your monthly costs.

▲ *As a part of your life-style, you may choose to either rent or buy a place to live. Name two advantages to renting.*

Furnishings. Finding a place to live is just the first step in living on your own. You will need some furnishings, too. Among other things, you will need a bed, a table and chairs, and some dishes. If you rent a furnished apartment, your job is much easier. In that case, you will need fewer things.

What if you rent an unfurnished apartment or buy your own home? Then you will have to get all of the furnishings. It can be very costly. But you will not have to get everything at once. You can get what you must have, then buy the rest over months or years.

Most people cannot buy everything they want. So you will need to plan what you want in your home. Look in magazines for ideas.

What should you think of when choosing furnishings? Think about how your home will meet the needs of your life-style.

How long do you expect to be in your home? Do you see yourself moving in a couple of years? If so, you will not want to spend a great deal of money matching your furniture with your home. Will you have children? If so, you will want furnishings that will stand up to a lot of use. You will want to avoid things that are fragile.

Begin with the furnishings you will need right away. Then add items over time. You will need a bed. That is the first purchase for most people. You might want a couch that can be made into a bed. Next, you will need a table and chairs. You may need some appliances such as a stove or refrigerator.

How can you furnish your place for the lowest cost? Your parents may have some things they no longer use. Household items such as linens and furniture go on sale at certain times every year. Look for these sales. Look in the newspaper ads for used furniture. Visit garage sales. Check used furniture stores. You will find some bargains if you shop around. In a few years, you will probably earn more money. Then you can replace your low-cost furniture.

▷ Clothing

Do you like nice clothes? Clothing can be expensive. But you can dress well without spending a lot, too.

Some people sew their own clothes. It does not cost much. If you do not sew, you can save money buying from discount stores.

Used clothing stores sometimes have good clothes at low prices. Often, the clothes look like new.

Department stores have all kinds of clothes at a wide range of prices. Some department stores offer good values at low prices. Some department stores sell designer fashions. Designer fashions are usually high priced. But the quality is often very good.

▶ *With some planning you can dress well without spending a lot of money. In what way did planning help this couple save money?*

You can save by buying clothing at the end-of-season clearance sales. Then you can put them away for the next year.

▷ Food

Do you like to eat in restaurants? Or do you prefer to eat at home?

Today, more people are eating out than ever before. One reason is that people have less time to cook because they work full time. When you eat out, you may choose from many types of restaurants. The amount of money you spend will depend on the type of restaurant you choose. You can go to fancy restaurants and spend $30 per person. Or you can go out to a fast-food restaurant and spend less than $10. Even fast food sometimes costs more than eating at home.

You will save money by eating at home. You can eat at home and still save time if you buy prepared foods. This is food that is ready to eat. You can buy it from delis. Potato salad and roasted chicken are examples of prepared foods.

Convenience foods are foods that are frozen, canned, or packaged. These foods cost less than prepared foods. But they take a little more time to get ready. Frozen foods need to be heated for a few minutes before you can eat them.

The cheapest way to eat at home is to prepare meals from scratch. Of course, you will spend more time cooking. You will spend more time shopping, too. But you will save a good deal of money.

If you have the time, you will save even more money by careful shopping. You can buy foods when they are on sale. You can also buy food in large quantities. Check the newspaper ads and cut out coupons. Plan your meals around the weekly specials at your local market.

▲ *Using coupons to buy food is one way to save money. What are three other ways?*

▷ **Transportation**

How do you get to school? If your school is close, you probably walk. If not, you may ride a bicycle or take a bus. When you begin working full time, how do you plan to get to work? Some people walk or ride a bicycle to work. This is usually the cheapest form of transportation. But some people live too far from their work to walk or ride a bicycle. So they take such public transportation as a bus, a subway, or a train.

In the United States, most people own cars. Some need a car. The rest may not need a car, but they want one. A car is handy. You can get to work or to a movie much faster in a car than you can by walking or riding a bicycle.

As you learned in Chapter 10, cars are expensive. The first expense is the purchase price. Then you must buy insurance. Gas and repairs are costly, too.

You can save money by joining a car pool. Then you may only have to drive your own car to work one or two days a week. You can ride in someone else's car the other days.

In your future life-style, you may want to own a car. What kind of a car will you want? Will you be happy to buy cars that are two or three years old? If so, you will save a lot of money. Buying a good used car will save you thousands of dollars. You can use the money you save for other things.

▷ Health Care

Having a healthy life-style will probably be very important to you. If you are healthy, you can work. You can enjoy your free time. Being healthy saves you money.

Health care can be very expensive. Even if you are not sick, you will probably have dental and doctor check-ups about twice a year. How can you plan for health expenses? These two things will help you afford health care.

- Preventative health care.
- Health insurance.

Here is a closer look at these things.

Preventative Health Care. There are several steps you can take to prevent getting sick or injured. This will save you money. For example, you know that wearing a seatbelt in a car can prevent injury. Not smoking will help keep you from getting cancer. Staying out of the sun will help prevent skin cancer. Thin people are often healthier than overweight people. They live longer, too. Eating right, exercising, and getting enough sleep will help you stay healthy.

Health Insurance. Of course, even a healthy life-style does not guarantee good health. Almost everyone becomes ill sometime. Health insurance will help pay for the expense of getting sick.

Some companies pay all of the health insurance costs for their employees. Other companies pay only part of the cost and the employees pay the rest. If you can, join a health insurance plan where you work. If you cannot do this, buy your own health insurance. Whether you or your company pays your health insurance, having it will save you money in the long-run.

▷ Recreation

You will probably want to set aside time in your life for recreation. Today's life-styles are often stressful. You need time to relax. You need more in life than work and other daily tasks. A **balanced life-style** leaves equal time for play as well as work. You will not mind working hard if you have time for fun later on.

As you learned in Chapter 11, most people use their leisure time for recreation. Some types of recreation are very expensive. Other types are free.

The extent to which you are involved in an activity can make it cheap or expensive. For example, owning your own horse can be very expensive. But it does not cost much to ride public horses on the weekend. Fishing can be expensive if you travel all over the country to find the best spots. But it will not cost much if you fish close to home.

◀ *Jogging is one type of recreation that is not expensive. Name three others.*

Most people can afford tennis, swimming, or photography. But if you want to, you can spend a lot of money on these activities as well.

The least expensive activities include such outdoor activities as bicycling, jogging, and hiking. Some low-cost indoor activities are reading, playing chess, or watching a movie. Pottery, crafts, and painting are artistic activities that do not cost a great amount.

Vacations are another type of recreation. If you can afford it, you can spend several thousand dollars on a vacation. You could spend six weeks touring Europe. More affordable vacations include touring the country or camping. Sometimes a vacation can simply mean staying home from work and relaxing. Many people like to take at least one vacation each year. Your costs will depend on the type of vacation you choose.

Continued on page 221.

★ **Tricks of the Trade** ★

Saving Money

The best way to save is to pay yourself first. This means you put money into a savings plan before you spend it on anything else.

Lee's Life-style

Lee assembles telephone parts. She is 21 and single.	**TAKE HOME INCOME:** $ 1,000 a month

	LIFE-STYLE COSTS PER MONTH:
Housing: She rents a three bedroom apartment with two roommates.	$250
Furnishings: The apartment is furnished. Lee likes to add her own furnishing now and then.	$50
Clothing: She does not spend much on clothes for work. She does like to buy some new clothes for evenings and weekend wear.	$100
Food: Lee usually prepares her own food during the week. She likes to go out for dinner on the weekend.	$300
Transportation: Lee lives near a bus stop. So she takes the bus to work and to shop.	$100
Health Care and Recreation: Lees has a group health policy through her work. She rides her bike and goes to aerobics class for exercise. She goes to two movies a month. She goes on one or two short vacations a year.	$100
Other Costs: Lee's other costs include household supplies and gifts.	$50
TOTAL LIFE-STYLE COSTS:	$950

▲ *Figure 12-1*
Your life-style costs will depend on your values and careful planning. Which things in Lee's life-style would you include in your plan? What changes would you include?

☐ Case Study ☐ ☐ ☐ ☐ ☐ ☐

When Jess dreamed about his future life-style, he thought about having many things. He wanted a fancy car, a house, three kids, and a vacation home.

When he got his first full-time job, Jess sat down and thought about his dream life-style. He listed all the things he wanted. And he estimated the cost for everything he wanted. Then he considered his income. He was amazed. The cost of his desired life-style was ten times more than his income!

Jess realized he needed to be realistic. It was going to take some planning to achieve the life-style he desired. Jess included only those things he needed most. By planning his spending, Jess knew he would be able to have a life-style he would enjoy.

▷ Saving for Unexpected Costs

No matter how well you plan, you will face unexpected costs. You may need to get your car repaired. You may want to spend money on magazines and movies. You may need to spend more for housing, medical expenses, or education. You may want to donate some money to worthwhile charities.

Plan for some extra costs by saving your money. Try to save some of what you earn each week or each month.

You may want to ask your employer to help you set up an automatic saving plan. With an automatic saving plan, part of your paycheck goes directly into your savings account. Then you can handle the other costs that will surely come along.

✔ Check Up ✔ ✔ ✔

1. List three planning steps that can help you reach your desired life-style.
2. What do you need to do if your estimated costs are greater than your estimated income?
3. How can you dress well without spending a lot?
4. What is the most expensive form of transportation?
5. What are two ways you can plan to meet your health expenses?
6. What are three affordable types of recreation?
7. Why should you include a saving plan in your life-style?

O Paying for the Cost of Your Life-style

Planning to pay for the cost of your life-style can be difficult. Many people assume they can afford more than they actually can.

Using credit can be very tempting. You can have what you want, when you want it. You do not have to wait until you save the full amount. Credit can seem like magic. It can make you feel as though you have a great deal of money. It can make you feel powerful.

Sometimes people lose control of their spending. They buy so much on credit that they cannot afford to make all their monthly payments. Then they must pay interest on the payments they do not make.

Make sure you buy no more than you can afford. Before you buy something on credit, ask yourself if you need the good or service right away. Could you do without it until you save enough to pay for it in cash? If you do buy on credit, try to pay off all that you owe each month.

Learn to budget your money. A **budget** is a plan to manage your money. Keep track of your monthly spending. Compare what you spend to your monthly salary. If you spend more than you make, you need to revise your life-style. Remember, be realistic. In the end, you must pay for everything you buy.

▷ Finding Money Management Help

If you have trouble managing your money, help is available. Here are six places you can go for money management help.

1. Schools.
2. Newspapers and magazines.
3. Government agencies.
4. Banks
5. Lawyers.
6. Other sources.

Schools. Many schools have consumer education courses. In these classes, students learn the best ways to buy and use goods and services.

Do not forget your teachers can help with your problems. Most teachers in business, homemaking, and industrial arts have studied consumer education. Your school counselor is another possible source of help.

Newspapers and Magazines. You can find information about money matters in newspapers and magazines. Most newspapers print daily or weekly articles on handling money. Several magazines, such as *Business Week, Forbes,* and *Fortune,* deal only with financial matters.

▲ *These magazines provide information about money matters. What are three other sources you can go to for help with money matters?*

Government Agencies. Many government agencies publish free or inexpensive booklets. These booklets will help you get the most for your money. You can find them at federal and county offices and at the library.

Banks. Many banks employ people to give free financial information to customers. Information is given on savings plans and bank loans. As a public service, some banks sponsor courses, called seminars, in money management. If you have money problems, ask at your bank if such a seminar is planned.

Lawyers. Sometimes money problems require legal help. Speak with a lawyer if you need a legal opinion. You will need to do this when making contracts, selling property, and collecting money. You will also need to do this if you are unable to pay the money you owe. You can find more information on legal help in Chapter 15.

Other Sources. Check the Yellow Pages of your phone book. Look under the name of your city or town. You may find agencies that can help you learn to manage your money.

★ Tricks of the Trade ★

Credit Card Record

Keep a credit card register as you do for your bank checks. When you use your credit card, write down the charge. This will help you keep track of how much you have spent on credit. It will help keep you from overspending.

✔ Check Up ✔ ✔ ✔

1. What are two ways to make sure you buy no more than you can afford?
2. What should you do if you spend more than you make?
3. What are six places you can find help managing your money?

Chapter 12 Review

Chapter Summary

- Daydreaming about the way you would like to live is the first step in planning your life-style.
- Looking at the way you live now will help you make choices about your future.
- Your life-style description will probably include some of today's life-style. It may also include many changes.
- A plan for your future needs to be realistic.
- Planning will help you afford your desired life-style.
- Many factors affect your living costs.
- Your living costs will depend on your choice of housing.
- Personal choices of clothing, food, and transportation affect your living costs.
- You need to plan for health care and recreation expenses in a balanced life-style.

Reviewing Vocabulary

Listed below are the important new words that were used in this chapter. Next to each word is the page on which you will find the word. Turn to that page and read the paragraph in which the word is printed in **bold** type. Write the word and its meaning. Then write a paragraph describing your dream life-style. Use all of the vocabulary words in your paragraph.

1. life-style (207)
2. personal values (208)
3. equity (214)
4. convenience foods (216)
5. balanced life-style (218)
6. budget (222)

Looking at the Facts

1. What are personal values?
2. Briefly describe the three planning steps you should follow to help you afford your dream life-style.
3. What are two ways of paying for a place to live?
4. What are three good reasons to rent a living place?
5. What are two good reasons to buy your own living place?
6. What basic furnishings will you need if you buy or rent an unfurnished living place?
7. Explain how your choice of food and clothing can affect your living costs.
8. List four ways people get to work.
9. What are three types of outdoor recreation?
10. What two things will help you afford health care?
11. How can you plan for unexpected costs in your life?
12. What are six sources of money management help?

Thinking Critically

1. Make a list of all the personal values you think you should consider before writing down a life-style description.
2. Thinking only about cost, do you believe it is better to rent or buy a living place? Explain your answer.
3. How can the kind of work you do affect your food and clothing costs?
4. Providing health insurance is a large expense for employers. If you could choose between higher pay or health insurance, which would you choose? Explain your answer.
5. Why do you think that so many people spend so much more than they can afford to?

Discussing Chapter Concepts

1. Is it more important to enjoy your work or to make a lot of money at your job? Why?
2. Assume that your life-style choice includes marriage and children. Discuss your ideas about ideal child-care arrangements. How will these arrangements affect your life-style?
3. Do you agree that recreation is an important part of life? Discuss your answers.
4. As a class, discuss an ideal life-style. Figure out the cost of such a life-style.

Using Basic Skills

Math
1. You are doing your shopping. Two brands of apple juice are on the shelf. Brand A is $1.50 for 12 ounces. Brand B is $2.75 for 24 ounces. How much will you save by buying the larger size?

Communication
2. You need a roommate to help you share your apartment expenses. Write an ad to describe the qualities you desire in a roommate.

Human Relations
3. Look at Lee's Life-style on page 220. Suppose Lee has decided to buy a used car. The payments will be $200 a month. Lee has asked you for advice on how she can afford the car. Write down suggestions for how she can save money.

Activities for Enrichment

1. Plan a trip to some city within the United States. Pick a city that is 700 to 1,000 miles from where you live. Contact a local travel agent for transportation costs for your trip. Compare the cost of traveling by train to traveling by air.
2. Keep track of your family's expenses for one week. Include food, clothing, and entertainment. What things would you include in your life-style?

Part Four
Life Skills

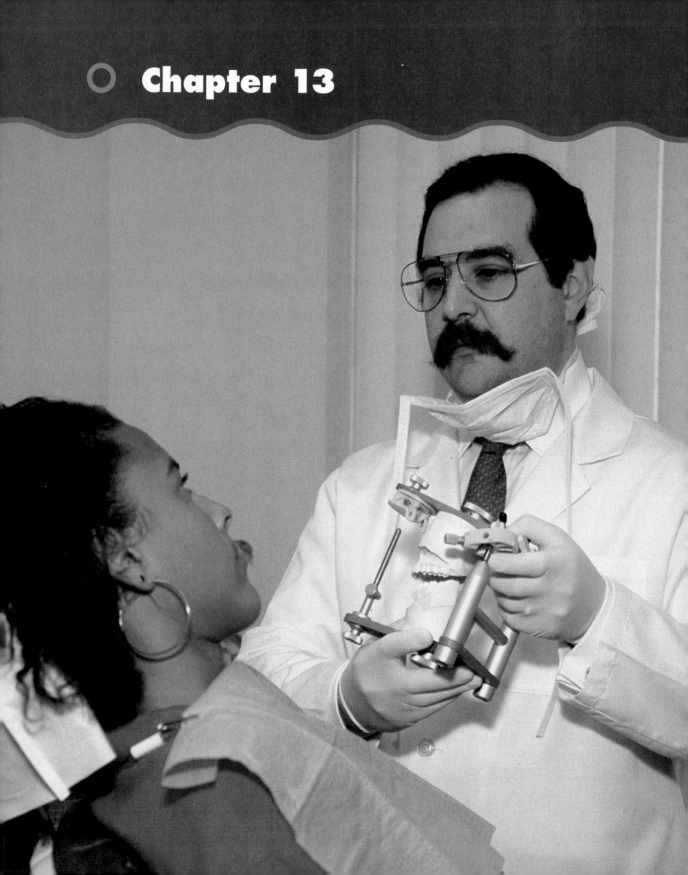

Protecting Your Health

Words to learn and use

Here are the new terms you will learn in this chapter. Challenge yourself. Read through the list to see if you know what they mean.

recommended daily allowance (RDA)
calorie
anorexia nervosa
bulimia
physical fitness
aerobic exercise
side effect
sunscreen
drug abuse
steroids
sexually transmitted disease (STD)

Build on what you know

You already know...
- your life-style affects your health.
- your diet and exercise affect your health.
- your environment affects your health.
- your health is your responsibility.

In this chapter you will learn...
- how to make good health part of your life-style.
- how to have a healthy diet and exercise program.
- how to control your personal health environment.
- how to take responsibility for your health.

Good health is more than just being free from sickness. Good health means having a healthy body, a sound mind, and a strong spirit.

Your health affects every part of your life. It affects how you feel, behave, and look. It affects how well you work. And it affects how well you get along with others.

Choosing a healthy life-style is up to you. In this chapter, you will learn about making healthy choices. Think about how you can put these ideas to work for you.

◯ Your Life-style and Health

Your life-style affects your health. Right now you may not think very much about your health. You may feel that you do not need to worry about it until you are older.

However, the habits people develop when they are young do affect their health. These habits include diet, exercise, and general health care. The sooner you form good health habits, the more likely you are to have a healthy life-style.

▷ Your Diet

You know it is wise to eat a *balanced diet*. A balanced diet includes food from the four basic food groups.

1. The milk and dairy products group.
2. The meat, fish, and poultry group.
3. The fruits and vegetables group.
4. The breads and cereals group.

Why should you eat food from every group? Each group has basic nutrients that you need for good health. They supply protein, fat, and carbohydrates. They also supply vitamins, minerals, and water.

Recommended Daily Allowances. How can you know how much of each food you should eat? Each person's needs are different. Scientists study how the body uses food. Then they make charts that show how much of each nutrient our bodies need.

Our daily nutrient needs are called our **recommended daily allowances (RDA)**. Many food labels give the percentage of RDA in a single serving of that food. These RDAs are just guides. Of course, everyone's needs are not the same.

Recent research suggests that we need fewer foods from the meat group. We may need more foods from the fruits and vegetables group. Certain foods in these groups may have more health benefits than others. Eating a balanced diet helps you get all the nutrients you need.

Water is the most important part of your diet. Nearly all foods contain water. Our bodies are about 60 percent water. The average adult body contains about 45 quarts of water.

Most people lose about three quarts of water a day. This water must be replaced so the body can function well. If you drink eight glasses of water a day, you will replace two quarts. You can get the rest of the water you need from the foods you eat.

Most of the food you eat should be high in the nutrients you need. And they should be low in sugar, salt, cholesterol, and fat.

NUTRITION INFORMATION PER SERVING

SERVING SIZE.........................1 OZ.   SERVINGS PER PACKAGE.................20

	1 OUNCE	WITH SKIM MILK
CALORIES	110	150
PROTEIN, g	3	7
CARBOHYDRATE, g	24	30
FAT, g	0	0
CHOLESTEROL, mg	0	0
SODIUM, mg	270	330
POTASSIUM, mg	80	280
PERCENTAGE OF U.S. RECOMMENDED DAILY ALLOWANCES (U.S. RDA)		
PROTEIN	3	12
VITAMIN A	25	30
VITAMIN C	25	25
THIAMIN	30	35
RIBOFLAVIN	30	40
NIACIN	25	25
CALCIUM	2	15
IRON	25	25
VITAMIN D	10	25
VITAMIN B_6	30	30
FOLIC ACID	35	35
PHOSPHORUS	8	18
MAGNESIUM	5	9
ZINC	3	7
COPPER	4	4

◀ *As a guide, many food labels give the nutrition information per serving. Is this cereal high in fat? Which of the RDAs is this cereal highest in?*

Try to avoid eating foods that are only empty calories. This means they supply calories but few nutrients. Many foods with lots of sugar contain empty calories. Sugar contains no important nutrients.

Avoid eating foods that are high in cholesterol. *Cholesterol* is a fatty, waxlike substance that helps your body produce substances it needs. Too much cholesterol can be unhealthy. Large amounts of cholesterol can build up on the walls of blood vessels making it hard for blood to pass through. Keep your cholesterol levels low by avoiding animal products such as eggs and red meat.

Most people eat far more salt than is healthy. Too much salt can cause high blood pressure. Cut down on salty snacks and do not put salt on your food.

You need some fat in your diet for good health. But too much can lead to heart disease and other health problems. Most foods contain more fat than you think. Avoid fat by learning to recognize high-fat foods such as butter, cheese, nuts, and eggs.

Our ideas about good eating habits change as we learn more about how our bodies use food. Choose food that will help you build and maintain a healthy body.

Weight Control. An important part of good health is weight control. New studies are changing our ideas about how much healthy people should weigh.

The ideal weight for you depends on your height, age, body frame, and gender. A healthy weight allows you to feel good. Being overweight strains your body and causes health problems.

Eating right can help you reach and maintain a healthy weight. Even if you are trying to lose weight, you still should eat a balanced diet. Your body needs the nutrients from each food group. This is why it is not safe to use diet aids to lose weight. Long-term use of these products robs your body of nutrients. A doctor or a weight loss clinic can help you plan a healthy diet.

A diet for weight loss needs to be low in *calories*. A **calorie** is a unit that measures the fuel value of food. To lose weight, you must eat fewer calories than your body burns. Your diet should also be low in fat. Less than 30 percent of the calories you eat should come from fat. There are nine calories in one gram of fat.

Recommended Weight for Females and Males							
Female				Male			
Hgt.	Small Frame	Medium Frame	Large Frame	Hgt.	Small Frame	Medium Frame	Large Frame
4' 8"	88– 94	92–103	100–115	5' 0"	101–109	107–117	115–130
9	90– 97	94–106	102–118	1	104–112	110–121	118–133
10	92–100	97–109	105–121	2	107–115	113–125	121–136
11	95–103	100–112	108–124	3	110–118	116–128	124–140
5' 0"	98–106	103–115	111–127	4	113–121	119–131	127–144
1	101–109	106–118	114–130	5	116–125	122–135	130–148
2	104–112	109–122	117–134	6	120–129	126–139	134–153
3	107–115	112–126	121–138	7	124–133	130–144	139–158
4	110–119	116–131	125–142	8	128–137	134–148	143–162
5	114–123	120–135	129–146	9	132–142	138–152	147–166
6	118–127	124–139	133–150	10	136–146	142–157	151–171
7	122–131	128–143	137–154	11	140–150	146–162	156–176
8	126–136	132–147	141–157	6' 0"	144–154	150–167	160–181
9	130–140	136–151	145–164	1	148–158	154–172	165–186
10	134–144	140–155	149–169	2	152–162	159–177	170–191
11	138–148	144–159	153–174	3	156–167	164–182	174–196
6' 0"	142–152	149–163	157–179	4	160–171	169–187	178–201

Adapted from Metropolitan Life Insurance chart on weight of males and females.

▲ *Figure 13-1*
Your recommended weight will depend on your height, age, body frame, and gender. According to this chart, what is your recommended weight?

The average woman eats about 1,600 to 1,800 calories a day. That means she should eat no more than 44 to 50 grams of fat. The average man eats 2,400 to 2,600 calories a day. He should eat no more than 67 to 70 grams of fat.

Did you know that a handful of potato chips contains about 6 grams of fat? Read food labels to learn how much fat is in the foods you eat. Meat and dairy products often contain many grams of fat. Bread, cereals, fruits, and vegetables have little or no fat. Eating foods low in fat will help you maintain a healthy weight.

Unhealthy Weight Control. Do you know someone who is always worried about gaining weight? Those who have a great fear of gaining weight may have an eating disorder. *Anorexia nervosa* and *bulimia* are two serious eating disorders. People with these disorders see themselves as fat, even when they are not.

Those with **anorexia nervosa** starve themselves to lose weight. Those with **bulimia** eat large amounts of food. Then they cause themselves to vomit to get rid of it.

These eating disorders are very unhealthy, both physically and emotionally. They can lead to serious illness and even death.

Never take dieting to these extremes. Diet is only one factor in maintaining a healthy life-style. It is just as vital to feel good about yourself.

Think of yourself as an attractive person. If you are trying to lose weight, set goals you can reach. Plan to lose only one or two pounds a week.

Do not plan your life around food. Focus on other things you enjoy doing and do well. Find some form of exercise that you like. It will help you reach a healthy weight. It will also improve your self-esteem.

Do not think of your diet as only a short-term change. Think of it as a change in your life-style. Be kind to yourself. Remember that your ideal weight makes you feel good.

Unhealthy "Health Foods." Reading food labels helps you choose healthy foods. But food labels can be misleading. Sometimes advertisers will put "No Cholesterol" on a food label. They want you to think the product is healthy.

But foods that do not contain cholesterol may still have large amounts of fat. For instance, microwave popcorn may be advertised as a health food because it has no cholesterol. But some bags of microwave popcorn contain 16 grams of fat. Products such as turkey hotdogs should be low in fat. But sometimes they include turkey skin, which is high in fat.

Do not be mislead by ads. Read the labels for RDAs, fat, sugar, cholesterol, and salt. Lard, butter, and coconut or palm oil are fats. Sucrose, fructose, and honey are sugars. Sodium is the most common word for salt.

▷ Exercise

Being physically fit is part of a healthy life-style. **Physical fitness** is a measure of your strength and how long you can do something without tiring. How fit are you? Can you run half a block or hike uphill without feeling out of breath? Are you strong enough to swim a few laps in a pool without tiring? If not, you may not be as fit as you should be.

It is up to you to take care of your body and keep it fit. Being fit will let you live a healthier life. And you can work more easily. Exercise is an important key to fitness.

Benefits of Exercise. Exercise helps you live longer. It gives you energy and strengthens your muscles. Strong muscles help your joints work smoothly. And strong joints that work well protect you from injury.

Some exercise strengthens your heart and lungs. This is called **aerobic exercise**. It makes your body take in more air. This increases your lung size. Aerobic exercise also makes your heart beat faster. This makes your heart muscle stronger. Brisk exercise, such as walking or jogging, helps build strong bones. Strong bones prevent the bone thinning that occurs as you get older.

▶ *Swimming is an aerobic exercise. What is one benefit of aerobic exercise?*

Exercise also increases the number of calories your body uses. Activity that raises your heart rate burns calories for several hours after you finish. This helps keep your weight at a healthy level.

Finally, exercise helps you think more clearly. It keeps you alert. It aids your ability to make decisions and solve problems.

Choosing an Exercise Program. There are many kinds of exercise. Before you begin an exercise program, be sure you are in good health. Check with your doctor if you have any questions.

Pick an exercise that you will enjoy. It is easier to stay with an activity you like. It may help to vary your exercise program with more than one kind of activity.

Some exercises, such as running, swimming, and riding a bike, strengthen your lungs and heart. Others, such as weight training, strengthen muscles. Walking is a good all-round exercise.

Exercise alone or with a friend. Find a program that works for you and stick to it.

Whatever exercise you choose, start slowly. If you do too much at first, your muscles and joints may hurt. Add a few minutes to your exercise time each day until you reach 20 to 30 minutes of lively exercise. Try to exercise at least three times a week.

★ Tricks of the Trade ★

Exercise Time

Set a regular time for exercise. You will find that your workouts are easier if you make them a regular part of your daily routine.

What if you do not have time to exercise 20 or 30 minutes? Then exercise more often for 10 to 15 minutes. Take ten minutes to go for a walk after lunch and dinner. Or ride your bike to the store instead of driving. You may not get all the benefits of the longer time. But it is better than not doing any exercise.

There are other ways to fit exercise into your life-style. When sitting in your car, do stretching exercises. If you drive to work, park several blocks away and walk. Or simply walk to work. Take the stairs instead of the elevator. Use part of your lunch time to exercise. Some employers provide gyms at work. Plan some exercise for after work or on weekends. Instead of watching TV after work, exercise. Play tennis, hike, or bike. Make a point to schedule time in your day for exercise. You will be more likely to exercise if you have a scheduled time set aside.

Choose any activity that you enjoy and can do your entire lifetime. Decide to be fit for life. You will enjoy being stronger and healthier.

▷ Health Care

A good diet and regular exercise help to keep you healthy. There are times, though, when you should see a doctor to help you stay in good health.

Get Regular Check-ups. A check-up is a physical exam. It is usually done once a year. The need for a check-up varies with each person. A regular dental check-up is also part of taking care of your health. A doctor can help you set a schedule that is right for you.

A check-up has two parts. The first part is a health history. The doctor will ask you questions about your health and life-style.

You will be asked about shots you have had to protect you from illnesses. Sometimes these shots need to be renewed. You will be asked questions about your diet and exercise program. Your doctor will ask about any illnesses or injuries you may have had. Your doctor will want to talk about your family's health history. This helps the doctor decide if you are likely to get certain diseases.

Give your doctor complete answers. The more a doctor knows about you, the better the health program you will have.

After your health history, your doctor will do a physical exam. Your blood pressure and weight will be checked. Eyes, ears, skin, and throat will be examined.

A woman will most likely be given a breast exam and a Pap smear test. In a Pap smear test, a doctor examines cell tissue taken from a woman's cervix. These tests help the doctor find any problems that can be treated early, such as cancer. Finding a problem early improves the chances of successful treatment.

If you have a minor injury or a cold, you can treat it yourself. But sometimes you will need to see a doctor if you are not sure how serious

▲ *Regular check-ups can help you stay in good health. What are the two parts of a check-up?*

your problem is. Ask for advice if you have pain for an unknown reason. Also, see a doctor for any symptom that does not go away. Pay attention to your body. You will probably know when something is wrong.

Follow your doctor's advice to benefit from each visit. Be sure you understand what your doctor has told you. Always ask questions. Ask the doctor to write down any instructions.

If your doctor prescribes medicine, use it properly. Some people stop taking their medicine when they begin to feel better. This can allow the illness to return. So take the amount prescribed. Take it at the right times and for as long as you are supposed to.

Use Only Prescribed Medicines. Take only the medicine your doctor gives you. Never take medicine prescribed for a friend. Also, taking more than one medicine at a time can be harmful.

Be sure to tell your doctor if you are taking any over-the-counter medicines. You may need to stop taking them while you take your prescribed medicine. If the prescribed medicine does not help, call your doctor.

The medicine prescribed may have a *side effect*. A **side effect** is a problem caused by a drug. You may find that your medicine makes you sleepy. This makes it unsafe for you to drive. Drinking alcohol is very dangerous if you are taking medicine. Some

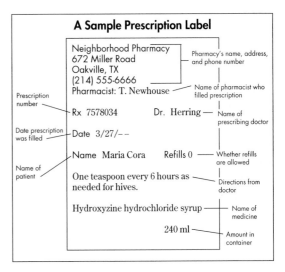

▲ *Figure 13-2*
If your doctor prescribes medicine, be sure to take it as directed. How much and how often should Maria Cora take this medicine?

medicines cause you to react to the sun. Ask your doctor what side effects to expect.

Think of your doctor as your partner. Work together with him or her to protect your health. Learn to check your body at home for early signs of cancer. Your doctor can teach you how to do this. Report any changes in your normal body functions to your doctor.

Develop Safety Habits. Safety habits protect your health, too. Wear a helmet if you are riding a bicycle or motorcycle. Buckle your seatbelt in a car. Wear any required safety equipment on your job. Avoid things that can damage your health.

Continued on page 239.

A Desire to Succeed

Gloria Estefan

Gloria Estefan is the star singer of Gloria Estefan and the Miami Sound Machine. Success has not been easy for Gloria.

She came to the United States from Cuba when she was two. She grew up in a ghetto in Miami. From the ages of 11 to 16, she took care of her bedridden father. She also cared for her sister and helped her mother learn English.

Gloria was a hard worker. She worked part-time at the Miami Airport. She also taught guitar lessons.

Gloria's mother encouraged her to sing. Gloria was invited by Emilio Estefan to sing with the Miami Latin Boys. Several years later, Gloria and Emilio married. The group was renamed Gloria Estefan and the Miami Sound Machine. They sold millions of records.

Then, in March of 1990, Gloria was in an accident. Her band's tour bus was hit by a truck. Gloria could not move her legs. She was in extreme pain. She had broken her back.

It took nearly two hours to get her to a hospital. During hours of surgery, the doctors put steel rods in her back to support her spine.

Gloria received thousands of cards and letters from fans. It made her desire to recover even stronger.

To get back into shape, Gloria worked out three days a week. The workouts were painful. But she did not complain. She felt lucky to be alive. She was determined to dance and perform again.

Once again, Gloria's hard work brought her success. Today, she is back doing what she loves. Her fans are thrilled to have her performing again.

Avoid Too Much Sun. New studies show that too much sun is harmful to your health. Sunburn damages your skin and is the leading cause of skin cancer. Getting a serious sunburn even once may increase your chances of getting skin cancer. The damage caused by each sunburn adds up over the years.

If you work outside, use a *sunscreen*. A **sunscreen** is a lotion or oil that protects your skin from the sun's damaging rays. Sunscreens are labeled with a sun protection factor (SPF). These are numbers from 2 to 40 that tell how much protection they provide. For example, a sunscreen with an SPF of 15 gives you 15 times your body's natural protection. The higher the number, the more protection you will get from the sun.

Use sunscreens any time you need to be in the sun between 10:00 a.m. and 3:00 p.m. If you are in the sun for several hours, you may also want to wear a hat to protect you.

Many people think that a suntan is healthy. But air pollution is destroying the ozone layer around the earth. The ozone layer protects us from the harmful effects of the sun. So we have less protection now than we did even ten years ago.

Do you know people who get a tan every summer? They are five times as likely to get deep face wrinkles before they are 40. If they also smoke, they are 12 times as likely.

▲ *A sunscreen will provide protection from the sun's damaging rays. What amount of sun protection does this lotion provide?*

It is more important now than ever to protect yourself from the sun. Form healthy habits so you can enjoy the sun and protect yourself from harmful sunburns.

✔ **Check Up** ✔ ✔ ✔

1. What does good health mean?
2. What are the four basic food groups?
3. What does RDA mean?
4. What is physical fitness?
5. Why should you have regular health check-ups?
6. What are three safety habits that can protect your health?
7. How has air pollution made the sun's rays more dangerous?

⃝ Your Personal Environment

A good diet, regular exercise, and good health care put you on the road to good health. Personal choices you make about your life-style also affect your health. Choosing to avoid smoking, alcohol, and drug abuse will add to your good health. Making wise choices about sex will also protect your health.

▷ Hazards of Smoking

Smoking has many health hazards. It is the main cause of lung cancer and other lung diseases. People who smoke have a greater chance of having heart disease. Smoking causes stomach and bladder diseases. It dulls your sense of taste and stains your teeth. It can cause cancer of the mouth. Just living with someone who smokes can be harmful to your health. Breathing *second-hand smoke* can lead to lung problems. Women who smoke while they are pregnant can damage the health of their babies.

Many employers will not allow you to smoke on the job. Many cities have banned smoking in public buildings.

Choosing not to smoke is an important choice in a healthy life-style. If you do not smoke, do not start. Most people find it hard to quit smoking once they form the habit.

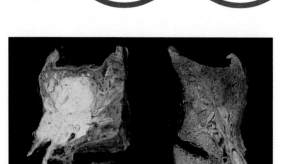

▲ *These two lungs show the difference between those of a smoker and a non-smoker. What are two other health hazards of smoking?*

If you do smoke, choose to stop. Breaking the habit may not be easy. But self-help groups or your doctor can help you quit. The health benefits are worth the work.

▷ Alcohol Abuse

Alcohol is the major drug problem in the United States. It is also the number one killer of teenagers.

Many teenagers drink and drive. Studies show that a teenager is in an alcohol related accident every ten seconds. About 12,000 teenagers are killed in these accidents each year.

Do not drink and drive. Do not risk riding with a friend who has been drinking. Your school or community may have a safe-ride program for people who are drinking. If not, call a friend or a parent to get you home safely.

Accidents are not the only health problems caused by drinking alcohol. Even drinking small amounts can affect your life-style. Drinking affects the way you react. It affects your attitude and behavior toward other people. You may do things when you are drinking that you would not usually do.

Long-term use of alcohol damages your body. It can damage your brain, liver, heart, skin, and major body systems. Drinking while pregnant causes birth defects.

The best way to avoid the problems caused by alcohol is to say no to drinking. This may be difficult. Drinking alcohol is part of many social activities. Your friends may want you to drink. But not drinking is your healthiest choice. Do not let your friends pressure you into drinking.

If alcohol becomes a problem for you, seek help. Your doctor can tell you how to find a self-help group.

▷ Drug Abuse

You read earlier that it may be dangerous to drive while taking some medicines. That is also true about driving and using drugs. **Drug abuse** is using drugs for reasons other than their intended purpose. People abuse drugs to make themselves feel better or to get "high." They use drugs to escape from their problems. Sometimes people think drugs help them perform certain tasks better.

But abusing drugs only leads to problems. People who think they can stop taking drugs any time they want to are fooling themselves. People become dependent on drugs. Drug dependence means that they need to keep taking the drug. They are unable to stop. Their bodies require larger and larger doses of the drug to get "high." Some drugs make people dependent on them after only one use!

Taking large doses of drugs or taking drugs for a long time is very harmful to your health. It can cause brain damage. It can cause mental problems that require years of treatment. It can cause kidney and liver damage. In some cases, it causes heart failure. Illnesses can be spread through unclean needles used to take drugs. These illnesses, such as AIDS, can lead to death. About 4,000 people die each year from drug abuse.

Use of drugs to improve as an athlete is dangerous, too. You may know an athlete who uses *steroids*. **Steroids** are drugs that build muscle and bone strength. But steroids are illegal. They can raise your blood pressure and cause liver damage. They can cause violent mood swings, depression, and even death.

Saying No to Drugs

Saying No Through Your Actions

- Be friends with people who do not use or approve of drugs.
- Stay away from situations where you think there may be drugs.
- If you are at someone's house or party where people begin using drugs, leave.

Saying No Through Your Words

When offered drugs, say:

- "No, thanks. I get high on life."
- "I don't do drugs."
- "If you were really my friend, you'd lay off — I'm not interested."
- "So long. I'll see you later."

▲ *Figure 13-3*
Saying no to drugs is the best way to protect your health. How would you say no to drugs?

Because of drug abuse, drug testing is becoming more common in our society. Athletes may be required to take drug tests before or after an event. Some employers now require drug tests of their workers. This is common if the work involves safety risks. Studies show that people taking drugs make more errors than other people.

Avoid drug abuse by only using medicine prescribed by your doctor for you. Do not use drugs to change the way you feel or to improve the way you perform. If drug abuse becomes a problem for you, seek help. Your doctor can put you back on the road to a drug-free life.

▷ Sexual Behavior

Protecting your health means making many choices. The decision about whether or not to have sex as a teenager is one of the most important choices you will make. Saying no to sex in your teenage years is the healthiest choice. If you choose to have sex now, you are risking your health and your future life-style.

Teen sex can result in pregnancy. Having sex also puts you at risk for getting **sexually transmitted diseases** (STDs). STDs are diseases you get through sexual contact. Some STDs have long-term effects. Some result in death.

Each year more than one million teenagers become pregnant. Only 10 to 20 percent of teenagers who are having sex use birth control.

Both the mother and the father are affected by a pregnancy. Pregnancy is stressful. Combined with the normal problems of being a teenager, pregnancy can be hard to cope with. Male teenagers are not free from the responsibility of pregnancy. Medical tests can prove who is the father of a child. The father can be held financially responsible for the child.

Protecting yourself from STDs is another reason to say no to sex. *One out of seven teenagers has an STD.* The risk of getting an STD is greater if you have sex with more than one person.

The symptoms of some STDs do not show up for several months. So a person can pass on the disease without knowing it. Some STDs are easily treated and cured. Other STDs are not easily cured. Some of the diseases make it difficult to have children later. They can also cause blindness and heart disease.

The most serious STD is AIDS. Researchers first thought this STD was only spread among homosexuals. They now know it is spread four ways.

1. Through sex. A person with the virus can give it to another through sexual contact.
2. Through a needle used to take drugs. A person with the virus can give it to another by sharing needles used to take drugs.
3. Through infected blood. A person can get AIDS by receiving blood from a person infected with AIDS.
4. Through an infected pregnant woman. A pregnant woman with AIDS can pass the virus to her baby.

AIDS is a fatal virus. It attacks the T-cells in the body. The T-cells are supposed to protect the body from disease. The virus weakens the T-cells so that the infected person's body cannot fight diseases.

Having sex is never totally safe. There is always the risk of pregnancy. But the risk of STDs can be reduced by being responsible. Safe sex means knowing your sex partner well. It means knowing about the person's past partners and about his or her sexual practices. It also means having sex with only one partner and using a condom for protection during sex.

Practicing safe sex is helpful. But it does not protect you completely. Saying no is the only protection you can be sure of.

★ Tricks of the Trade ★

How AIDS is Not Spread

AIDS is *not* spread through casual contact. You cannot get AIDS from toilet seats, water fountains, or if someone sneezes near you.

▷ Handling Stress

Making choices that will affect the rest of your life is a big responsibility. Sometimes it is hard to make the right choice. Making tough choices can make you feel stressed.

Stress is tension. It can be caused by problems in your life, changes, sickness, or other events.

Stress can be both helpful and harmful. It can help you make decisions or get things done. However, too much stress can make it hard for you to function. It may cause you to feel sad or depressed. Or it may cause you to feel restless and unable to sleep.

Everyone has stress. Learning how to handle stress is part of a healthy life-style. Eating well, exercising, and getting enough rest will help you handle stress.

Planning your life so you do not have too much to do at one time helps you avoid stress. Taking time for yourself and doing something you enjoy also helps. Doing something that makes you laugh helps relieve stress. Sharing your problems with a friend or a person you trust always helps you feel better.

If stress becomes a serious problem in your life, ask your doctor for help. Dealing with stress early will help you live a healthier, happier life.

▶ *Handling stress will help you stay healthy. How are these people handling stress?*

☐ Case Study ☐ ☐ ☐ ☐ ☐ ☐

At the beginning of the new year, Vicky took a good look at her life-style. She thought it was time for some changes. She decided she would lose weight and start an exercise program.

The next day, Vicky ate only cottage cheese for breakfast, lunch, and dinner. She played tennis. Then she went for a three-mile run. She was feeling good about herself.

But the next morning Vicky was exhausted. Her muscles ached. She felt tired, grumpy, and hungry.

When she told her friend how she felt, her friend smiled. She told Vicky that she could not change her life-style overnight. A healthy life-style should be for a lifetime. If she worked on it slowly and sensibly, she would be more likely to succeed.

Handling Stress

1. What am I feeling?

2. What happened to make me feel this way?

3. When I had this feeling before, how long did it last?

4. What can I do to feel better?

5. Should I talk to someone? To whom?

 Figure 13-4
When you are feeling stressed, ask yourself these questions. They will help you feel better. How else can you relieve stress?

✳ Tricks of the Trade ✳

Relieving Stress

When you feel stressed, take five deep breaths. As you breath out, feel the tension leave your body.

✔ Check Up ✔ ✔ ✔

1. What is the number one killer of teenagers in this country?
2. What does long-term use of alcohol do to a person's health?
3. What are three hazards of drug abuse?
4. What is an STD?
5. How can you learn to handle stress?

Chapter 13 Review

Chapter Summary

- Your life-style affects your health.
- A balanced diet supplies the basic nutrients you need for good health.
- A healthy diet helps you maintain a healthy weight.
- Physical fitness is part of a healthy life-style.
- Regular check-ups are part of a good health care program.
- Wise choices about the use of cigarettes, alcohol, and drugs will protect your health.
- Responsible sexual behavior is part of a healthy life-style.
- Learning to handle stress is part of a healthy life-style.

Reviewing Vocabulary

Listed below are the important new words in this chapter. Next to each word is the page on which you will find the word. Turn to that page and read the paragraph in which the word is printed in **bold** type. On a separate piece of paper, write the word and its meaning. Then write sentences using the words. Each sentence should be a statement about a healthy life-style. You may use more than one of the words per sentence.

1. recommended daily allowance (RDA) (230)
2. calorie (232)
3. anorexia nervosa (233)
4. bulimia (233)
5. physical fitness (234)
6. aerobic exercise (234)
7. side effect (237)
8. sunscreen (239)
9. drug abuse (241)
10. steroids (241)
11. sexually transmitted disease (STD) (242)

Looking at the Facts

1. What are the four basic food groups?
2. How much water should you drink each day?
3. What factors determine the right weight for each person?
4. What are two eating disorders?
5. What are five benefits of exercise?
6. What are the two parts of a check-up?
7. What are two health hazards of smoking?
8. Why do people abuse drugs?
9. What are two risks of being sexually active?
10. What are two things you can do to handle stress?

Thinking Critically

1. Why is it important for your health to eat certain foods?
2. Why do you think people are so concerned about gaining weight?

3. A friend of yours wants to begin an exercise program. He does not have much money or time. What type of exercise program would you suggest?
4. Why should you not take medicine prescribed for someone else?
5. Your town is considering passing a law that bans smoking in restaurants. What are two reasons you could give in support of this law?
6. Explain why good health is a personal responsibility.

Discussing Chapter Concepts

1. A doctor keeps a record of your visits. Some people feel it is wise to keep your own medical records. What are some reasons for keeping your own records?
2. Suppose you have decided to change your exercise or eating habits. List some things you can do to help you reach your goal.
3. How can stress be healthy? What do you think is the best way for you to handle stress?

Using Basic Skills

Math
1. Suppose that eight ounces of milk supply 25 percent of the RDA for calcium. How many ounces of milk must you drink to get 100 percent of the RDA of calcium?

Communication
2. Interview three people about smoking. Ask them whether or not they ever smoked cigarettes. Ask them the reasons why they did or did not smoke. Write down your findings.

Human Relations
3. Suppose someone offers you drugs. Write down how you will say no to their offer.

Activities for Enrichment

1. Make a poster that advertises a healthy life-style. For example, you might choose to make an anti-smoking poster. Use pictures and colored markers to make your advertisement.
2. Keep a food diary and an activity diary for three days. Locate charts in your library that give the calories of the foods you eat. Find other charts that show the number of calories you burned by each activity. Estimate the number of calories you eat each day and the number of calories you burn. Which estimate was higher?
3. List all the healthy life-style choices you have made during your life. Describe why you made these choices. Then, make a second list of health goals you would like to reach in the future. Describe why these goals are important to you.

Social Issues at Work

Words to learn and use

Here are the new terms you will learn in this chapter. Challenge yourself. Read through the list to see if you know what they mean.

> discrimination
> national origin
> disability
> sexual harassment
> peer pressure

Build on what you know

You already know...
- you may have to deal with discrimination.
- you may interview for many jobs.
- you will face social issues at work.
- sometimes you need to speak up for yourself at work.
- some people are leaders.

In this chapter you will learn...
- what discrimination is.
- what questions you can be asked in an interview.
- how to handle social issues at work.
- when and how to speak up for yourself at work.
- how to lead by example.

We all have to face social issues at work. Social issues are the problems that come from dealing with others. Because most jobs involve working with others, social issues are often likely to occur.

Social issues you may face include discrimination, peer pressure, socializing with co-workers, and using drugs. In this chapter you will learn more about these issues and how to handle them.

⭕ Discrimination

What is *discrimination*? Where do you find it? Can it happen to anyone? **Discrimination** means treating someone unfairly because he or she belongs to a certain group. You may be a victim of discrimination because of your race, skin color, or religion. You may also be a victim of discrimination because of your gender, age, or *national origin*. **National origin** is the country your family came from.

Discrimination can be found in any social setting. You could find it at work. You could find it at school. You could find it in your community.

Throughout history, many groups have been discriminated against. In the past, it was hard to do something about it. Today we have laws that make discrimination illegal. These laws help victims of discrimination. The purpose of these laws is to be sure people are judged on their abilities and not on the group they belong to.

▷ Discrimination and the Job Interview

When you go to a job interview, you will be asked questions. These questions help the employer decide whether you have the ability to do the job. There are many questions the employer may ask. They are questions about your ability to do the job.

There are some questions the employer should not ask. The answers could be used to discriminate against you. Do you know what these questions are? Here are questions you may and may not be asked in a job interview.

Name. The employer may ask you these questions about your name.

- What is your full name?
- Have you worked under another name?
- Should we check under another name to find out about your work record? (If you answer yes, you may be asked to explain.)

You should not be asked these things about your name.

- What is your real name, if it was changed by court order or otherwise?
- What is your maiden name?

Address or Length of Residence. Sometimes employers ask questions about where you live. The employer may ask how long you have lived in a city or state.

Birthplace. The employer may not ask you questions about your or your parents' birthplace. The employer also may not ask you for proof of your birthplace. This includes a birth certificate.

◄ *During an interview there are many questions an employer may and may not ask you. What is one question an employer may not ask about your name?*

Age. You may be asked if you are of legal age for certain types of employment. Otherwise, the employer may not ask questions about how old you are or your birth date.

Religion. The employer may not ask you questions about your religious beliefs. This includes questions about what religious holidays you observe during the year.

Race or Color. The employer may not ask you questions about the color of your skin. He or she also may not ask you questions about your family members' skin color.

Photograph. The employer may not ask you for a photo of yourself. But he or she may ask for a photo for identification after you are hired.

Marital Status. The employer may ask whether your spouse (husband or wife) works for the company. The employer may not ask these questions.

- Are you married?
- Do you have children, or do you plan to have children?
- Who cares for your children?
- Are you single or married?
- Does your spouse work?
- What is your spouse's name?

Health. An employer may only ask you if you have physical or mental problems if they affect your present ability to do the job. The employer may not ask you about your past health.

Citizenship. *Citizenship* means you are a citizen of a certain country. The employer may ask you these questions about citizenship.

- Are you a citizen of the United States? (The employer can ask for proof that you are a citizen *after* you are hired.)
- If you are not a citizen, do you intend to become a United States citizen?
- If you are not a citizen, are you living in the United States legally?
- Do you intend to remain in the United States?

The employer may not ask you these questions about citizenship.

- What country, other than the United States, are you a citizen of or were born in?
- Were you born in the United States?
- On what date did you become a citizen?
- Were your parents or your spouse born in the United States?
- On what date did your parents or spouse become a citizen of the United States?

★ **Tricks of the Trade** ★

Interview Questions

While you are in a job interview, do not worry about remembering what you legally may and may not be asked. Focus on doing a good job of answering the questions being asked. If you realize after the interview that you were asked an illegal question, you can always file a complaint.

Education. The employer may ask questions about your education. He or she may also ask about your foreign language skills. But the employer may not ask how you learned a foreign language.

Experience. The employer may ask about your work experience. The employer may also ask about your travel experience.

Arrests. In some states, the employer may ask if you were ever found guilty of a crime. He or she may also ask if you are being charged with a serious crime. The employer may not ask about arrests in which you were charged but not convicted.

Relatives. The employer may ask for the names of your relatives who work for the company.

◀ On an application, an employer may not ask any questions that can be used to discriminate against you. How could questions about clubs that you belong to be used to discriminate against you?

Notice in Case of an Emergency. The employer may ask who to contact in case of an emergency. They may ask for the person's name and address. The employer may not ask for a *relative* to contact in case of an emergency.

Military Experience. The employer may ask about your U.S. military experience. But the employer may not ask to see your military records.

Organizations. The employer may not ask for a list of *all* the clubs you belong to. This is because some club names may associate you with groups that are illegally discriminated against. This law protects you from being discriminated against because you belong to a certain club.

References. The employer may ask how you found out about the position. He or she may also ask for references. *References* are people an employer can speak with to find out about your work habits. These references may not be asked certain questions. They may not be asked about your race, national origin, or your family background. This law varies from state to state.

Continued on page 255.

Heron Corporation
APPLICATION FOR EMPLOYMENT

DATE		19	PERSONAL (Please print using ball point pen)			

FULL NAME	First	Middle	Last		Social Security Number	
PRESENT ADDRESS	Street	City	State	Zip	How long	Telephone No.

If no phone, how may we contact you?	Are you 18 years of age or older? ☐ Yes ☐ No

List activities or commitments that may interfere with attendance requirements

List handicaps or health problems that should be considered in job placement.

Have you ever applied for employment to the K mart Corporation or a subsidiary before?	☐ Yes ☐ No	If "yes," where?	Approximate Date Mo. ____ Yr. ____	How referred to us?
Have you ever been convicted of a felony?	☐ Yes ☐ No	If "yes," when? Mo. ____ Yr. ____	Explain	

IDENTITY AND EMPLOYMENT ELIGIBILITY VERIFICATION

When requested, can you provide genuine documentation establishing your identity and eligibility to be legally employed in the United States? ☐ Yes ☐ No	Will Visa or Immigration status prevent lawful employment? ☐ Yes ☐ No

EMPLOYMENT INTERESTS AND SKILLS

SCHEDULE DESIRED	☐ DAY ☐ EVENING ☐ ANY HOURS		FULL TIME ☐	PART TIME ☐	SEASONAL ☐	
AVAILABLE HOURS:		Sunday	Monday	Tuesday	Wednesday	Thursday	Friday	Saturday
	DAY							
	EVENING							

DATE AVAILABLE FOR WORK —   TOTAL HOURS PER WEEK DESIRED —   SALARY EXPECTED—

TYPE OF WORK PREFERRED	EXAMPLES. Service Employee Checkout Service Employee Food Dept. Apparel (Women's – Men's – Children's) Camera/Jewelry Sporting Goods Mechanic Stockroom, etc.	1. Position desired	Years experience in this work
		2.	
		3.	

EDUCATION

SCHOOLS	NAME AND ADDRESS OF SCHOOL OR COLLEGE	Dates Attended From	Dates Attended To	MAJOR STUDIES	Last Grade Completed	Graduation Date
HIGH SCHOOL						
COLLEGE TRADE OR BUSINESS SCHOOL						

THE CIVIL RIGHTS ACT OF 1964 PROHIBITS DISCRIMINATION IN EMPLOYMENT PRACTICE BECAUSE OF RACE, COLOR, RELIGION, SEX OR NATIONAL ORIGIN.
(An Equal Opportunity Employer)

▲ *Figure 14-1*
Here is a standard application for employment. Does this application ask any questions that should not be asked?

▷ Handling Discrimination in an Interview

Suppose you are in an interview. The employer asks you a question that he or she should not ask. What should you do? Ask how the question relates to your ability to do the job. This will let the person know that you understand your rights.

It can be hard to stop employers from asking illegal questions. You may find that you answer a question you should not have been asked. If so, you may want to contact the Equal Employment Opportunity Commission (EEOC) to find out more about your rights. Check with your librarian for local branches of the EEOC. You may also contact the Civil Rights Office in your state.

▷ Discrimination Based on a Disability

If you are *disabled*, it is important to know your rights. A **disability** limits how well a person may be able to do some things. A special law, called the *Americans with Disabilities Act,* prevents discrimination against disabled people in the workplace. Employers may not discriminate against you in any of these areas.

- Hiring procedures.
- Promotion.
- Ending a job.
- Pay.
- Conditions of employment.

The employer should give you the chance to compete fairly with others. A disability should not prevent you from advancing in the workplace. If you have questions about the law, check with the EEOC.

Who Is Protected? To be protected by the Disabilities Act, you must be disabled. You also must be able to do the important tasks of the job. This act protects the disabled from discrimination in four ways.

First, you are protected if you have physical or mental limits. These limits may make it hard to do things that others take for granted.

Second, you are protected if you were disabled in the past. For example, you had cancer but now you are cancer free.

Third, you are protected if people think you might be disabled in the future. For example, you may have had a bad back. But you were treated, and now you are fine. An employer might not want to hire you. He or she is afraid your back will disable you in the future.

Fourth, you are protected if you have a responsibility to a disabled person. For example, you may take care of a disabled person. You should not be denied a job because of this. The employer should not assume that this responsibility will make you miss work. But the employer does not have to give you time off that other employees do not get.

Services Employers Need to Provide. What employers are covered by the Americans with Disabilities Act? Most employers that buy and sell goods and services are covered.

Under this act, the employer may be required to provide the things you need to do the job. For example, you may be sight impaired. If so, you might need someone to read to you. You may also need special training manuals.

If you need such special equipment or help, you must ask for it. The employer only has to provide what you ask for. But your employer does not have to provide anything that is a *financial burden* to the company. For example, suppose the equipment you need is expensive. The employer may not have enough money for the equipment. In this case, the equipment would be a financial burden.

The law decides what is a financial burden. It does so on a case-by-case basis. What may be a financial burden to one employer may not be a burden to another. The law allows you to buy your own equipment if you choose to.

▶ *The Americans with Disabilities Act protects disabled people from discrimination when they apply for a job. What are the four ways you are protected under this act?*

☐ Case Study ☐ ☐ ☐ ☐ ☐ ☐

Mac relies on a wheelchair to get around. He was just hired for a new job. The first day that Mac arrived at work, he found that his desk was too low for his wheelchair. He became angry. He went to his boss and complained. He told his boss he could not work with the equipment he was given. His boss explained that Mac had to tell him what he needed. He would be glad to provide what he needed. Mac realized his mistake. He had assumed his boss would know what he needed.

▷ Discrimination Based on Race, Color, Religion, Gender, or National Origin

Under the Civil Rights Act, you cannot be discriminated against because of your race, color, religion, gender, or national origin. The employer may not discriminate against you in any of these areas.

- Hiring procedures.
- Promotion.
- Ending a job.
- Pay.
- Conditions of employment.

You may feel you were discriminated against. If so, you should contact the EEOC. There are time limits for filing a charge after the incident. Some states give you up to 180 days to file a charge. Other states give you up to 300 days. If you have any questions about discrimination and the law, check with the EEOC. They will inform you of your rights.

▲ *The passing of the 1964 Civil Rights Act was an important victory for many people. It, in part, forbids discrimination by employers on the basis of race, color, religion, gender, or national origin. Why would such an act be important?*

▷ Sexual Harassment

Sexual harassment may happen to you or someone you know. It is important to know what it is and what to do about it.

To *harass* someone means to annoy someone constantly. **Sexual harassment** occurs when someone makes unwanted sexual advances. It also occurs when a person's sexual talk or actions offend someone. Some people allow sexual harassment to continue. They do this because they feel threatened by the harasser. The harasser may discriminate against them if they do not give in. Anyone can be a victim of sexual harassment. People sometimes do not report it because they are afraid. They may feel no one will believe them. Or they may think they will get in trouble for reporting it.

No one has the right to harass you. Seek help right away if this happens to you.

What You Can Do. There are actions you can take to stop harassment. Follow these seven steps.

1. Do not ignore the problem. It usually will not go away by itself.
2. Tell the person to stop.
3. Give your boss your complaint in writing.
4. Ask your boss to write down what he or she is going to do about the problem. Ask for a copy.
5. Contact the EEOC or the Civil Rights Office in your state. Ask for a list of local agencies that can help you.
6. If the problem continues, you may wish to get legal advice.
7. You may wish to seek counseling to help you handle your problem.

▲ *Telling sexual jokes that offend others in the workplace can be a form of sexual harassment. What is another form?*

✔ Check Up ✔ ✔ ✔

1. What is discrimination?
2. Can an employer ask you about your past health history?
3. What law protects the disabled when they apply for a job?
4. What is sexual harassment?

O Handling Social Issues on the Job

You will face many social issues on the job. Some, like discrimination, will involve you whether you want them to or not. Other social issues you will have more control over. You can decide what part they will play in your job. Your decisions can determine your success at work. Here are three such major issues you may deal with on the job.

- Peer pressure.
- Socializing with co-workers.
- Drugs.

▷ Peer Pressure

Peer pressure is the influence people in your group can have on you. A peer may be someone about your age. It may be a co-worker who has a similar job or rank in the company. Your peers can have a very strong influence on you.

Most people want to be liked and accepted by their peers. That is what makes peer pressure hard to resist. Peer pressure can cause you to do things you might not otherwise do.

You may have peer pressure on the job. You might feel pressure to leave early because everyone else does. Or you might take food without paying for it because everyone else does.

When you ignore the rules, you risk losing your job. Telling your boss that you did something wrong because everyone else did it is a bad excuse. It can destroy the trust your boss has in you. Learning to avoid peer pressure on the job is important. You will be seen as a valued employee who can think for yourself.

▲ *Peer pressure is the influence people in your group can have on you. What peer pressure is this employee resisting?*

Peer pressure often happens because your peers want you to join them. They may not like it if you tell them they are doing something wrong. If this is the case, you have a choice to make. You can go along with your peers, even when they are doing something wrong. Or you can be *independent.* This means you make your own decisions. And you are responsible for your own actions. It means that you do not follow your peers if you think they are wrong.

Being independent can be lonely at times. The pressure to get along with your peers can be great. But it is better to be a *little* lonely than to be in a *lot* of trouble.

▷ Socializing with Co-workers

Sometimes your co-workers will invite you to socialize after work. Once in a while, this can be fun. It can also lead to friendships at work.

What should you be careful of when you socialize with co-workers? Avoid complaining about work. This may make you feel negative about your job.

Here are some things you should do if you are going to see your co-workers after work.

- Plan a fun activity that will take your mind off your job.
- Do not gossip about co-workers.
- Avoid negative talk about the job or the company.

What about dating your co-workers? This is always a difficult issue. Some employers discourage this. People have even been fired for dating people they work with.

It can be difficult to work with someone you are dating. When your relationship does not go well, it can affect your work. This can cause problems for both of you. It can make it very difficult to do your work properly. It can also cause problems for your co-workers. It can make it difficult to work as a team. Before dating someone at work, think it over carefully.

▷ Drugs in the Workplace

Alcohol and other drug use at work is not allowed. If you are caught using these drugs, you may be fired. Company policies vary, but employers will take action. Many employers have begun drug testing programs. They do this to discourage employees from using drugs. They know that drug users may be more likely to do these things.

- Make mistakes.
- Have accidents.
- Hurt themselves or others.

If you feel you have a drug abuse problem, check with your personnel manager. Some companies offer programs to help drug abusers. They do this because they believe these three things.

◀ *Many employers offer programs to help drug abusers overcome their problems. What is one reason employers might do this?*

1. Workers are valuable.
2. It is better to help workers with problems than to fire them.
3. Employees who overcome drug abuse problems are more productive.

One program designed to help workers is the Employee Assistance Programs (EAP). The program helps correct employees' drug abuse and other personal problems.

This is how the program works. The employee who is abusing drugs is given two choices. He or she can enter the EAP. Or he or she can face being suspended or fired from work. The employee that enters the program gets help with the drug abuse problem. He or she also gets help with any other personal problems that need to be solved. Then he or she returns to work once the problem is overcome. The employee is then seen as a valued worker.

If there is no EAP available, check the Yellow Pages in the phone book. Look under these headings.

- Drug Abuse and Addiction.
- Alcoholism Information and Treatment Centers.

✓ **Check Up** ✓ ✓ ✓

1. What is peer pressure?
2. When you ignore rules at work, what do you risk losing?
3. Name two things you should not do when you socialize with co-workers after work.

O Speaking Up for Yourself

Something unfair may happen to you at work. You may be unhappy about a new rule. You may feel that your boss does not give you help when you need it. What should you do?

Speaking up for yourself is a skill you have to learn. When you have to speak up for yourself, be positive. Be sure you talk to the person that can help you with the problem. Address the problem clearly. Have a solution in mind. Use the You Win, and I Win approach you learned in Chapter 5.

There are many reasons for speaking up for yourself. Learning why it is important to speak up for yourself will encourage you to do so. Here are three of the most important times to do so.

1. When you are treated unfairly.
2. When you need more help or you do not understand.
3. When change is needed.

Here is a closer look at each of these reasons.

▶ *Sometimes you may want to suggest changes that need to be made in the workplace. What is one benefit of improving the employees' working space in this kitchen?*

When You Are Treated Unfairly. There may be times when you are treated unfairly on the job. Sometimes this may happen because of a misunderstanding. For example, your boss may give you extra work to do. And he or she may not realize you already have extra work to do. Sometimes the treatment may be intended. For example, your co-worker may try to make you do his or her work. Either way, you may need to talk to your employer about it. If you are in a union, you could talk to the union steward. He or she may help you resolve the problem. If you do not speak up, the problem can become worse.

When you talk about the problem, do not blame someone else. Try to be understanding. This will help your employer see things your way.

When You Need More Help or Do Not Understand. You may be shy about asking for help at work. Perhaps you are afraid that the boss will think you are not good at your job.

When your boss instructs you in a task, it is important that you understand. If you do not understand, ask questions. Otherwise, the boss may think you understand when you do not. This could lead to mistakes.

When Change Is Needed. Sometimes changes need to be made in the workplace. Perhaps a policy is not working. Maybe one of your co-workers is always in a bad mood. Or

★ **Tricks of the Trade** ★

Speaking Up

Sometimes you may feel afraid to speak up. If so, imagine speaking to your boss. See the situation working out exactly as you would wish. See your boss giving you a positive response. Picture yourself succeeding. This will help you feel confident about speaking up.

maybe you find a better way to handle customer complaints. You feel that a change could make you feel more positive about your job. And it would help the company's business.

When you have the chance to improve your workplace, speak up. Working to improve things helps you feel better about the job. And your co-workers will respect your interest in the company.

✔ **Check Up** ✔ ✔ ✔

1. Name three reasons for speaking up for yourself.
2. Why are people sometimes shy about asking for help when they need it?
3. When should you try to change the workplace?

A Desire to Succeed

Martin Luther King, Jr.

Are you afraid to speak up? Martin Luther King, Jr. was not. His words moved a nation. He spoke out against racial discrimination.

Martin Luther King, Jr. was born in 1929 in Atlanta, Georgia. At 15, King entered college. He studied to become a minister. In 1955, he received his Ph.D. from Boston University. Then he moved to Alabama and became a pastor.

King became involved in the civil rights movement in 1955. He led a nonviolent protest against a bus line in Montgomery, Alabama. A law there made blacks sit in the back of buses. Only whites could sit in the front of the bus. King worked to change laws that separated blacks from whites.

King convinced people of the need for equal rights. He was often arrested and jailed for his part in the movement. But that never stopped his work.

In 1963, King and other civil rights leaders led a march on Washington. More than 200,000 people took part. Here King made his famous "I Have

a Dream" speech about equal rights. King said he hoped one day all people would be free and equal. The movement led to the passage of the Civil Rights Act. The act prevents discrimination in public places and in the workplace. In 1964, King was awarded the Nobel Peace Prize for his work.

In 1968, King was shot and killed. His death caused violent riots in the U.S. He was clearly a great force in the country. He will be remembered as a great leader of the civil rights movement.

○ Leading by Example

Anyone can be a leader, depending on the situation. A *leader* is someone who guides or directs others. You are a leader in some area of your life. Perhaps you are a good athlete. Maybe you work with children. Or you might be good at fixing things. The talents you have help determine the areas in which you will lead.

Leadership is a social issue that you will deal with at work. Sometimes you will be the leader. And sometimes others will lead you. When you work as part of a team, you will take turns leading.

Sooner or later you will probably be a leader at work. You might be asked to train a new person. Or you might be asked to solve a problem. When you lead, you have certain responsibilities. You should be responsible enough to lead by example.

Have you ever noticed that people pay more attention to what you do than to what you say? What if your boss told you never to make personal phone calls at work? But the next day, you heard him talking to his friend. What would you think? You might be angry that you have to obey rules that your boss ignores.

If you are a leader, remember that others are watching you. The role of the leader is to set a good example.

When you are not leading, be a good follower. Try to make the leader's job easier. Whether you are leading or following, someone is watching you. Set a good example!

▲ *At some point in your career, you will probably be a leader. What is one thing to remember when you are a leader?*

✔ Check Up ✔ ✔ ✔

1. What is a leader?
2. Who can be a leader?
3. What is the best way to lead?

Chapter 14 Review

Chapter Summary

- Social issues are the problems that you face when dealing with others.
- There are certain questions an employer may not ask you in a job interview.
- The Americans with Disabilities Act protects disabled people when they apply for a job.
- You may not be discriminated against on the basis of race, color, religion, gender, or national origin.
- Sexual harassment is when someone makes constant, unwanted sexual advances. It is also when a person's sexual talk or actions offend someone.
- Peer pressure is the influence your peers have on you.
- You have to be responsible about how you socialize at work.
- Drug abuse on the job can lead to dismissal.
- It is important to learn to speak up for yourself in a positive way.
- Good leaders lead by example.

Reviewing Vocabulary

Listed below are the important new words that were used in this chapter. Next to each word is the page on which you will find it. Turn to that page. Read the paragraph where the word is printed in **bold** type. Write a sentence using each word.

1. discrimination (250)
2. national origin (250)
3. disability (255)
4. sexual harassment (258)
5. peer pressure (259)

Looking at the Facts

1. It is illegal to be discriminated against on the basis of what five things?
2. May an employer ask you where you were born in an interview?
3. Are there any questions an employer may ask you about your race or color?
4. Tell four groups of people who are protected by the Americans with Disabilities Act.
5. Does an employer have to provide equipment that a disabled person has not asked for?
6. Name five things you can do about sexual harassment.
7. How can you avoid peer pressure?
8. What should you be careful of when you socialize with co-workers?
9. What is one reason why an employer may help an employee overcome drug abuse?
10. Name three reasons why you should speak up for yourself in the workplace.
11. What is the role of the leader?

Thinking Critically

1. You are in a job interview. The interviewer has just asked you an illegal question. How will you answer?
2. A friend tells you that she is having a problem at work. Her boss told her she will not get a raise if she will not go out with him. What will you tell her?
3. You work in a factory. The air conditioning does not work very well. In the summer, it is hard to work because it is so hot. What will you do about this problem?
4. You are the shift leader at Lou's Pizza. You told your crew that they can only eat when they are on break. You are hungry. Your break is still an hour away. Probably no one will notice if you eat before your break. What will you do?

Discussing Chapter Concepts

1. Do you think discrimination is a big problem in this country? Explain your answer.
2. Should employers be able to ask you about your health in general? Why or why not? What if your job involves working with heavy equipment?
3. Should employers have to provide disabled employees with equipment? Why or why not?
4. Why is peer pressure so powerful?

Using Basic Skills

Math
1. A co-worker wants you to leave 15 minutes early on Friday with him. You get paid $6.00 an hour. How much money will the company lose in terms of your time if you leave early?

Communication
2. Your boss has treated you unfairly. You were the only one who was not allowed to leave early on a long holiday weekend. Tell what you will say to your boss. Use the guidelines for speaking up for yourself.

Human Relations
3. You are working in a clothing store. Some of your co-workers are gossiping. You notice that a customer near them needs help. Tell how you will lead by example.

Activities for Enrichment

1. With a classmate, ask each other the interview questions discussed in this chapter. Answer yes or no depending on whether the question may or may not be asked.
2. Talk to two working adults. Find out if they had to speak up for themselves in the workplace. Was it because they were treated unfairly, they needed more help, or a change was needed?

Handling Legal Matters

Words to learn and use

Here are the new terms you will learn in this chapter. Challenge yourself. Read through the list to see if you know what they mean.

contract
party
competent parties
countersign
consideration
felony
misdemeanor
bail
contingency basis

Build on what you know

You already know...
- you will sign contracts as an adult.
- you should obey the law.
- you may need a lawyer sometime.

In this chapter you will learn...
- why you make many contracts.
- what to do if you are arrested.
- how to find a lawyer.

People who live together need rules to get along. Your family has rules. You must do certain chores. You cannot stay out late at night. Rules help prevent arguments and trouble. They help your family get along.

Laws are rules made by a city, state, or country. They help everyone who lives there get along. Laws are made by our governments. To do something against the law means to break the rules made by the government. Laws are enforced by the courts. If you break a law, you may have to pay a fine. Or you may have to go to jail.

As an adult, you are responsible for your actions. So you may have dealings with the law. In this chapter, you will learn about the law and how it affects you.

⚪ Contracts

The word *legal* means anything that has to do with the law. The *legal system* is made up of laws, processes, and people. The legal system protects our rights and safety. Judges, courts, and lawyers are part of the legal system.

There are two major kinds of law in the legal system.

- Public laws.
- Private laws.

Public laws tell us how to behave toward people in our community. These laws protect the health and safety of the public. Traffic laws and criminal laws are public laws.

Private laws tell people how to behave toward each other. Private laws are also called *civil laws*. These laws help prevent trouble, arguments, and misunderstandings between people.

Contracts are an important part of civil law. A **contract** is a legal agreement between two or more people. You may have a contract with a person or a company. Two companies may have a contract with each other.

The legal term for a person who enters into a contract is **party**. Each party in a contract agrees to do something or to pay something. For example, a carpenter may agree to fix your porch. In return, you agree to pay him or her $100. You and the carpenter are the parties who have the contract.

Contracts may be *informal* or *formal*. Informal contracts are spoken. There are no papers signed. Informal contracts usually deal with small amounts of money. You make informal contracts every day. For example, you have an informal contract with the dry cleaner. He or she agrees to clean your clothing. You agree to pay the person. You have an informal contract at a restaurant. The restaurant agrees to deliver a meal. You agree to pay for it.

▲ *Informal contracts are spoken agreements that concern small amounts of money. What are the two parties in this contract agreeing to?*

Formal contracts are written. They usually deal with large amounts of money. For example, when you buy a house, you must have a formal contract. Such formal contracts are usually written with the help of a lawyer.

As an adult, you will make many contracts. For example, you will sign a contract when you rent an apartment. This contract is called a lease. You will sign a contract when you agree to make car payments. You may even sign a contract with the company you work for. For example, you may agree not to work for your company's competition if you leave your job. This contract could last for months or years. You may also sign a contract agreeing not to tell about company secrets or projects.

Know what your rights and responsibilities are when you sign a contract. If you do not understand the legal terms that contracts contain, ask what they mean. You should also understand the parts of the contract.

▷ Required Contract Elements

You want a contract to be *binding*. This means the contract is legal and cannot be broken. All parties must keep their agreement. A contract must have five elements to be binding.

- Mutual agreement.
- Competent parties.

- Legal purpose.
- Consideration.
- Correct legal form.

Mutual Agreement. All parties must agree to the terms of the contract. Each party agrees to accept what the other party offers. Suppose a carpenter agrees to accept $100 to fix your porch. You agree to let him or her do the work.

All parties must enter the contract because they want to. You cannot be forced into a contract. If anyone threatens you, or forces you to sign, the contract is not binding. It may be broken.

Competent Parties. A contract is binding only when the parties are *competent*. **Competent parties** are people who are responsible for their actions.

The legal term for people who *cannot* understand a contract is *incompetent*. A contract with an incompetent person is not binding. How do you know a person is incompetent? A court may decide that a mentally handicapped person is incompetent. Someone who drinks heavily or who is temporarily insane may be incompetent.

Minors are also incompetent to enter into a contract. A *minor* is someone who is not old enough to have certain rights. In most states, people under 18 are minors. A contract is not binding if any of these people enter into it.

☐ **Case Study** ☐   ☐   ☐   ☐   ☐   ☐

Andy is 15 years old. He bought an expensive stereo on sale at a local store. When he brought it home, he put on some music. After listening to it for a while he decided he did not like the stereo's sound. He decided to return the stereo to the store and get his money back.

The store did not give refunds on sale items. However, Andy's contract was not binding. He was a minor and he did not need the stereo in order to live. The store was forced to accept the stereo and refund his money. The store should have asked Andy's parents to countersign the contract.

Minors can break some of the contracts they have with adults. But the adults must keep their part of the contract. So the adults may ask the minor's parents to *countersign* the contract. To **countersign** means to sign a contract in support of someone else. If someone countersigns a contract for you, they must keep the agreement if you fail to do so.

Minors cannot break contracts when they agree to pay for things they must have in order to live. These things include food, shelter, clothing, and medical care.

Sometimes minors lie about their age. If they do lie, the law says they cannot get out of the contract. They will have to pay for what they agreed to buy. They may even have to pay more money to make up for the trouble they cause. This is called paying damages. To avoid such problems, most store owners ask minors to show proof of their age.

▲ *Sometimes minors can break informal contracts. Other times the law will hold them to their agreements. This minor is buying asthma medicine. Can she break her contract with the druggist?*

Legal Purpose. You must have a purpose for making a contract. But the purpose must be legal for the contract to be binding. For example, a contract to buy a house is binding because it is for a legal purpose. But suppose gambling is illegal in your state. You win a great deal of money from someone. You cannot legally collect your winnings. The purpose of the contract (gambling) was not legal.

In some states, it is illegal to do some types of work without a license. For example, a builder may need a

▲ *Some kinds of workers need a license before they can work. A contract with an unlicensed worker is not binding. Can a contract with this carpenter be enforced?*

license before building a house. If you make a contract with an unlicensed builder, it is not binding. You cannot make the builder finish the work.

Consideration. In a contract, one party promises to do something. The other party agrees to give something in return. This payment for the promise to do something is called **consideration.**

Consideration is usually money. But it may be property or jewelry. Sometimes consideration is very small. Suppose an electric company wanted to put a power line over Mr. South's farm. Mr. South agreed. Mr. South did not want money. So the company gave him $1 as consideration. The dollar makes the contract legal.

Correct Legal Form. The law says that certain contracts must be in writing. Here are the types of contracts that must be in writing.

- Installment contracts.
- Contracts to buy or sell land or buildings.
- Contracts to pay the debt of another person. (You agree to pay if the other person does not.)
- Contracts to sell personal things worth more than $500. (This amount varies from state to state.)
- Contracts that will not be carried out for one year.

Continued on page 275.

THIS AGREEMENT, made the 12th day of May, 19   , by and between CRESTWOOD REALTY CORPORATION of Crestwood, Texas, and hereinafter called the OWNER, and JAMES M. LEW, hereinafter called the ARCHITECT, WITNESSETH, that whereas the Owner intends to build a one-family dwelling in Crestwood, Texas, of approximately 16,500 cubic feet in volume, and will furnish a survey of the property to the Architect, NOW, THEREFORE, the Owner and the Architect, for the considerations hereinafter named, agree as follows:

The Architect agrees to perform for the above-named work the following professional services:

Prepare plans and specifications suitable for the construction of said dwelling and for obtaining the approval of local building authorities having legal jurisdiction. Architect will furnish three sets of plans and specifications to Owner. Additional sets will be furnished to Owner at cost.

The Owner agrees to pay the Architect the sum of Three Thousand Dollars ($3,000), payable as follows:

As a retainer upon signing of this agreement	$1,000
When preliminary designs and plans are approved	$1,000
When plans and specifications are completed and three sets are furnished to Owner	$1,000

The Owner and the Architect further agree that the Standard Conditions of Agreement between Owner and Architect as now published by the American Institute of Architects shall be part of this agreement insofar as they are applicable hereto.

The Owner and the Architect hereby agree to the full performance of the covenants contained herein.

IN WITNESS WHEREOF, the said parties have executed this Agreement on the day and year first above written.

CRESTWOOD REALTY CORPORATION

_____ _____ President
Witness

_____ _____ Architect
Witness

▲ *Figure 15-1*
Formal written contracts must must be in the correct legal form. They must have certain pieces of information. Name seven elements in this contract that make it binding.

Written contracts must be in the correct legal form like the contract in Figure 15-1. That is, they must include these seven things.

1. The date the agreement was made.
2. The place the agreement was made.
3. The names and addresses of the parties who sign the contract.
4. The purpose or reason for the contract.
5. The consideration to be paid.
6. The signatures of both parties.
7. The signatures of witnesses (when this is required by law).

▷ Precautions When Signing

Some people have trouble understanding contracts. So they do not read them all the way through. If you sign a contract, make sure you read and understand it. Follow these suggestions.

1. Be sure the amount of money or compensation is correct.
2. Be sure you are signing the agreement you want to sign.
3. Be sure there are no mistakes. If there are mistakes, the contract may not be binding.
4. Be sure all five elements are in the contract. If one is missing, the contract may be broken.
5. If part of the contract is written in small print, read that part, too. You need to understand everything in the contract.

★ Tricks of the Trade ★

Understanding Contracts

Before signing a contract, read it carefully. Then, ask the other party to explain its meaning in his or her own words. Ask questions until you fully understand the contract.

---

6. The contract should be signed by both parties. Keep a copy of the contract in a safe place.

You can have a lawyer check a contract before you sign it. Contracts that involve large amounts of money should be written by a lawyer.

✔ Check Up ✔ ✔ ✔

1. What are the two major types of laws?
2. What are the two types of contracts?
3. What are the five elements needed to make a contract binding?
4. What is consideration?
5. What are two groups of people who are incompetent to enter into a contract?
6. To be in legal form, what six things are needed in a written contract?

◯ Criminal Law

As you know from page 270, public laws tell us how to behave toward people in our community. Criminal law is a type of public law. Criminal laws protect your safety. They protect your rights. These laws tell how to punish people who commit crimes.

Criminal laws vary from state to state. The punishment for lawbreakers varies, too.

Two groups of people are treated differently from other people who break the law. These are mentally incompetent people and minors. Mentally incompetent people cannot tell right from wrong. The courts call in an expert to decide if someone is mentally incompetent. The expert will then state whether or not the person is mentally competent. A mentally incompetent person will not have to go to trial.

Minors are treated differently from adults under criminal law. They may not fully understand the result of what they do. Minors charged with a crime are tried in juvenile court. A juvenile court handles only the cases that involve minors.

The punishment for minors is different than it is for adults. Minors cannot be punished by death. They cannot be put in prison for life. But in special cases, a judge may try a minor as an adult. This happens when the crime is very serious.

▷ Types of Crimes

A serious crime is called a **felony**. Murder, rape, armed robbery, and arson (setting fires) are felonies. Felonies are punished by large fines or prison sentences. In some states the punishment may be death. Figure 15-2 tells what rights you lose *for the rest of your life* if you are found guilty of a felony.

A less serious crime is called a **misdemeanor**. For example, traffic violations and disturbing the peace are misdemeanors. So is petty theft. *Petty theft* means stealing something of little value. Misdemeanors are punished by small fines, short jail terms, and/or community service.

▲ *When you run a red light, you break the law. A traffic violation is what kind of crime?*

Rights Lost Due to a Felony Charge

If you are convicted of a felony charge you lose these rights for the rest of your life.

1. The right to vote.
2. The right to hold many public offices.
3. Many job opportunities. A felony charge is put on your credit reference reports. It is also on police records.
4. The right to a position in the armed forces.
5. The right to a veterans administration pension.
6. The right to become an officer in a small business investment company.
7. The opportunity to be an investment advisor.
8. The right to a pension or civil service pension.
9. The right to postgraduate training in such areas as law, medicine, and nursing.
10. The right to hold office in any labor union.

◀ *Figure 15-2 Being convicted of a felony can have serious effects on your life. What is one part of your life that would be affected by a felony charge?*

People who commit misdemeanors may be put on *probation*. During this time they are not in jail. But they must report to a probation officer.

Corporate crimes take place in businesses. Forgery and fraud are corporate crimes. Forgery is the dishonest changing of a written record. A report card is an example of a written record. So is a check. If you change these records, you are committing forgery.

▷ Arrest Procedures

Our legal system protects innocent people. Courts treat everyone as if they are innocent until they are proven guilty. This is only fair to the person who has been arrested for a crime. After all, he or she may be really innocent.

If you are ever stopped by the police, stay calm. Do not panic. The officers will ask you for identification. They may ask other questions. Answer their questions completely. You have a right to ask, "Am I under arrest?" or "Why are you arresting me?"

If they say you are under arrest, do not argue. Do not try to fight. You might be charged with resisting arrest. Tell the police you will have nothing to say until you see a lawyer. You have the right to remain silent.

The officer may search you for a hidden weapon. Police officers must have a search warrant to search your home. This gives them legal permission to search. They must give a judge a good reason for the search. They must believe they will find something illegal in your house.

Continued on page 279.

A Desire to Succeed

Elizabeth M. Watson

Police officers used to be called "the boys in blue." But now there are women in blue, too. In Houston, Texas, the top "man behind the badge" is a woman.

Elizabeth M. Watson became Houston's police chief in 1990. She was the first woman to head a large police force. This was a remarkable success. Twenty years earlier, female officers were not even allowed to go on patrol. They worked only in the police station offices.

In 1971, the law changed. Employers could not refuse women jobs. This law included police departments.

Watson became a police officer in 1972. On her wedding day in 1976, she was promoted from beat officer to a detective. In 1981, she became a lieutenant.

Becoming a lieutenant was an important achievement. But Watson did not stop there. She became Houston's first female police captain in 1984. In 1987, she became deputy chief and took over the West Side Command Station.

Many people in Watson's family are police officers. Her grandfather was a police officer. So were several of her uncles and cousins. Her husband, Robert, is on the Houston police force, too.

Doing her job well is important to Watson. She is proud of her success. She is also proud to be a role model for women. "I am deeply committed to policing," explains Watson. "If in the course of doing that I serve as a role model to other women, I am doubly honored."

Your Rights. If you are arrested, the officers must read you your rights. This means they must tell you things you can do while under arrest. You have the right to stay silent. You do not have to answer questions without a lawyer.

Booking. If you are arrested, you will be *booked.* This means you will be charged with a crime. If you are arrested after midnight, you may not be booked right away. This means you may have to stay in jail until you are booked the next morning.

Your personal things will be taken from you. They will be returned to you when you leave jail. The officers will make a list of these things. They will ask you to sign the list. Sign it. But do not sign anything else.

Do not talk about your arrest with other people in the jail. Do not talk about why you were arrested. Only talk to your lawyer.

Setting Bail. When you are arrested, you must be charged with a crime. If you are not charged, you must be let go. If you are charged, the court will set *bail.* **Bail** is money given to the court. When bail is paid, you can leave jail until your trial. Bail is a guarantee to the court that you will not leave town or miss your trial. If bail is not paid, you must stay in jail. The amount of bail varies with the crime. The more serious the crime, the higher the bail amount.

The bail money is held by the court until the trial is over. Then it is returned to you. If you do not come to the trial, the court keeps the money.

You may not have the money to pay bail. If not, you can call a bail bondsman who will pay your bail. You must pay the person a fee. This is usually 10 percent of the amount of the bail. After the trial, the bail money is returned to the bail bondsman.

Appearing in Court. You can defend yourself in court. But this is not usually a good idea. Most people do not know enough about the law to defend themselves. If you can, you should hire a lawyer. The lawyer will gather information about your case. He or she will tell you to plead guilty or not guilty. If you tell the court you are not guilty, you will have a trial. The court will then decide if you are guilty or not.

Our court system does everything it can to protect innocent people. Innocent people have a chance to prove they are not guilty.

✔ **Check Up** ✔ ✔ ✔

1. What are two ways minors charged with crimes are treated differently from adults?
2. What are the two major types of crimes?
3. What is bail?

O Using Legal Services

At some time, you may need a lawyer. These times are included here.

- If you plan to sign a contract dealing with a large amount of money.
- If you are arrested.
- If you are in an accident in which there is injury or property damage.
- If you need help to collect money someone owes you.
- If someone wants to collect money from you. But you feel you do not owe them money.

- If you have a tax problem dealing with a large amount of money.
- If you start or close a business.
- If you file for divorce.
- If you are adopting a child.

Many lawyers practice only one kind of law. One lawyer may be an expert on criminal law. Another may know contract law. Before you look for a lawyer, think about your case. What kind of expert do you need? Is your case a civil or criminal case? How much money is involved in your case?

▶ *You may one day need the help of a lawyer. Give four examples of times you may need a lawyer.*

For help with a contract, a small legal firm or legal clinic can help you. If you are charged with a crime, you need a criminal lawyer. Try to get the best lawyer you can.

▷ Finding a Lawyer

You can find a lawyer in several ways. You can ask friends or family members to suggest one. You can look in the Yellow Pages of the telephone book. Look for the state legal association. It may have a toll-free number. It can tell you which lawyers in your area can help you with your case.

You can also use the Yellow Pages to find lawyers in your area. Look under the heading *Attorneys* in the phone book. Call several firms and ask about their fees. This method will not tell you much about their experience, though.

A private attorney is usually very expensive. The services of a legal clinic cost less. A legal clinic is a group of lawyers who work for lower fees. They hire law students and other assistants to help them handle the case.

Maybe you cannot afford a legal clinic. If not, you can get special free legal services. The Legal Aid Society can help you with civil cases. Public defenders can help you with criminal cases. They are lawyers who help people who cannot pay legal fees. The court assigns public defenders.

▷ Paying Legal Fees

Before you hire an attorney, ask what he or she charges. A good time to do this is at your first meeting. Ask for an estimate for your case.

There are three ways lawyers set their fees. They may charge a flat fee for certain common services. For example, a lawyer may charge $100 to look over a business contract.

A lawyer may charge an hourly rate every time you meet. The lawyer may also charge an hourly rate when he or she does research on the case. Hourly rates may start at $40 per hour. But they may go as high as several hundred dollars per hour.

Some lawyers work on a **contingency basis**. This means the attorney is paid only if he or she wins the case. You will pay the lawyer a percentage of the money you win. Suppose you win $100,000. You have agreed to pay the lawyer 25 percent (one-fourth the amount). You will pay the attorney $25,000. ($100,000 ÷ 4 = $25,000.)

When do lawyers work on a contingency basis? Maybe you have a good case. But you cannot pay a large legal fee. The lawyer may work on a contingency basis. In malpractice and personal injury cases, lawyers may work on a contingency basis.

If you have a divorce or criminal case, you must pay the lawyer's fee. You cannot pay the attorney on a contingency basis.

☐ **Case Study** ☐ ☐ ☐ ☐ ☐ ☐

John worked on an auto assembly line. One day at work he had a serious accident. A cable on the assembly line broke. A large car part fell on his leg. John's leg was badly injured. He was in the hospital for four weeks. He could not go back to work for five months. When he went back to work, he still had to use crutches.

The insurance company offered John a cash settlement for his injury. But the offer did not fully cover all John's expenses. John decided to see an attorney. His father recommended the legal office of Murray and Clark. Ms. Murray thought that John had a good case. She agreed to take it on a contingency basis.

▷ **Going to Small-claims Court**

For legal cases that deal with small amounts of money, you can go to small-claims court. You do not need to hire a lawyer for these cases. The lawyer will probably cost more than you can win.

Small-claims cases usually deal with amounts less than $1,000. You go to small-claims court if someone owes you money. For example, if you have an argument with your landlord, you may go to small-claims court.

In small-claims court, you do not have a lawyer. You talk to the judge about your case yourself. Small-claims court does not cost very much. Usually there is only a small filing fee. This may be as low as $5. Often you can go to court at night. This is more convenient for people who work.

▲ *Some legal cases can be handled in small-claims court. Name one type of case.*

◀ For some legal cases, you do not need to hire a lawyer. You may go to small-claims court instead. Would you hire a lawyer in this case? Why or why not?

You must be prepared when you go to small-claims court. Put together all the papers that are important to the case.

Suppose your landlord tells you to move. He says you did not pay your rent on time. He also says your dog is not allowed in the apartment. You will need a copy of your rental agreement. This will show whether there is a rule against pets. You will need your canceled rent check. This will show you paid your rent on time. You can also call witnesses. You may have a friend who heard you talk to the landlord. He heard the landlord say it was okay to have a dog.

Tell the judge what happened as clearly as you can. Stick to the point. Do not waste time. As soon as the judge has heard both sides, he or she will make a decision. Usually you will not have to wait.

✔ Check Up ✔ ✔ ✔

1. Give three ways to find an attorney.
2. What are the three types of lawyers fees?
3. When will you go to small-claims court?

Chapter 15 Review

Chapter Summary

- Laws are rules that are made by governments.
- A contract is a legal agreement between two or more parties.
- There are five elements that make a contract binding. They are mutual agreement, competent parties, legal purpose, consideration, and correct legal form.
- Crimes are committed when people break public laws.
- Felonies and misdemeanors are two major types of crimes.
- Most people will need a lawyer at some time in their lives.
- You may need a lawyer to review a contract or to represent you in court. You may need a lawyer to collect money, start a business, get a divorce, or adopt a child.
- For minor civil cases, you may not want a lawyer. You can present your case yourself in small-claims court.

Reviewing Vocabulary

Listed in the next column are the important new words that were used in this chapter. Next to each word is the page on which you will find the word. Turn to that page and read the paragraph in which the word is printed in **bold** type. Write the word and its meaning. Then write a sentence of your own using each word.

1. contract (270)
2. party (270)
3. competent parties (271)
4. countersign (272)
5. consideration (273)
6. felony (276)
7. misdemeanor (276)
8. bail (279)
9. contingency basis (281)

Looking at the Facts

1. Name two major types of law.
2. What is the difference between a formal and an informal contract?
3. What five elements make a contract binding?
4. Name two groups of people who cannot make binding contracts.
5. What is consideration?
6. What are the two major types of crimes?
7. Give three examples of times you may need a lawyer.
8. What kinds of cases would you take to small-claims court?

Thinking Critically

1. You have agreed to build a fence for your neighbor. You will supply the materials to build the fence. The neighbor will pay you for the job and the materials when you are finished. You decide to write up a contract for the work. What will you include?

2. Your co-worker has been arrested. He has been caught stealing $5 from the cash drawer at work. What type of crime has been committed?
3. Why should you not get angry when you are arrested? Even if your arrest is a mistake?
4. Why do courts set bail?
5. Why do you think small-claims courts were started?

Discussing Chapter Concepts

1. Your best friend is buying a new car. He wants to borrow money from you for the down payment. When you ask him to sign a contract for the money, he gets angry. He promises he will not let you down. What do you do?
2. Some people say the contingency basis is a good way to set legal fees. Some say it is a bad way. What do you think? Why?
3. Should the court be allowed to sentence minors who commit a murder to the death penalty? Why or why not? Would the age of the minor change your response? What if the minor was 9 years old instead of 16?

Using Basic Skills

Math

1. Suppose you hire a lawyer who charges $50 an hour. The lawyer does 40 hours of work for you. How much will you be charged?

Communication

2. Work with a partner in your class. Write up a formal contract for helping your partner study for a math test. Include everything you need to make the contract binding.

Human Relations

3. A friend borrows $175 from you. She promises to repay you in one month. Two months later she says she cannot pay you back. But you know she just bought a new stereo. What can you do to get your money back?

Activities for Enrichment

1. Read the newspaper for stories that deal with arrests and trials. Cut them out of the paper. Bring them to class. Discuss the types of crimes that were committed. Also discuss the punishments that were given out. Did the punishments seem fair?
2. Watch the news on TV. Look for stories that deal with arrests and trials. Make a list of the stories. Was the crime a felony or misdemeanor?
3. Sit in on a small-claims court session. Or watch "The People's Court" on TV. What kinds of cases did you hear? In what ways did both parties come prepared for small-claims court? How would you have presented the case?

Living with Change

Words to learn and use

Here are the new terms you will learn in this chapter. Challenge yourself. Read through the list to see if you know what they mean.

change
trends
labor supply
environment

Build on what you know

You already know...
- change is constant.
- change can be positive or negative.
- it can be difficult to cope with change.
- sometimes you avoid change.

In this chapter you will learn...
- why change is constant.
- why good self-esteem helps you cope with change.
- how to handle change.
- how to overcome barriers to changing.

Change is anything that causes you to alter your life. Everyone must deal with change. You may change jobs. You may move from one place to another. You may learn new skills.

Change can be positive or negative. It can be expected or unexpected. It can be exciting or scary. But it always helps you grow.

How you view change depends on your outlook on life. Your self-esteem will help you cope with change. Everyone is capable of dealing with change. Sometimes coping with change is just a matter of learning to overcome certain barriers. This chapter will help you become better at handling change.

O Change Is Constant

Change is the only constant thing in life. It often forces you to do things or think about things in a different way.

You will make some changes because you are ready to do so. For example, you may move to a new apartment that you like better than your old one.

You will make other changes because you have to. For example, you may be forced to find a new job because you are laid off from your old one.

In this section, you will look at several areas in which you may experience change. You will see what types of changes you may experience. And you will learn how you can deal with them.

▷ Change in the Workplace

The average job lasts just over five years. You may hunt for a new job eight times or more in your life! Does this feel exciting? Or does it feel scary? It probably feels a little of both!

As you learned in Chapter 8, the economy influences the job market. So one main reason people change jobs is because of changes in the economy. When the economy slows down, people spend less. Fewer goods and services are produced. Not as many workers are needed. Unemployment rises.

Suppose you work for a company that supplies an automaker with dashboards. If the demand for autos goes down, the demand for dashboards goes down. This could lead to layoffs in your shop. You may like your job. You may not wish to leave. But if you are laid off, you would be forced to look for work elsewhere. So jobs that are here today may not be here tomorrow.

There is opportunity in change, though. In the early twentieth century, for example, there were many blacksmiths. When people started using cars for transportation instead of horses, fewer blacksmiths were needed. But many new jobs were created in the auto industry! Here, change closed one door but opened another.

Here is a more recent example of opportunities in change. There are not as many bank tellers today as there were ten years ago. Automated teller machines have replaced many human tellers. But now repair people are needed to maintain and fix automated tellers. The skills needed to be a repair person are different from those needed to be a teller.

◀ *You will face changes in the workplace. What change has occurred in this workplace in the last 50 years?*

Many people looking for a new job must learn new skills. Once they have a new job, they may still have to update their skills. In some fields you may have to do this every few months!

Companies are always competing to get more customers. So they change their goods or services to make them better. This means that the people producing those goods or services must learn new skills. The people selling them must learn the new features and benefits.

Even if your job is secure now, continue to update your skills. People who update their skills show initiative. So they are often chosen for special training and duties. It is also often easier for them to find a new job if they must do so.

▷ Trends

One way to prepare for change is to look at *trends*. **Trends** are the general changes that are taking place in our society.

Studying trends will help you predict what the workplace of the future will be like. There are some exciting trends to look for over the next ten years. Here are some of them.

- More women in the workplace.
- A labor supply shortage.
- A need to care for the elderly.
- A global economy.
- More concern for the environment.
- Increased importance of speed and convenience.

Women in the Workplace. There are more women in the workplace today than in the past. In fact, women are entering the workforce in large numbers. They are starting businesses twice as fast as men.

With both men and women working, people spend less time in the home. They have less time to take care of their homes and children. This creates more jobs that involve daycare, housecleaning, and personal shopping services.

The Labor Supply. The **labor supply** is made up of all the people who are willing and able to work. The number of entry-level workers in the U.S. today is falling. How will this affect you? If you start your own business, you may have trouble finding good workers. If you are looking for a job, though, there may be less competition.

Because of the labor shortage, many businesses have looked to different labor sources. McDonald's, for example, began hiring the elderly and the disabled. You have many years to go before you are elderly! But you might have a disability that prevents you from working in some areas. You could find job opportunities in the fast-food industry.

Care for the Elderly. The number of elderly in the U.S. is rising. This means there will be a greater need for services for the elderly. This includes health care services.

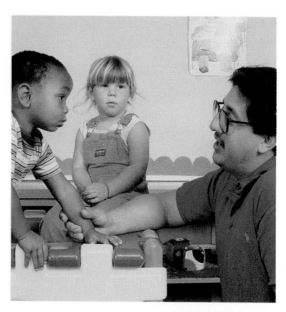

▲ *Studying trends often opens the door to new opportunities. What trend provided a need for more daycare centers?*

Think of some of the things the elderly cannot do for themselves. They may find it hard to shop, run errands, or get to appointments. Which of these services could you provide? You may want to become a health care worker who cares for the elderly.

The Global Economy. Changes that occur in the global economy can affect you. The amount of business the U.S. does with other countries is increasing. The U.S. buys goods and services from other countries. It depends on other nations for such things as oil. It invests in other countries, and other countries invest in the U.S. Changes in the global economy will affect the workplace.

These changes could create a demand for your company to produce new goods or services. It may provide more opportunities for workers who speak a foreign language. It may create opportunities for workers who can operate foreign machinery. Be aware of the global economy. You may create new business opportunities for yourself.

The Environment. Everything that surrounds you makes up your **environment**. Many people today are becoming more concerned about the environment. They are conserving energy sources and fighting pollution. They are recycling such things as glass, plastic, and aluminum.

This concern for the environment could be an opportunity for you. Automakers, for example, are making more fuel-efficient cars. Fast-food restaurants have begun to use paper plates and cups instead of styrofoam. Some companies make recycling bins for home use. You may find a job making or selling products that help to protect the environment.

▲ *The increasing concern for the environment has resulted in new jobs such as this one. What are two other jobs that may have resulted from this trend?*

▶ *People today demand speed and convenience. How does this pizza business fulfill these demands?*

Speed and Convenience. People's life-styles are busier today. So they are demanding that things be faster and more convenient. For example, people once had to wait several days to receive mail. Now they can get it overnight. They can get letters faxed to them in a matter of minutes.

People used to wait a week or more for new eye glasses. Now they can have them in an hour! Even the Internal Revenue Service gives refunds in a few days with electronic filing!

How does this need for speed affect you? You could start a business or service that saves people time. You could do painting or wallpapering. You could clean pools, carpets, or even pets! Have you ever thought of being a chimney sweep or a lawn care specialist? What could you do that a busy person has no time to do for himself or herself?

> # ✓ Check Up ✓ ✓ ✓
>
> 1. Define change.
> 2. What is one way to prepare for change?
> 3. How can a labor shortage help you if you are looking for a job?

⭘ Self-esteem and Change

As you learned in Chapter 5, your self-esteem is the way you feel about yourself. Your level of self-esteem affects how you deal with change. If you have positive self-esteem, you may find change challenging and fun. You will see it as something that helps you grow. If you have low self-esteem, you may not believe you are able to change. You may stay in a negative situation because you think you cannot change.

If you feel that your self-esteem is low, you can raise it. How? You can realize that you have control over your own life. No matter who you are, you can learn new skills. You can look for another job. You can find relationships that will help you grow. You are never too young or too old to do any of these things! You can always make yourself and your life better.

▷ You Are Valuable

Being *valuable* means you feel you have worth. Seeing yourself as valuable will help you deal with change. You will know that you can contribute to any situation. You will believe that you can change.

Have you ever noticed how different people handle the same problems differently? One person who loses a job may get depressed. Another may look at a job loss as a chance to find a better job. Which person sees himself or herself as more valuable?

To find value in yourself, do three things.

1. Believe in yourself.
2. Know that strength does not come from being with someone else who is strong. Strength comes from inside yourself.
3. Trust yourself.

Here is a closer look at each of these points.

Believing in Yourself. To deal with change, you must believe that you have strength. You can face the challenges change brings. This involves more than just belief. It involves action, too.

For example, if you lose your job, you can take action by going to many job interviews. Let the employer know that you can handle the challenges of the position. Tell the person your skills and background that qualify you for the job. Your attitude will show your belief in yourself and your abilities. And your actions will help you take advantage of change.

Continued on page 295.

A Desire to Succeed

Wally Amos

You probably know Wally Amos by his picture on Famous Amos cookies. But he was not always famous! And he was not always known for good cookies. His ability to cope with change helped him succeed.

As a young boy, Wally Amos ate his aunt's chocolate chip cookies. He loved the cookies. But he did not look into a career as a baker. Instead, he went into the music business. He became an agent, trying to get work for musicians.

As an adult, Wally often made "Toll House" cookies. Soon he was changing the recipe and baking his own version of cookies. His cookies were so good, he thought they might help his work.

When Wally visited music producers, he passed out cookies to break the ice. Everybody loved the cookies. But he had little success in getting his clients work.

Wally became discouraged with the music business. It was time for a change. He started thinking of other businesses he would like to work in. He did not have much money. But his friends in the music business loaned him $25,000 to start the Famous Amos Chocolate Chip Cookie Company.

Wally made the change from agent to baker. He used the skills he had learned in the music business. He put on a flowered shirt and a Panama hat. He handed out his cookies on the street. He threw parties to promote his cookies. He truly became Famous Amos.

By dealing with change, Wally created a new opportunity for himself. Believing in himself led to his success.

Case Study

John decided he wanted to lose ten pounds. To do this, he knew he needed to make some changes. He needed to change the way he ate and exercised. John believed he had the strength to make these changes.

He began to eat foods that were low in fat. He took two-mile walks each day instead of watching TV. He also took up tennis. A month later he had lost four pounds! He only had six more pounds to go.

John felt good about being able to make the changes he needed to make. He felt that he looked better. This boosted his self-esteem. And feeling this good made it easy for him to lose the last six pounds.

Strength Comes from Within. Sometimes people believe that strength comes from others. They think that others are better than they are at dealing with problems. So they look to other people to help them solve their problems. But this keeps them from building inner strength.

People who find strength from others do not take responsibility for their own lives. They do not feel they have the power to make changes by themselves. They do not trust their abilities. They want others to be responsible for changing their lives.

Being responsible for yourself and your actions is part of believing in yourself. Other people can offer advice. But you still must have the strength to change your life. After all, you are the only one who will live with the changes that are made. And you know best what is right for you.

▲ *Seeing yourself as a valuable person will help you deal with change. What are two things that will help you find value in yourself?*

Trust Yourself. Trusting yourself is a key in learning to value yourself. You learn to trust yourself by listening to your "inner voice." Some people call this inner voice *intuition.* Some simply call it their *gut feeling.*

You probably have always known when something was right for you and when it was wrong. You may not have followed this inner voice. But it was there all the same.

You develop more trust in yourself when you successfully solve problems. Solving a problem is like climbing to the top of the mountain. At first, you are not quite sure how you will do it. But each step brings you closer to your goal. You gain confidence in yourself. You trust your abilities. When you finally reach the top of the mountain, you know that *you* did it! The success gives you self-confidence. And the self-confidence helps you trust your "inner voice." You will trust yourself to do what is right for you.

▲ *By listening to your "inner voice," you will learn to trust yourself. Why is it important to trust yourself?*

★ **Tricks of the Trade** ★

Building Self-esteem

Give your self-esteem a boost. Write positive statements about yourself. Then tape them to your bathroom mirror or someplace where you will see them often. Read these statements every morning and night. They will give your self-esteem a boost!

✔ **Check Up** ✔ ✔ ✔

1. How does self-esteem relate to your ability to deal with change?
2. Why is it important to understand that you have value?
3. What are three things to do to find value in yourself?
4. What is your "inner voice"?

○ Barriers to Changing

Everyone can change. Yet some people *think* they cannot. They have barriers to changing. A *barrier* blocks your ability to get at something. For example, you may have seen a barrier that blocks you from getting to a certain street. This is a physical barrier.

There are emotional barriers, too. You can have emotional barriers inside of yourself. They block you from making positive changes in your life. Here are the four most common barriers to change.

- Fear of a disability.
- Fear of success.
- Fear of taking risks.
- Fear of failure.

Each of us may experience one or some of these barriers from time to time. But these barriers become a problem when we cannot manage to get over them. Luckily, these barriers can be overcome.

▷ Fear of a Disability

Sometimes people think that their disabilities prevent them from learning. But disabilities do not have to hold anyone back. They can be viewed as positive challenges instead of negative barriers.

For example, consider Mary, who is hearing impaired. Mary cannot hear the spoken word. But she must still communicate with others. So she learned sign language to communicate with other hearing-impaired people. In addition, she became very good at reading people's body language! And, of course, she can read and write. So her disability helped her expand her knowledge. It opened a door of opportunity that helped her belief in her abilities.

Any disability will challenge you to do something better. Remember, disabilities are not barriers to changing. They are challenges that open new doors.

✱ Tricks of the Trade ✱

A Stress Reliever

If changes in your life are creating stress, try one or two of these stress-relievers. Listen to relaxing music. Go for a fast walk. Talk to a good friend. Read a good book. Create something. Take a bubble bath. Give yourself a gift. Make yourself happy! Feel good about the changes in your life.

▷ Fear of Success

Some people think that success sets them apart from others. They think their family and friends will not accept them because they are "different." So if your friends and family do not value success, you yourself may fear it.

To overcome your fear, you may have to become more independent. You may have to learn that others' opinions of you do not matter. Tell yourself that it is all right to be good at something. Your friends and family may be jealous of you. If so, they may have some learning of their own to do.

Learn to reward yourself for your successes. For example, when you get a good grade on a test, do something special for yourself. Valuing your own success will help you look forward to change.

▲ *Reward yourself for your success. Why is this important?*

▷ Fear of Taking Risks

Many of the things you do involve risk. When you love someone, for example, you risk not being loved back. When you hope, you risk disappointment.

If you fear taking risks, you may lack practice at it. But you cannot change without taking risks. If you never risked anything, you would never learn or grow as a person. You may feel safer if you do not risk. But you will be less able to handle change.

To become comfortable with taking risks, try taking small risks first. If you fear answering questions in class, try it just once a day. Do it even when you are not sure you are right. Volunteer to learn a new task at work. Ask someone to go out, even if you think the person might say no. Each time you take a risk, you will feel less fear in doing so.

▷ Fear of Failure

You may not want to try things because you fear that you cannot learn to do them well. Remember, though, that everyone is capable of learning. The only failure is in *not* trying to learn.

People do not all learn at the same rate. You may need more time than others. You may respond better to pictures than to spoken directions. You may have a disability that requires you to use different learning materials. Whatever your situation, you can learn. Your success may simply depend on your method of learning. Ask your high school counselor about methods that will best help you succeed.

▲ *Taking risks builds confidence. What are two other benefits of taking risks?*

✔ Check Up ✔ ✔ ✔

1. Name four barriers to change.
2. How can a disability help you?
3. What is one reason why some people are afraid to succeed?
4. How can you get over a fear of taking risks?

Chapter 16 Review

Chapter Summary

- Change is constant.
- Handling change is easier if you do not try to change everything at once.
- Studying trends can help you prepare for change.
- The level of your self-esteem affects how you deal with change.
- Seeing yourself as valuable will help you deal with change.
- You can find value in yourself by doing three things. Believe in yourself. Know that strength comes from within. And trust yourself.
- You can overcome barriers to changing.
- Four barriers to changing are fear of a disability, fear of success, fear of taking risks, and fear of failure.

Reviewing Vocabulary

Listed below are the important new words that were used in this chapter. Next to each word is the page on which you will find the word. Turn to that page and read the paragraph in which the word is printed in **bold** type. Use each word in a sentence that describes change.

1. change (287)
2. trends (289)
3. labor supply (290)
4. environment (291)

Looking at the Facts

1. What is the only thing that is constant in life?
2. Why is it important to study trends?
3. List six trends that may affect you in the future.
4. Name two ways to raise your self-esteem.
5. How will understanding that you have value help you deal with change?
6. Why do you need to believe in yourself in order to deal with change?
7. Why is it important to find strength from within instead of from others?
8. How can you build trust in yourself?
9. What does having a barrier to changing mean?
10. Name four barriers to changing.

Thinking Critically

1. You tell your friend that the store you have been working at is closing soon. You are not worried because you know how to handle change. She asks you what the secret is. What will you tell her?
2. Your friend tells you he does not like his job. He has decided he does not like where he lives, either. He also wants to lose some

weight. He has also signed up for a speed reading class. What can you tell your friend about handling change successfully?

3. Your company has just told you that they are laying off 100 employees. You are one of them. You are worried. You do not think you can find a new job. Your self-esteem is low. Your friend tells you that you must raise your level of self-esteem. How will you do this?

4. You want to learn to use your computer. But you are afraid to take a computer class. You fear you will do poorly in the class. Which barrier to learning are you faced with?

Discussing Chapter Concepts

1. Of the six trends discussed in this chapter, which do you think you would be most likely to take advantage of? How?

2. Discuss one change you have made in the last month.

3. Do you think it is all right to let others solve your problems for you? Why or why not?

4. Tell about a time that you had a barrier to changing. Why do you think you had this barrier? Were you able to overcome it?

5. Some people handle change by not dealing with it at all. They let "fate" control their lives. Why is this not a good plan?

Using Basic Skills

Math

1. You would like to change how much money you save in a year. Last year you saved $240. You want to save twice as much this year. You will save an equal amount each month. How much will you have to save a month?

Communication

2. Read the classified ads for jobs that are available. Pick three jobs that appear most often. Write down what trend might have caused these job opportunities.

Human Relations

3. Your friend will not sit next to you in keyboarding class because he keyboards more slowly than you do. He says he feels embarrassed because he cannot keep up with you during timed drills. What will you say to him about people's ability to learn?

Activities for Enrichment

1. Make a poster that shows your self-esteem. Use both words and pictures.

2. Interview three people who work. Ask them how trends have affected their work. Share your information with the class.

3. Make a list of risks you have taken in your life. Make a second list of risks you would like to take in your life.

~~~~~ **Epilog** ~~~~~

Life in the Year 2010

~~~~~

Changes, changes, changes! Today's world is changing fast, even as you read these words! New jobs are being created. New technology is giving us more information. New advances in health care are helping people live long, healthy lives.

Think of the life you are leading right now. Then think of what the future will bring! Here is what a day in your life might be like in the year 2010.

~~~~~

You leave for work early in the morning. Your company, W & B Inc., has a flextime program. This allows you to work ten hours a day, four days a week. The company does this to cut down on commuter traffic. It allows you to spend more time with your family.

You take the commuter train to work. You take your child with you. W & B offers a daycare service. They know that two-income families have a great need for daycare.

Your spouse, Jamie, works at home as a word processor. A computer allows Jamie to communicate with the office. Jamie can also send and receive work through the computer. A fax machine allows Jamie to send written material instantly to the office. Once a week, Jamie goes into the office to take care of any business that cannot be done from home.

Jamie saves several hours a week by not commuting to work. These hours are used to study for a second career as a proofreader.

You work for a manufacturing plant. The plant makes parts for airplanes. The work is done by robotics. Your job is to control the robotics.

Before you begin work, you check the computer mail. This is a computer with a wide screen that posts the daily meetings and company notices.

There is a message about a meeting with your boss today. You will discuss how to improve the workplace. There is also a training session posted for tomorrow evening. You will learn to use the new equipment. On Friday you will play in the company softball game.

You work through the morning. The plant is clean, well lit, and comfortable to work in. You work behind glass walls. You can watch the machines from your work area. You remember when there were twice as many people working at the plant. Robotics have reduced the number of people needed to do the job.

You break for lunch at noon. The plant has a cafeteria. So you do not have to go out for lunch. You can eat lunch with your child.

You work until 6:00. Then you and your child take the train back to your home. You live in a condominium. A careful savings plan allowed you to afford your own home.

You arrive home to find a delivery truck in the driveway. Your spouse has faxed a grocery list to the supermarket. The supermarket delivers the food for free.

After you eat dinner, you separate your garbage in the recycling bins. You have three crates for glass, paper, and aluminum. You are only allowed to throw out three crates of garbage a week to be recycled. This helps you think about what you buy and throw away.

By 9:00 you sit down at the T.V. Tonight you decide to watch a movie. You dial the movie request line. You ask for the movie. You are charged a small fee. But it is cheaper than going out to the movies. As you relax, you wonder what life will be like in the year 2020!

Appendix A
Sources of Career Information

Choosing a career is one of the most important decisions you will make. Making a career choice takes careful planning. You will have to do some research to decide what career is best for you. Luckily, it is easier to research careers now than ever before. More information on careers has been printed in the last ten years than in the previous three hundred years!

Your school and public libraries are both good sources of career information. Some school libraries have a special section on career information. These sections are often called career information centers.

If your school has a career information center, that is the place to start your research. If there is no career center, start with the library's card catalog.

Looking up the subject *careers* in the card catalog will give you a list of books on careers. If you want information on a certain career area (such as business or health care), look up that topic in the catalog.

▷ Government Publications

The U.S. Department of Labor provides information on careers. Their books are in most libraries. Here are three of their books.

1. The *Dictionary of Occupational Titles.*
2. The *Occupational Outlook Handbook.*
3. The *Guide for Occupational Exploration.*

Dictionary of Occupational Titles (DOT). The *DOT* describes more than 20,000 jobs. The *DOT* is well organized and easy to use. The jobs are listed in groups. The groups are based on the job task. For example, all clerical and sales jobs will be listed in the same group.

All jobs in the *DOT* have code numbers. The code numbers relate to the type of work that the job involves. Under each code number, the job title is listed. A brief description of the work is given for each job code.

▲ *The Dictionary of Occupational Titles*

All jobs are listed in an alphabetical index. The index is in the back of the book. To find a job, simply look up the name in the index. There will be a code number for that job. You can then turn to the front section of the book. It is arranged by code numbers. You can find the job description you want using the code number.

Occupational Outlook Handbook (OOH). The *OOH* is a major source of career information. It provides information on hundreds of jobs. The *OOH* can be found in most school libraries. Public libraries also keep copies.

▲ *The Occupational Outlook Handbook*

The table of contents lists all the jobs described. Use the table of contents to look up various jobs. Each job description gives these things.

- Work done on the job.
- Working conditions.
- Tools and equipment used on the job.
- Job locations in the country.
- How much education and training a job requires.
- Job outlook.
- Average earnings.
- Related jobs.
- Sources of additional information.

Guide for Occupational Exploration (GOE). The *GOE* will help you learn what jobs relate to your interests, aptitudes, and abilities.

▲ *The Guide for Occupational Exploration*

The information is organized by interest groups. Within each interest group are worker trait groups. The groups have information about the things listed here.

- Kind of work done.
- Skills needed.
- Interests and aptitudes.
- Education and training.

▷ Career Information Center (CIC)

The *CIC* is a multi-volume set found in your school or public library. More than 3,000 jobs are described in the *CIC*. It is organized by job clusters. Here is the information it gives.

- How to prepare and apply for jobs.
- Entry-level job requirements.
- Job-search skills such as writing resumes, letters of application, and interview hints.
- The latest developments in different job fields.

▷ The Telephone Book

Another source of career information is in the front pages in the telephone book. They contain phone numbers and addresses of many local agencies that can provide career information. Here are some of the agencies listed.

- City Chamber of Commerce.
- Community Service Organizations.
- Consumer Protection Agency.
- Counseling and Guidance Services.

▶ *Career Information Center*

- City and State Employment Services.
- Job Services.
- Schools offering adult education.
- Vocational Schools.

▷ Other Resources

Here is a list of other resources that give career information.

Books on Job Descriptions
- *Encyclopedia of Careers and Vocational Guidance.*
- *Occupational Briefs.*

Books on Vocational, Trade, and Technical Schools
- *Lovejoy's Career and Vocational School Guide—A Handbook of Job Training.*

Books on Military Information
- *U.S. Army Career Education Guide.*
- *The Navy Career Guide.*
- *Air Forces Information.*

Books on Jobs for the Disabled
- *Your Handicap—Don't Let It Handicap You.*
- *Directory for Exceptional Children.*

Books for Minorities
- *Equal Employment Opportunities for Minority Groups and College Graduates: Locating, Recruiting, Employing.*
- *Placing Minority Women in Professional Jobs.*

Books on Career Decision Making
- *Effective Personal and Career Decision Making.*
- *Career Skills Assessment Program.*
- *Decision Making for Career Development.*
- *Guided Career Exploration.*

You can find many of these resources in your school or public libraries. You can also go to your school guidance office for information. Most bookstores have books on careers.

Appendix B
Career Support Information

The information in this Appendix will help you before and after you get a job. If you want to know more about the information given here, check with your teacher. He or she will give you a copy of *Entering the World of Work*. It talks about each of these things in greater detail.

Abbreviations Often Used in Newspaper Ads

a.m. = morning
appl. = applicant
appt. = appointment
asst. = assistant
ATTN = attention
ben. = benefits
co. = company
c/o = in care of
dept. = department
EOE = equal opportunity
       employer
etc. = and so on
exc. = excellent
exp. = experience
FT = full time
gd = good
hr. = hour
hrs+ = at least that many hours
immed. = immediate
incl. = included
info = information
lic = license or licensed
M-F (Mon.-Fri.) = Monday through
       Friday

mfg. = manufacturing
mgr. = manager
min. = minimum
nec. = necessary
ofc. = office
oppor. (oppty.) = opportunity
PC = personal computer
pd. = paid
ph. = phone
p.m. = afternoon or evening
pos. = position
pref. = preferred
PT = part time
qual. = qualified or qualifications
ref. = reference
rep. = representative
req. = required
sal. = salary
sec. = secretary
w/ = with
wk. = week
WP = word processing
wpm = words per minute
yrs. = years

▲ *These abbreviations will help you read the want ads.*

Job Lead Cards

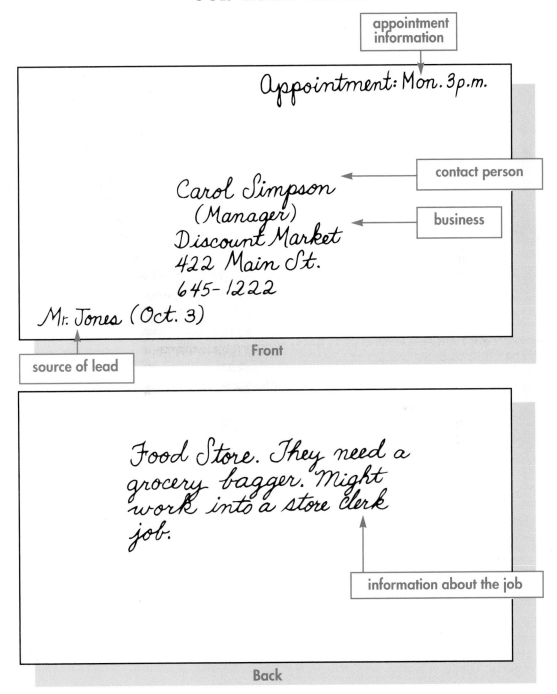

▲ *Job lead cards help you remember important information and keep track of your job interviews.*

Social Security Application

DEPARTMENT OF HEALTH AND HUMAN SERVICES
SOCIAL SECURITY ADMINISTRATION

Form Approved
OMB No. 0690-0066

FORM SS-5 — APPLICATION FOR A SOCIAL SECURITY NUMBER CARD (Original, Replacement or Correction)

Unless the requested information is provided, we may not be able to issue a Social Security Number (20 CFR 422-103(b))

INSTRUCTIONS TO APPLICANT ▶ Before completing this form, please read the instructions on the opposite page. Type or print, using pen with dark blue or black ink. Do not use pencil. SEE PAGE 1 FOR REQUIRED EVIDENCE.

		First	Middle	Last
NAA	NAME TO BE SHOWN ON CARD			
NAB	FULL NAME AT BIRTH (IF OTHER THAN ABOVE)	First	Middle	Last
ONA	OTHER NAME(S) USED			

1

2 STT MAILING ADDRESS   (Street/Apt. No., P.O. Box, Rural Route No.)

CTY	CITY (Do not abbreviate)	STE	STATE	ZIP	ZIP CODE

3 CSP CITIZENSHIP (Check one only)

☐ a. U.S. citizen

☐ b. Legal alien allowed to work

☐ c. Legal alien not allowed to work

☐ d. Other (See instructions on Page 2)

4 SEX SEX

☐ MALE

☐ FEMALE

5 ETB RACE/ETHNIC DESCRIPTION (Check one only) (Voluntary)

☐ a. Asian, Asian-American or Pacific Islander (includes persons of Chinese, Filipino, Japanese, Korean, Samoan, etc., ancestry or descent)

☐ b. Hispanic (Includes persons of Chicano, Cuban, Mexican or Mexican-American, Puerto Rican, South or Central American, or other Spanish ancestry or descent)

☐ c. Negro or Black (not Hispanic)

☐ d. Northern American Indian or Alaskan Native

☐ e. White (not Hispanic)

		Month	Day	Year	AGE	PRESENT AGE	PLB	PLACE OF BIRTH	CITY (Do not abbreviate)	STATE OR FOREIGN COUNTRY (Do not abbreviate)	FCI
6 DOB	DATE OF BIRTH				**7**		**8**				

9 MNA	MOTHER'S NAME AT BIRTH	First	Middle	Last (Her maiden name)
FNA	FATHER'S NAME	First	Middle	Last

10 PNO

a. Has a Social Security number card ever been requested for the person listed in item 1?   ☐ YES(2) ☐ NO(1) ☐ Don't know (1)

b. Was a card received for the person listed in item 1?   ☐ YES(2) ☐ NO(1) ☐ Don't know (1)

▶ IF YOU CHECKED YES TO A OR B, COMPLETE ITEMS C THROUGH E; OTHERWISE GO TO ITEM 11.

SSN c. Enter the Social Security number assigned to the person listed in item 1.   ☐☐☐ — ☐☐ — ☐☐☐☐

NLC d. Enter the name shown on the most recent Social Security card issued for the person listed in item 1.

PDB e. Date of birth correction (See instruction 10 on page 2)   MONTH DAY YEAR

11 DON	TODAY'S DATE	MONTH	DAY	YEAR	**12**	Telephone number where we can reach you during the day. Please include the area code.	HOME	OTHER

ASD **WARNING:** Deliberately furnishing (or causing to be furnished) false information on this application is a crime punishable by fine or imprisonment, or both.

IMPORTANT REMINDER: WE CANNOT PROCESS THIS APPLICATION WITHOUT THE REQUIRED EVIDENCE. SEE PAGE 1

13 YOUR SIGNATURE

14 YOUR RELATIONSHIP TO PERSON IN ITEM 1   ☐ Self ☐ Other (Specify) _____

WITNESS (Needed only if signed by mark "X")

WITNESS (Needed only if signed by mark "X")

DO NOT WRITE BELOW THIS LINE (FOR SSA USE ONLY)

DTC (SSA RECEIPT DATE)	NPN	DOC
NTC	CAN	BIC	IDN	ITV	☐ MANDATORY IN PERSON INTERVIEW CONDUCTED

TYPE(S) OF EVIDENCE SUBMITTED

SIGNATURE AND TITLE OF EMPLOYEE(S) REVIEWING EVIDENCE AND/OR CONDUCTING INTERVIEW

DATE

DCL   DATE

Form SS-5 (11-86)
5/84, 1/85 and 8/85 editions may be used until supply is exhausted   3

▲ *You will need a social security card to begin working. You probably have one if you or your parents filed an income tax form last year. If you recently arrived in the U.S., you will need to fill out an application for a social security card.*

Personal Fact Sheet

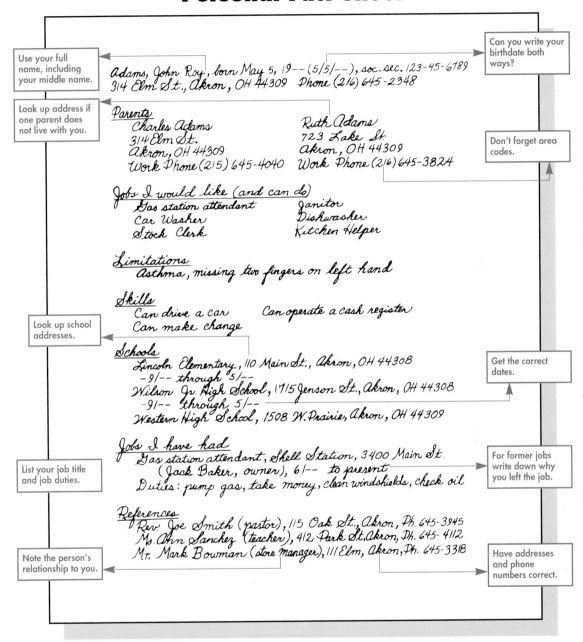

Use your full name, including your middle name.

Can you write your birthdate both ways?

Look up address if one parent does not live with you.

Don't forget area codes.

Look up school addresses.

Get the correct dates.

List your job title and job duties.

For former jobs write down why you left the job.

Note the person's relationship to you.

Have addresses and phone numbers correct.

Adams, John Roy, born May 5, 19—– (5/5/—–), soc. sec. 123-45-6789
314 Elm St., Akron, OH 44309   Phone (216) 645-2348

Parents
Charles Adams   Ruth Adams
314 Elm St.   723 Lake St.
Akron, OH 44309   Akron, OH 44309
Work Phone (215) 645-4040   Work Phone (216) 645-3824

Jobs I would like (and can do)
Gas station attendant   Janitor
Car Washer   Dishwasher
Stock Clerk   Kitchen Helper

Limitations
Asthma, missing two fingers on left hand

Skills
Can drive a car   Can operate a cash register
Can make change

Schools
Lincoln Elementary, 110 Main St., Akron, OH 44308
–91–– through 5/––
Wilson Jr. High School, 1715 Jenson St., Akron, OH 44308
–91–– through 5/––
Western High School, 1508 W. Prairie, Akron, OH 44309

Jobs I have had
Gas station attendant, Shell Station, 3400 Main St.
(Jack Baker, owner), 61–– to present
Duties: pump gas, take money, clean windshields, check oil

References
Rev. Joe Smith (pastor), 115 Oak St., Akron, Ph. 645-3945
Ms. Ann Sanchez (teacher), 412 Park St., Akron, Ph. 645-4112
Mr. Mark Bowman (store manager), 111 Elm, Akron, Ph. 645-3318

▲ *Take a personal fact sheet with you when you apply for a job. This will help you remember details and keep dates straight.*

Letter Requesting an Application Form

800 Main Street
White Plains, IL 63105
March 14, 19--

Joe's Steak House
815 Garden Street
Jonesville, IL. 67890

Dear Sir or Madam:

When I graduate from White Plains High School in May, I plan to move to Jonesville.

I have worked part time as a waitress and would like to work at Joe's Steak House. Please send me an application form.

Yours truly,

Linda Hill

▲ *You can ask for an application form in a letter like this one.*

Job Application Form

APPLICATION FORM

Joe's Steak House   **815 Garden Street**   **Jonesville 67890**

PLEASE TYPE OR PRINT CLEARLY

Hill   Linda   Ann   123-46-6789
Last Name   First   Middle   Social Security Number

800 Main St., White Plains,   IL   36105   (609) 963-1421
Address   City   State   Zip   (Area Code)   Home Phone

In case of an emergency,   Louis Hill   (609) 963-8486
whom should be called? _____
                                      Name   Telephone Number

What job or jobs are   Waitress (part-time)
you applying for? _____

What special skills   Get along well with people
do you have? _____

Education: Circle Highest Grade Completed   1 2 3 4 5 6 7 8 9 10 11 12 13 14 15 16 17 +

List schools you have attended:

Grade School (last attended)

Adams   100 Oak St, Ventura, CA   Sept., 19-- -June, 19--
Name of School   Address   Dates You Attended

Junior High School (last attended)

Lakeview   530 4th St., White Plains, IL Sept., 19-- – June,19-- Yes
Name of School   Address   Dates You Attended   Did You Graduate?

High School (last attended)   will graduate

White Plains 700 Mill St., White Plains, IL Sept.,19-- -present   5/--
Name of School   Address   Dates You Attended   Did You Graduate?

Colleges or Trade Schools Attended

_____   _____   _____   _____
Name of School   Address   Dates You Attended   Did You Graduate?

_____   _____   _____   _____
Name of School   Address   Dates You Attended   Did You Graduate?

Employment History (list most recent job first):

Chicken Betty's White Plains, IL   Oct, 19-- -Sept., 19--   5⁰⁰ hr.
Employer   Address   Date of Employment   Salary or Wage

7-11 Store   900 State, Marion, IL June, 19-- -Sept., 19--   4⁵⁰ hr.
Employer   Address   Date of Employment   Salary or Wage

_____   _____   _____   _____
Employer   Address   Date of Employment   Salary or Wage

References (not related to you):

Mr. Harold Sims   3741 Carol St, Santa Barbara, CA (805) 259-3414
     Name   Address   Telephone

Ms. June Taylor   1601 Menor, White Plains, IL   (609) 684-1439
     Name   Address   Telephone

Ms. Ann Thach   412 L St. Marion, IL   (609) 687-1341
     Name   Address   Telephone

Signed   *Linda Ann Hill*

▲ *Your personal fact sheet (page 311) will help you fill out an application form.*

Letter of Application

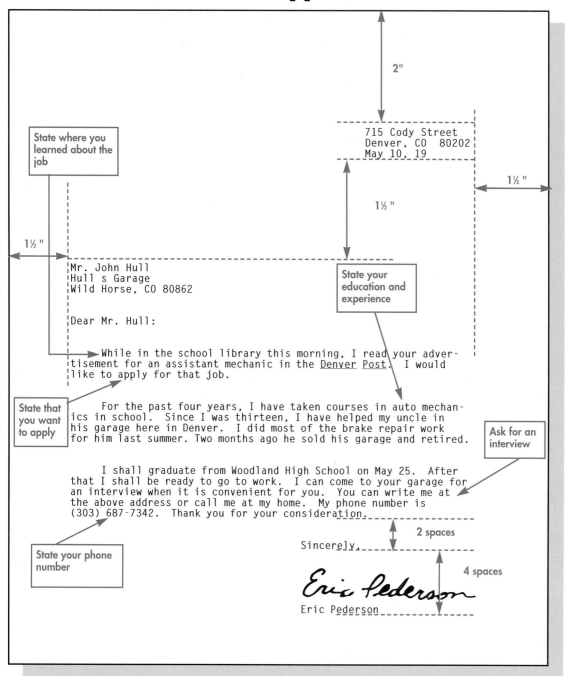

2"

715 Cody Street
Denver, CO 80202
May 10, 19

1½ "

1½ "

State where you learned about the job

1½ "

Mr. John Hull
Hull s Garage
Wild Horse, CO 80862

Dear Mr. Hull:

State your education and experience

While in the school library this morning, I read your advertisement for an assistant mechanic in the <u>Denver Post</u>. I would like to apply for that job.

State that you want to apply

For the past four years, I have taken courses in auto mechanics in school. Since I was thirteen, I have helped my uncle in his garage here in Denver. I did most of the brake repair work for him last summer. Two months ago he sold his garage and retired.

Ask for an interview

I shall graduate from Woodland High School on May 25. After that I shall be ready to go to work. I can come to your garage for an interview when it is convenient for you. You can write me at the above address or call me at my home. My phone number is (303) 687-7342. Thank you for your consideration.

Sincerely,

2 spaces

4 spaces

Eric Pederson
Eric Pederson

State your phone number

▲ *A letter of application should be typed neatly, just like any other important business letter.*

Resume

KAY ANDERSON
314 Mission Drive
Wichita, Kansas 67213

(316) 369-2305

<u>JOB OBJECTIVE</u>

Waitress or Hostess

<u>SKILLS</u>

Follow directions well   Get along well with others
Have good handwriting   Operate a cash register
Type 40 words a minute   Have good calculator skills

<u>EDUCATION</u>

Will graduate from Wichita West High School in May, 19--. My
courses include:

Home Economics	3 years
English	3 years
Math	3 years
Typing	1 year

<u>WORK EXPERIENCE</u>

<u>Cashier</u>, Northside Hardware Store, 2400 W. Douglas Street,
Wichita, KS (May, 19-- to present)

<u>Desk Clerk</u>, Western Motel, 320 Hydraulic, Wichita, KS (May,
19-- to September, 19--)

<u>PERSONAL INFORMATION</u>

Date of birth: September 16, 19--
Interests: Photography, swimming, reading
Transportation: Drive my own car to school and work
Traits: Dependable, good at following directions,
                      always on time
Limitations: Limited vision in right eye

<u>REFERENCES</u>

Mrs. Arleen Jacobs   Dr. Louise Fisher
Wichita Electric Co.   Snyder Medical Clinic
444 Camden Street   510 West Redford
Wichita, KS 67213   Wichita, KS 67213
(913) 762-1438   (913) 762-7827

Mr. Arnold Smith   Miss Lynne Morrison
Marion High School   720 Newton Avenue
Marion, KS 66861   Newton, KS 67114
(913) 828-1640   (913) 438-1492

▲ *On a resume, you can add personal traits and skills that you might not write on an
application form.*

Questions Often Asked in an Interview

The interview is an exchange of information. It is helpful both to the employer and to you. The employer tries to learn what you are really like. You have a chance to see if you really want the job. In most cases, the employer asks you questions. You can also ask questions.

Questions the Employer Might Ask

1. Why would you like to work for this company?
2. Do you want a permanent or temporary job?
3. What job would you most like?
4. What do you want to be doing in five years?
5. What **qualifications** do you have for this job? (This just means what skills and experience you have that will help on this job.)
6. What subjects in school did you like best? Least?
7. Do you prefer working alone or with others?
8. How do you use your free time?
9. What can you do best? What can you not do?
10. What jobs have you had? Why did you leave?
11. What pay do you expect?
12. Have you had any serious illnesses?
13. Do you smoke?
14. How many days of school did you miss last year?
15. What grades did you get in your schoolwork?
16. What hours can you work?
17. How will you get to work?
18. Do you take part in sports at school? Are you on a team? (Some employers think if you are on a team you will not have time to work.)
19. Are you willing to work overtime when needed?
20. What questions would you like to ask me?

Questions You Might Ask

1. What are the duties on this job?
2. What are the hours?
3. Would I be working with someone else?
4. If I need help, whom can I ask?
5. What is the pay?

▲ *Prepare for the interview by knowing the answers to these questions.*

Thank-you Letter

142 Circle Drive
Brockton, MA 20403
May 14, 19—

Mr. Charles North
276 Mill Street
Brockton, MA 20403

Dear Mr. North:

I want to thank you for interviewing me yesterday afternoon.

The job interests me very much, and I believe I can do a good job for you. Even if I don't get the job, though, I appreciate the opportunity to be interviewed.

Sincerely yours,

Rebecca Cole

▲ *A letter of thanks makes a good impression on the employer.*

W-4 Form

------------Cut here and give the certificate to your employer. Keep the top portion for your records. ------------

Form **W-4**
Department of the Treasury
Internal Revenue Service

Employee's Withholding Allowance Certificate
▶ **For Privacy Act and Paperwork Reduction Act Notice, see reverse.**

OMB No. 1545-0010

19 --

1 Type or print your first name and middle initial   Last name

Tamara   J.   Wilson

2 Your social security number

408-10-1452

Home address (number and street or rural route)
111 Timberlane Dr.

City or town, state, and ZIP code
Mooresville, NY, 11000

3 Marital status

☒ Single   ☐ Married
☐ Married, but withhold at higher Single rate.
Note: *If married, but legally separated, or spouse is a nonresident alien, check the Single box.*

4 Total number of allowances you are claiming (from line G above or from the Worksheets on back if they apply) **4** *1*

5 Additional amount, if any, you want deducted from each pay . . . . **5** $

6 I claim exemption from withholding and I certify that I meet **ALL** of the following conditions for exemption:
  • Last year I had a right to a refund of all Federal income tax withheld because I had **NO** tax liability; **AND**
  • This year I expect a refund of **ALL** Federal income tax withheld because I expect to have **NO** tax liability; **AND**
  • This year if my income exceeds $550 and includes nonwage income, another person cannot claim me as a dependent.

If you meet all of the above conditions, enter the year effective and "EXEMPT" here **6** 19

7 Are you a full-time student? (**Note:** *Full-time students are not automatically exempt.*) . . . . **7** ☐ Yes ☐ No

Under penalties of perjury, I certify that I am entitled to the number of withholding allowances claimed on this certificate or entitled to claim exempt status.

Employee's signature ▶ *Tamara J. Wilson*   Date ▶ *March 2,* 19--

8 Employer's name and address (**Employer:** Complete 8 and 10 **only if sending to IRS**)

9 Office code (optional)

10 Employer identification number

▲ *An Employee's Withholding Allowance Certificate gives your boss information that will affect your income taxes. It is called a W-4 form.*

All new employees must fill out a W-4 form. Your boss will ask you to fill out one when you start work.

Each time you are paid, your employer will keep a small part of your wages. Then this money will be used to pay your taxes. The W-4 will help your boss know how much to keep for your taxes.

As a young, single person your W-4 will probably be easy to complete. Write in your name, address, and social security number.

Check the box marked "single." On line 4, the form asks for "total number of allowances you are claiming." Enter "1." Sign and date the form at the bottom. See the example above.

Lower income workers may have no tax money held back at all. Ask your boss if this might be true for you. If so, fill in the boxes on line 6.

Are you married? Do you have more than one job? Do you have other income? In these cases, ask if you should fill out a W-4 worksheet.

Resignation Letter

1020 Hill Street
New City, MO 63201
May 17, 19— —

New City Auto Company
2366 Center Street
New City, MO 63201

Dear Mrs. Adams,

I would like to stop work at the New City Auto Company on May 31. I plan to begin working at the Jones Truck Lines on June 1, 19— —.

I have enjoyed working with you and everyone else here. I have learned a great deal about cars during the last two years.

Thank you very much for all you have done for me.

Very truly yours,
John Doss

▲ *Sometimes you may need to write a letter saying you are quitting your job. This is called a resignation letter.*

Paycheck Stub

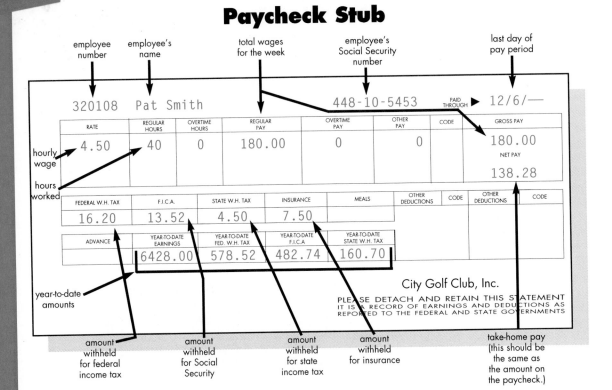

▲ The paycheck stub tells the total wages for the pay period and what has been deducted from the wages.

W-2 Form

1 Control Number			**OMB No. 1545-0008**		

2 Employer's Name, Address, and ZIP Code	**3** Employer's Identification Number	**4** Employer's State Number

The City Golf Club
8700 River Drive
Pittsburg, IL 66762

3 Employer's Identification Number
26-492-8745

4 Employer's State Number

5 Stat. Employee ☐   Deceased ☐   Legal Rep. ☐   942 Emp. ☐   Subtotal ☐   Void ☐

6 Allocated Tips   **7** Advance EIC Payment

8 Employee's Social Security Number	**9** Federal Income Tax Withheld	**10** Wages, Tips, Other Compensation	**11** Social Security Tax Withheld
448-10-5453	$622.00	$6968.00	$523.30

12 Employee's Name, Address, and ZIP Code

Pat Smith
8500 River Drive
Pittsburg, IL 66762

13 Social Security Wages
$6968.00

14 Social Security Tips

16

17 State Income Tax	**16** State Wages, Tips, Etc.	**19** Name of State
$174.20	$6968.00	IL
20 Social Security Tax Withheld	**21** Local Wages, Tips, Etc.	**22** Name of Locality

Form W-2 Wage and Tax Statement 19--
36-2515832 APP. 4/84

Copy B To be filed with employee's FEDERAL tax return
This information is being furnished to the Internal Revenue Service

Department of the Treasury
Internal Revenue Service

▲ *The W-2 form is completed by your employer. It is used to report earnings, social security tax, and other information. Attach Copy B to your federal tax return.*

Income Tax Return

| Form **1040EZ** | Department of the Tresury – Internal Revenue Service **Income Tax Return for Single filers with no dependents** (0) | **19 - -** | OMB No. 1545-0675 |

Name & address

Use the IRS mailing label. If you don't have one, please print.

PAT SMITH
Print your name above (first, initial, last)
8500 RIVER DRIVE
Present home address (number and street). (If you have a P.O. box, see instructions.)
PITTSBURG, I1 66762
City, town, or post office, state and ZIP code

Please read the instructions for this form on the reverse side.

Presidential Election Campaign Fund
Do you want $1 to go to this fund?

Note: Checking "Yes" will not change your tax or reduce your refund.

Please print your numbers like this:

| 0 | 1 | 2 | 3 | 4 | 5 | 6 | 7 | 8 | 9 |

Your social security number

| 4 | 4 | 8 | | 1 | 0 | | 5 | 4 | 5 | 3 |

Yes No
[X]

Report your income

			Dollars	Cents
1	Total wages, salaries, and tips. This should be shown in Box 10 of your W-2 form(s). (Attach your W-2 form(s).)	**1**	6 968	00
2	Taxable interest income of $400 or less. if the total is more than $400, you cannot use Form 1040EZ.	**2**	10	00

Attach Copy B of Form(s) W-2 here

3	Add line 1 and line 2. This is your **adjusted gross income**.	**3**	6 978	00
4	Can you be claimed as a dependent on another person's return? [X] Yes. Do worksheet on back; enter amount from line E here. [ ] No. Enter 2,540 as your standard deduction.	**4**	2 540	00
5	Subtract line 4 from line 3.	**5**	4 438	00
6	If you checked the "Yes" box on line 4, enter 0. If you checked the "No" box on line 4, enter 1,900. This is your **personal exemption**.	**6**	0	00
7	Subtract line 6 from line 5. If line 6 is larger than line 5, enter 0 on line 7. This is your **taxable income**.	**7**	4 438	00

Figure your tax

8	Enter your Federal income tax withheld. This should be shown in Box 9 of your W-2 form(s).	**8**	622	00
9	Use the **single** column in the tax table on pages 32-37 of the Form 1040A instruction booklet to find the **tax** on the amount shown on **line 7** above. Enter the amount of tax.	**9**	592	00

Refund or amount you owe
Attach tax payment here

10	If line 8 is larger than line 9, subtract line 9 from line 8. Enter the **amount of your refund**.	**10**	30	00
11	If line 9 is larger than line 8, subtract line 8 from line 9. Enter the **amount you owe**. Attach check or money order for the full amount, payable to "Internal Revenue Service."	**11**		

Sign your return

I have read this return. Under penalties of perjury, I declare that to the best of my knowledge and belief, the return is true, correct, and complete.

Your signature *Pat Smith*   Date *April 1, 19 - -*

For IRS Use Only — Please do not write in boxes below.

For Privacy Act and Paperwork Reduction Act Notice, see page 31.

Form **1040EZ** (19--)

▲ *Most beginning workers use the 1040EZ form to report income and figure income tax.*

◯ Glossary

A

ability　A skill that has already been developed. (190)

aerobic exercise　Exercise that strengthens your heart and lungs. (234)

anorexia nervosa　A serious eating disorder in which the victim has a fear of being overweight. It often leads to extreme weight loss from self-starvation. (233)

apprenticeship　A training program that offers a way to learn through hands-on experience. (116)

aptitude　A knack, or potential, for learning certain skills. (190)

atlas　A large book of maps. (202)

attitude　Your way of looking at the world and the people in it. (82)

B

bail　Money given to the court so that an accused person can be freed from jail until trial. (279)

balanced life-style　Equal time for both work and play. (218)

body language　Using the body to communicate meaning. (6)

budget　A plan to manage your money. (222)

bulimia　A serious eating disorder in which the victim has a fear of being overweight. The victim eats large amounts of food, then vomits in order to get rid of it. (233)

C

calorie　A unit that measures the fuel value of food. (232)

career　The work a person does during his or her life. (127)

career goals　What a person wants to achieve during his or her working life. (128)

cash drawer　The name for the drawer where the money is kept in a cash register. (30)

central processing unit (CPU)　A computer's control center. (48)

change　Anything that causes you to alter your life. (287)

collision insurance　Insurance that pays for damage to your car if you hit something. (178)

communication　The sending and receiving of messages that both the sender and receiver understand in the same way. (5)

competent parties   People who are responsible for their actions. (271)

compromise   Both parties give up something to resolve a conflict. (86)

comprehensive insurance   Insurance that pays if your car is damaged by fire, hail, or flood. It also pays if someone breaks into your car. (000)

condominiums   Privately owned housing units joined like apartments. (162)

confidentiality   Protecting others' right to privacy. (103)

conflict   The result of a dispute. (85)

conflict resolution   Bringing people who are in conflict into agreement. (86)

consideration   The payment one party to a contract gives the other in return for a promise to do something. (273)

consumer   A person who buys goods and services. (73)

contingency basis   Fee arrangement under which an attorney is paid only if he or she wins the case. (281)

contract   A legal agreement between two or more people. (270)

convenience foods   Frozen, canned, or packaged foods. (216)

cooperation   Working together to achieve common goals. (106)

countersign   To sign a contract in support of someone else. (272)

courtesy   Being considerate of others. (105)

cursor   A mark on the computer screen that shows you where you are working. (46)

D

data   Facts or information. (134)

deductible   The amount an insurance policyholder must pay. (178)

defensive driver   A driver who is alert and thinking ahead when he or she drives. (179)

disability   A factor that limits how well a person may be able to do some things. (255)

discount   A reduced price. (29)

discrimination   Treating someone unfairly because of such factors as race, skin color, religion, sex, age, or national origin. (250)

distractions   Things that take your mind off a subject. (9)

drug abuse   Using drugs for reasons other than for their intended use. (241)

E

emotional block   Something that emotionally bars you from understanding a message. (9)

empathy   Being able to understand how someone else feels. (83)

enunciation   Speaking each syllable clearly. (12)

environment   Everything that surrounds you. (291)

equity   The share of your home that you really own. (214)

eviction   Forcing a renter from the landlord's property. (158)

F

felony   A serious crime punishable by a large fine, a prison sentence, or even death. (276)

field   An area in which one has special skills or training. (127)

formal education   The learning that takes place in school. (112)

fraction   A part of a whole number. (36)

G

goods   Products that you buy. (73)

H

hardware   The parts of the computer system that you can touch. (46)

home study programs   Education courses that can be taken at home. (117)

human relations skills   Skills that help you get along with other people. (81)

I

inflections   The rising and falling tones in a person's voice. (7)

informal education   Learning that you do on your own. (120)

initiative   Using your energy to do what needs to be done without being told. (98)

installment   A regular monthly payment made over a period of time. (177)

J

job   A collection of duties that a person does to earn a living. (127)

L

labor contract   A written agreement between the union members and the company's management. (70)

labor supply All the people who are willing and able to work. (290)

labor union A group of workers who join together to get higher pay and better working conditions. (70)

landlord A person who owns rental property. (151)

lateral move Moving to a job that is at the same level as your old job. (128)

lease A legal contract between a landlord and a tenant. (152)

leisure time Free time. (188)

liability insurance Insurance that covers you if you cause an accident. It pays the expenses of those who suffer injury or damage. (178)

life-style The way you live. (207)

light-rail vehicles Electric railroad cars. (170)

loyalty Being faithful. (103)

M

mass transit Transportation that carries many people. (170)

medical insurance Insurance that pays your medical bills if you are injured in your car. (178)

misdemeanor A less serious crime punishable by a small fine, a short jail term, and/or community service. (276)

mobile homes Homes that can be moved from one place to another. (162)

modem A special piece of computer equipment that connects a computer to a telephone line. It allows communication between computers. (49)

mouse A piece of computer equipment that moves a pointer around on the screen. (49)

N

national origin The country your family came from. (250)

negotiate To try to reach an agreement through discussion. (86)

O

occupational organizations A group of people who do the same kind of work. (122)

P

pace The speed at which you speak. (12)

party A legal term for a person who enters into a contract. (270)

passport Document that identifies you as a citizen of a country. (201)

peer pressure The influence people in your group have on you. (259)

percent A number divided into 100 parts. (27)

personal values Ideas about your life that are important to you. (208)

physical fitness A measure of your strength and how long you can do something without tiring. (234)

pitch How high or low your voice sounds. (13)

plotter A piece of computer equipment that makes graphs. (49)

previewing Reading only those parts that outline what the writing contains. (15)

private transportation Travel in vehicles that are owned by individuals. (172)

promotion An advancement to a higher-level job. (128)

pronunciation The way a word sounds. (12)

public transportation Transportation for public use that is owned and run by private companies or the government. It includes buses, subways, and trains. (170)

R

recommended dietary allowances (RDA) Daily nutrient needs. (230)

recreation Activities you do during your leisure time. (188)

reimburse To pay back. (32)

respect Holding someone or something in high regard. (105)

responsible Being reliable. (99)

S

scanner A tool that reads data and saves it in a computer. (45)

security deposit The amount the renter gives the landlord when the lease is signed. (152)

self-control The ability to control your actions. (100)

self-esteem The way you feel about yourself. (83)

services Things that you pay other people to do for you. (73)

sexual harassment Constant unwanted sexual advances. (258)

sexually transmitted disease (STD) Disease that passes from one person to another through sexual contact. (242)

shipping charge The cost of sending the goods to the customer. (30)

side effect A problem caused by a drug. (237)

skimming Reading something very quickly and picking out the main points. (15)

software Instructions that tell a computer how to do a certain task. (51)

spectator sports Sports that you enjoy by watching them. (194)

standard English The formal style of writing and speaking you learned in school. (11)

steroids Illegal drugs that build muscle and bone strength. (241)

subleasing The process in which the tenant leases a place to someone else. (152)

sunscreen A lotion or oil that protects the skin from the sun's damaging rays. (239)

system unit The main part of a computer. (47)

T

tenant A person who rents an apartment or house. (152)

topic sentence A sentence that states a paragraph's main idea. (15)

trade A job that requires manual or mechanical skill. (116)

trade schools Schools that help people learn job skills. (114)

transfer skills The skills that you can use in any job or field. (133)

trends The general changes that are taking place in our society. (289)

U

uninsured motorist insurance Insurance that covers you if you are injured by a driver who does not have insurance. (178)

utilities Services such as heat, gas, and water. (155)

V

values Beliefs that are important to you. (97)

visas Special travel permits that are needed in order to travel in certain countries. (201)

volume How loudly you speak. (13)

vocational student organizations Student clubs that allow students to learn about an occupation. (120)

Y

youth hostel A place where traveling students can stay overnight. (201)

○ Index

Roger B. Bean, 163, 265

Ben & Jerry's All Natural Ice Cream/ Lee Holden, 104

Bettmann Archive, 38, 72, 88, 136

David Cornwell, Honolulu, HI, 294

David Falconer/Frazier Photolibrary, 106

Ford Motor Company, 180

David R. Frazier Photolibrary, 119, 135, 168, 198, 206, 289, 299, 303

Ann Garvin, 10, 115, 121, 134, 140, 146, 163, 244

Stan Gorman, 16, 17, 75, 87, 91, 92, 101, 161, 179, 209, 258, 259, 276, 283, 295

Grand Illusions/Rick Burdette, 324

Greyhound Dial Corporation, 169

Houston Police, 278

Bob Hunt/Peoria Chiefs, 194

KCBS-TV, 18

Bob McElwee, 57

Methodist Medical Center of Illinois, 213

Microsoft/D.T.S., 50

NASA, 286

National Multiple Sclerosis Society, 192

Brent Phelps, 135, 219, 298, 326

Elena Rooraid/PhotoEdit, 141

© Barry Rosen/Outward Bound, 197

St. Bartholomew's Hospital/Science Photo Library, 240

Bill Shirkey, 231, 232, 237, 242, 245, 254, 274, 277, 308, 309, 310, 311, 312, 313, 314, 315, 316, 317, 318, 319, 320, 321, 322

Alberto Tolot, 238

UAW Solidarity, 85

UPI Bettmann, 160, 257, 264

U.S. Department of Interior, 118

Warner Brothers International Television Distribution, 210

Dana White Productions, Inc., vi, vii, viii, ix, x, xi, xii, 1, 4, 7, 9, 13, 17, 19, 24, 27, 34, 35, 37, 39, 42, 44, 49, 54, 55, 60, 64, 65, 67, 71, 74, 80, 82, 83, 90, 96, 98, 102, 107, 110, 117, 122, 123, 126, 129, 131, 137, 139, 150, 151, 155, 157, 166, 168, 175, 186, 189, 190, 196, 200, 201, 203, 208, 216, 217, 223, 228, 234, 236, 239, 248, 251, 253, 256, 261, 262, 268, 270, 272, 273, 280, 290, 291, 292, 296, 304, 305, 323, 325, 327

Duane R. Zehr, 112, 135, 154, 163, 214

The publisher would like to thank the following individuals, schools, businesses, and organizations for their assistance with photographs in this book: Armstrong's Home & Garden; Century Freeway Women's Employment Program; Conrad Johnson (Atlantis Studios); Glendale Public Library, California; Jack-In-The-Box Restaurant; National Medical Enterprises; Recycle America; Thomas Richards & Company; Santa Monica High School; Santa Monica Hospital Medical Center; Westside Center for Independent Living; Natalie, Michael, and Andrew White; Windward School.

Models and fictional names have been used to portray characters in stories and examples in this text.